D1154771

# RELIGION AND STATECRAFT AMONG THE ROMANS

ALAN WARDMAN

**GRANADA**
London

To

The Immortal Gods

Granada Publishing Limited
Frogmore, St Albans, Herts AL2 2NF
and
36 Golden Square, London W1R 4AH
117 York Street, Sydney, NSW 2000, Australia
61 Beach Road, Auckland, New Zealand

Published by Granada Publishing 1982



*British Library Cataloguing in Publication Data*

Wardman, Alan
Religion and statecraft among the Romans.
1. Rome—Religious life and customs
2. Rome—History—Empire, to ca. 395
I. Title
303.2'24'0937' (expanded) DG109

ISBN 0 246 11743 5

Typeset by V & M Graphics Ltd, Aylesbury, Bucks
Printed by Richard Clay (The Chaucer Press) Ltd, Bungay, Suffolk

# *Contents*

Preface iv

1 INTRODUCTION: GODS, TEMPLES AND PRIESTS 1

2 THE LATE REPUBLIC 22
*Expansion* 24
*The Second Punic War* 33
*The Civil Conflicts* 42
*Some Contemporary Views* 52

3 AUGUSTANISM 63
*Augustus and the Republican Tradition* 67

4 THE LATER AUGUSTANISM 80
*Imperial Cult* 81
*Emperors and Subjects* 90
*Theory in Brief* 103

5 RELIGIONS FROM THE EAST 108
*The Oriental Religions* 109
*Imperial Persecutions* 123

6 THE FOURTH CENTURY 135
*Christians' Progress* 136
*Pagan Revivals* 149
*Christian Interpretations* 161

CONCLUSION 169

Notes 175
Bibliography 204
Index 215

# *Preface*

The purpose of this book is to show what different cults and religious practices contributed to various political systems – first oligarchy, then moderate and extreme monarchy – in the late Roman Republic and Empire. It discusses the effect of religion on the political conduct of rulers and on social organization within the Roman world; it links these with some of the theoretical issues about the political value of religion which were raised though seldom resolved by contemporaries. Part of the book is therefore concerned with interpreting the gods as signposts to men's thinking about the objectives of the state and of the ideal citizen.

It will be seen that this study is not a history of religion nor of politics, but it assumes on the reader's part an acquaintance with the outlines of both. My aim is to bring the different subjects together, in the conviction that they have been kept apart too long. Students of religion have written excellent general accounts of the subject as well as detailed studies of particular deities; and historians (in the ordinary sense of the word) have done even more to characterize the structure of Roman society at different periods. The modern emphasis is on political, administrative, economic and military history, in which religion has little more than a walking-on part. The public role of religion has been undervalued, and I suggest that the gods of Rome (*all* the gods) should have more lines to utter than they are allowed in the usual quota of footnotes or part-chapter.

The chronological limits of this study are the late third century BC and the end of the fourth century AD. These extremes have distinct characteristics in both politics and religion. At the beginning of the period the Rome which fought against Hannibal's Carthage was ruled by a polytheistic aristocracy, the members of which could hold both types of office, the religious and the political. With a few exceptions religion had no separate personnel. The Empire of the fourth century presents us with a striking contrast; it is governed by a monotheistic autocracy with a powerful clergy set apart from the ruler's civil and military servants. We have then to account for a movement from civic polytheism professed by oligarchs and their subjects to a universalist religion set in a form of absolute rule. It seems right to say that religion became more, not less, important over the period as a whole. And this fact, once it is admitted, adds to the difficulty and interest of the subject; it means that the Roman world offers us a different experience from that which has seemed characteristic of Europe since the Enlightenment. Instead of secularization Rome had, if not an expansive, at least an accommodating heaven; we may venture to say that the typical Roman mode is a kind of 'ouranization', the characteristic of piling new heavens on top of the old. The increase of deities was arrested, it is true, by the success of Christianity with its exclusive God. The one successor-god was hostile to the innumerable divinities of the pagan past. But any loss in numbers was made up in power. Throughout antiquity as we have defined it the deity did nothing but grow, advancing first by diffusion and then, at long last, by concentration.

Within the civic polytheism of pagan Rome three factors are especially prominent: the conception of the gods' relationship to the community, the functions of a god's dwelling, and the role of the priestly groups which represent the state in its approach to the deity. My aim is to show how these enduring religious institutions were thought to be of use and value to the activity of the whole community and to the public life of various groups, the generals of the republic, the emperors, army officers, freedmen, matrons and provincials. The introduction sets out a modest grammar of these elements, the gods, temples and priests, which are basic to polytheism; in subsequent chapters too I have tried to show how religion varied or changed in this three-fold medium.

The main narrative begins with a study of events in the history of the late Roman Republic, from the war against Carthage to the civil war between Caesar and Pompey. Other chapters discuss the conservative revival known as Augustanism; the spread of emperor-worship and the fortunes of some traditional cults under the Empire; Roman attitudes to eastern religions; and the changes in the fourth century AD when Christianity was officially accepted and civic polytheism began to recede from the political scene. In these different phases I have tried to explain why religion mattered to the state and to assess the main contemporary response.

No one historian could possibly hope to become acquainted with the greater part of the secondary literature on this large subject. My hope is that the scholarship in this work will be enough to sustain at least some of the arguments. For a brief summary of these the interested reader should glance at the conclusion.

I am grateful for permission to reprint passages from Virgil, *The Aeneid*, translated by W. F. Jackson Knight (Penguin Classics, Revised edition,

1958), 7.170–76, copyright © G. R. Wilson Knight, 1956; and from Tacitus, *Histories*, translated by Kenneth Wellesley (Penguin Classics, Revised edition, 1972), p. 53, copyright © Kenneth Wellesley, 1964, 1972. Reprinted by permission of Penguin Books Ltd.

I am also grateful to my colleagues and friends, Jane Gardner and Tessa Rajak, and to my wife, Judith Wardman, who all took time and trouble in giving me advice on matters of substance and presentation. I am also indebted to Doreen Janes, secretary of the Classics Department of Reading, who typed the manuscript.

Alan Wardman
Reading

CHAPTER ONE

# *Introduction: Gods, Temples and Priests*

In the course of her long history Rome developed new political habits and institutions in order to meet the changed conditions of the world she came to rule. We think of the main phases as the early monarchy, the Republic, the early principate and the later Empire, and these terms remind the historian of the different forms of government, which were so many adaptations to the needs imposed by expansion abroad and the stresses of internal conflict. Throughout the changes, however, there were many traces of continuity, even if the traditional names of things were not always a guide to their changing function. The Romans of the Republic, for example, had they been able to survey the fourth century AD, would still have recognized familiar organs of state like the senate, though experience of the Republic would not have helped to unravel the mysteries of its importance in the later period. The religious experience of Rome cannot be enshrined in such well-defined structures. But in one respect at least religion had a close resemblance to politics. Both in cult and in practice there was a tenacious conservatism, with the result that the polytheists of the Republic would have discovered old gods as well as new within the hospitable complexity of the later Empire. The strength of such traditions makes it advisable to describe in general terms the divine order as it was conceived by polytheistic Rome, and to explain the public functions of the temples which housed the gods and of the priests who served them.

Some modern interpreters have found it useful to describe the Roman conception of deity in terms of a contrast between numinous spirit and the more fully personalized god in human form;[1] such numinous powers may be lacking in anthropomorphic clarity but they are nonetheless endowed with specific functions. In any case, by the third century BC (when most of the Italian peninsula was under Roman control and influence) the Romans of the middle Republic acknowledged divine beings of widely differing types. Some were numinous spirits (in the sense mentioned above, with supernatural power) and had probably survived from an early period of settlement into the more urban and more military state. Such powers as Robigus, Furrina, Consus and Ops lacked personality in the anthropomorphic sense, but their importance was marked by dates in the calendar and their festivals were still observed. Robigus for instance was the spirit concerned with the rust or mildew which can spoil the corn, and the appropriate festival, the Robigalia, was held on 25 April.[2] A festival such as this one was still an enjoyable occasion even though its meaning became obscure and it seemed less relevant to a society that was being urbanized through expansion and conquest. By the first century BC many of these numinous powers had become obscure, even to a sympathetic antiquarian like Varro. Later still they were turned into objects of ridicule by Christian polemicists who were convinced that paganism with its archaic festivals was trivial and absurd. But they had the power of survival and citizens went on celebrating their rites even when they were unable to give an account of their origin or purpose.

The counterpart of numinous spirit is the divine being in human form. God the anthropomorph (so Varro maintained) was not known to the earliest Romans and did not make his presence felt as a symbolic statue for many years. Presumably Varro's theory would be rejected by those who think that the Romans, like other Indo-European societies, knew some gods, such as the sky-god, Jupiter, as individual beings from early times.[3] And even if we accept that it is valid to posit a distinct period of numinous spirit, it would not be prudent to assume too sharp or too exclusive a separation between a more primitive beginning, a state of pre-deism, and a later, more complex phase of anthropomorphic gods.

For present purposes it is enough to emphasize the fact that the god in human form with a cult-statue was the clearest sign of Roman civic polytheism. In antiquity this form of religion was not confined to the city-states of Greece and Rome. It denotes the cult of gods or deities who are the guardians of the society which gives them worship and who may also be functionaries in a wider order of things. In such systems a god's local status is not always on a par with his religious function in the more general sense. In Sumeria, for example, the god Enlil became supremely important to mankind as a whole, but locally he was no more than the protective deity of the minor state, Nippur.[4] The Romans of the developed city-state would have been baffled by a discrepancy of this kind, a contrast between the god's lesser place in history and his grand role in cosmology. Their sense would have been that Jupiter's importance as a sky-god, as the equal of Zeus or as the despot of a poetic Olympus, was concordant with his local significance at Rome; and of the numerous towns in Italy which had a Jupiter-cult Rome itself was considered (above all by the Romans) to be the terrestrial home of the god. It was tempting for poets and others to see Jupiter as the Roman Zeus because there was a long tradition of borrowing anthropomorphic practices and habits from Greeks and Etruscans. In this way some Roman gods were assimilated to Greek, so that Ceres, for example, acquired the attributes and the myth of Demeter. Aesculapius on the other hand was a wholly Greek import, a medical deity who might heal or even avert disease, a foreign god with no pre-existing counterpart on the Roman or Italian scene to whom he was assimilated. Other gods came from towns which Rome had defeated in war; a Juno was taken from Veii to be housed at Rome, even though this goddess was already known at Rome, and the god Vortumnus probably arrived when the general Fulvius Flaccus triumphed over Volsinii.[5]

The divine order, with its host of anthropomorphic and numinous gods, has several remarkable features. All the gods are to co-operate in the supreme task of civic polytheism, to protect and favour the city which has installed them and pays them respect. The people has its chosen gods to be cherished for their partiality, since it is presupposed that favours granted to Rome imply the downfall or defeat of another state. We might say (to take up once more the distinction made earlier) that the functional gods of the earliest Roman religion are always being joined by anthropomorphic deities whose states have loomed large in more recent events. A Roman savant[6] referred to the foreign gods (the *novensiles*) as gods who were so named because they were new to Rome 'for the Romans used to distribute the cults of conquered cities among private families or award them state recognition.' The system is therefore both conservative and acquisitive. The polytheon (a better term than pantheon) is entirely open, like a temple with an infinite number of niches. It does not wish to forget by exclusion of the past or to omit a god of importance to the present. The system cannot be made complete since it is always possible for Rome to come into contact with the new gods of other societies who should be won over or who may suit a Roman need. The gods form a series all the members of which are slightly different, as the system tolerates new arrivals who may well bear the name of an established god with a change of epithet. Rome knew more than one Juno, and Mars was a familiar Roman deity long before his Augustan incarnation as Mars the Avenger. In spite of such similarities there is no clash within the system; the new god, even though he may seem to be a kinsman of those already present, does not drive out a decayed relative. This tolerance made it possible for Rome to introduce and accept strange gods as well as those who might seem less remote from her own political experience, the imported gods of the eastern religions as well as the home-produced variety, the deified emperors.

It is difficult for those who are used to monotheism or a theistic philosophy to detect any sign of order within this multitude of deities and divine powers. It seems at first sight to be no more than an anarchy of traditions and novelties. There is indeed some correspondence or symmetry between the world of gods and aristocratic society. The greater civic deities might be described as so many patricians or nobles, with plebeian dependants or clients among the less important or the immigrant gods.[7] This comparison is based on the patron-client relationship, which is a key to the political activities of worshippers and citizens. But the analogy should not be pressed since gods are not patrons of other gods in the way that great men attach lesser mortals to themselves. Perhaps the analogy, to be convincing, should be expressed differently. Just as clientship is a bond which attaches most of the inhabitants to a few citizens, so too there is a bond which makes all citizens the clients of the gods. But the analogy would still be unhelpful; it compares clientship in the literal sense with what can be no more than a metaphorical clientship; and (even if that is overlooked) it takes no account of the fact that political clients owe allegiance to a few particular citizens, whereas for religious purposes citizens are the dependants of all the gods, even if they have a special devotion to a few or to one in particular. As the argument from a social and political parallel does not take us very far we may be tempted to use a theme taken from literature, to ask whether or not an Olympian[8] model may help to explain relationships within the polytheon. I mean by 'Olympian model' the kind of family with a paternalistic head which is familiar in the Homeric poems or in the *Aeneid*. But though Rome's greatest god, Jupiter Optimus Maximus, has the name in common with the deity who decides the course of the *Aeneid*, he is not dominant over other gods in the same imperious way. The civic sky of Rome is inhabited by far more gods than the Olympus portrayed by the poets.

Internal coherence is not to be expected of a system which welcomes new members in the Roman way. But there are signs of relative importance, some of which became a lasting feature of the calendar. Juno and Jupiter were both deities with special days in each month, Juno having the Calends and Jupiter the Ides. The official year[9] began with prayers to a Jupiter who, though not in time the first of Rome's Jupiters, came to surpass the others, the Capitoline Jupiter. He was also to be honoured on the important occasion when a general was about to leave the city in order to lead an army in war. Technically the consuls could not begin their year of office before they had paid the traditional worship to Jupiter. Even though certain gods continued to dominate and were not seriously challenged by new arrivals, the system allowed considerable flexibility. There were fashions among gods, some of whom experienced varying political fortunes. Neptune did not really advance to the political forefront until the period of civil war, with its naval battles, after the death of Julius Caesar. The case of Venus is even more remarkable; the cult became important to the politician-generals of the late Republic, especially to the Julian family, for Venus, as the mother of Aeneas, was the patron of Rome before the Romans, a guarantee of patriotism and antiquity.[10]

It is clear that other communities, most obviously those in Italy of Latin or allied culture, acknowledged gods with the same name as gods at Rome. The habit of assimilation provided more instances, since Greek religious culture was thought to be broadly identical; Athena therefore was the counterpart of Minerva, Ares of Mars, and so on. It is a matter of considerable interest to know how Romans valued such gods in other communities, to decide whether they thought them as important as their own. Does Cicero, for instance, reflect a general opinion when he justifies a Roman decision (made in 133 BC) to consult the Ceres of Henna? His reason is that the Ceres of Henna was prior to the Ceres of Rome, and so he alleges it was right for the Romans as a religious people to send an embassy overseas to honour the goddess there, despite the wonderful temple of Ceres in Rome itself. But Rome's official genuflexion before another Ceres was probably connected with the fact that Henna had been occupied by rebellious slaves, and so decreeing a visit to the temple abroad was a sign of Rome's determination to proclaim the rebels' defeat. Again, what are we to make of Cicero's invocation of Juno when he assumes that an offence committed by Verres against the shrines of Juno on Malta and Samos is also an act of sacrilege against the Juno Regina of Rome? In this particular instance Cicero has good reason to plead as he does, in order to accuse his adversary of as much religious misconduct as possible. But since the god was civic and local first, and universal (if at all) second, it seems likely that in general the Roman deity counted for much more. It is doubtful whether Romans would naturally assume that the relationship between these distant Junos was the close and intimate connection that an Athenian, for example, would readily discover between the local Dionysiac festivals in Attica and the greater festival of Dionysus, the Lenaia, which was held in Athens itself. They would not easily accept that a violation of distant Junos would also bruise their own civic deity of the same name, though there was a tradition, not unimportant in politics, of behaving with decorum towards the similar deities of other peoples.[11]

In discussing this last example from Cicero we are in effect comparing the deity of a world-power with the deities of defeated states which had remained or had become provincial. The relationship between Junos is bound to express something of the difference between the peoples who offer cult. The Romans of Rome can afford to make a patronizing gesture of respect to the Juno-figures who have made the mistake of living elsewhere, and the inhabitants of Malta and Samos cannot afford *not* to look up to the victor goddess, as a supremo among Juno-figures. Cicero's readiness to see a likeness between Junos is therefore founded on an inequality in the standing of the different communities, and can only be made at a relatively late stage in the history of civic polytheism. It might be argued that there is an earlier stage, marked by a 'common belief in the equality of sovereign parochial gods, each within his own domain. But this belief is apt to break down, and, with it, the restraint that is imposed by it.'[12] At the supposed early stage, then, 'neighbour parochial gods' are allowed the right to control their own territory, and the deities are equal because the communities are powerless to invade or occupy one another's territory. Thus gods are first comparable when the different communities are close together and weak, and they are also comparable later when they are made to bridge great distances and to overcome dissimilarities in power. They begin as equal and alike and move towards a condition of being alike though unequal.

Rome had encountered many cities with deities that were apparently identical to her own; some were left in their defeated residence, others, like the Juno of Veii, were invited to leave and were promised a new home even before capture. This would suggest that in some cases at least the difference in domicile was all-important, that locality prevailed over identity of name. Another cult relevant to this discussion is the worship of Jupiter Latiaris[13] on the Alban mountain. The Latin festival in honour of this god had been founded in days when Rome was a weak power, but as Rome became stronger she took over the management of the festival; perhaps this federal Jupiter had for a time at least a useful political function as the subordinate ally of Rome's own magnificent Jupiter. If so, the Roman consuls who honoured the neighbouring Jupiter would see their prayers and actions as beneficial to Rome in much the same way as they regarded the procession to Jupiter on the Capitol; both sets of religious acts were forms of magnification of Rome. The statesmen of Rome might well have appreciated the sort of reasoning used by Hobbes, that although Jupiter is king of all the earth, 'yet may he be king of a peculiar, and chosen nation.'[14]

The conservative flexibility of the system had certain advantages for political leaders who could claim (or thought they could claim) an association with a deity or group of deities. The more Rome succeeded in expanding (a process which continued throughout the civil wars and afterwards), the more it was felt that the gods had shown their approval of Roman piety. The proof that a community was truly religious was thought to be success in agriculture, politics and war. The Roman past was made even more exalted as men looked back on it with pride and a feeling that the present too would be improved if it could appear to be connected with the past through one or more gods. Venus, as I indicated above, was important to Pompey and Caesar and seemed to associate them with a time before the foundation of Rome. Augustus, once he was deified, played the part of Venus (in this sense) to many of the successor-emperors in the principate; and at a late stage Diocletian made himself and his associates the adjutants of the ever-enduring Jupiter and Hercules. Historical mythology[15] of this sort raised the imagination of the present to dwell upon a hallowed past, such as Venus' protection of Aeneas or Augustus' restoration of the Republic. Its weakness was an inability to define the future except by an appeal to the magnified promise of the past. The deficiency became glaring when this form of civic polytheism was challenged by Christianity, which offered a distinct interpretation of the future.

The gods (to discuss briefly the nature of Roman practice) affected the political and social life of the community in many ways. Gods had their birthdays, often the day on which their temple was dedicated, and their festivals, when in theory the citizens would attend a sacrifice and a celebration. Political business, as in the senate, was often preceded by a sacrifice and sometimes by a religious procession. Although some gods were more important than others, the acknowledgement of a new god did not condone indifference to another cult. Such indifference (as I shall show) was an inevitable part of the system but it was not encouraged in theory and was often checked in practice. It was at all times necessary to carry out the proper rites so that the divine order, 'the peace of the gods', should be preserved. A fault in ritual, even if it was unintentional, was an offence against the gods and had to be made good by repeating the ritual in the proper way.

Civic religious activity was rooted in a feeling of awe for the gods, and a sense that sacrifice should be ritually correct, accompanied with the right victims. Prayer was mostly conditional and petitionary; it promised rewards to the god, a temple or an offering, if an enterprise were successful. The preoccupation with correctness is apparent in the formula which betrays the sense that the right god can be difficult to name; by the words 'whether you are a god or a goddess ...' the Roman avoided the dangers of an over-precise declaration and yet announced his sense that deity was present. Sexing a god could be dangerous and was anyway beyond the strict call of devotion. The Romans considered that the sense of awe (*religio*) should be controlled and organized. It was important to prevent immoderate religiosity or an excess of zeal. Thus *religio* tended to be used not only to denote the sense that an obligation to the gods had arisen but also to imply that the right steps had been taken. So far, anxious scruple may seem to be the underlying attitude. But merely to lull such a feeling would not do more than stop the unnerving of a community. The festivals and games provided the citizens with the opportunity for collective celebration and enjoyment of a positive kind. Many of these occasions had in an expressive sense 'the emotional association of a national anthem.'[16] Fear of the gods' anger was a vital part of public religious sentiment, but there was an expectation that in time it would disappear and be replaced by confidence and gratitude. One and the same term, supplication, was used to describe the prayer to the gods to avert further calamity and the thanksgiving of relief over success or victory.

The developed, hypertrophied even, sense of awe led the Romans to be receptive, if not curious, about the gods from elsewhere. This feeling made Rome as acquisitive of gods as she was of territory and provinces. The readiness to accept new gods arose from the religious sense that the gods might show themselves in different forms at any time or place. But what started as religious accretion could at times seem to peter out in neglect or indifference. The expanding system was bound to install and retain so many deities that some would inevitably be forgotten. Piety therefore produced too many gods for civic consciousness to need or bear. When the Romans felt guilty, as they did after the civil wars, they tended to blame their failures on their wickedness, their indifference to the gods. But this mood, though understandable, was a Roman misconception, a failure to understand their divine order. The whole system was a mixture of innovation and obsolescence; some indifference or neglect of the gods was bound to occur and was as essential to the system as the initial proliferation of gods. I do not mean to say that the Romans had not experienced feelings of guilt when they blamed their political failures on neglect or indifference to the gods or divine ritual. The point is that as the system increased the number of gods so too it multiplied the opportunities for indifference and made it more likely that neglect would occur.

The system of gods was characterized by conservatism, adaptability and obsolescence. It is likely that in the earliest Rome, long before the critical historian can be as sure of his facts as he begins to feel with the third century BC, the sacral rhythm of the year was intended to secure agricultural prosperity and success in war.[17] The agricultural festivals stayed in the calendar and were celebrated long *after* Rome had become less immediately dependent on the produce of the adjacent land. The goddess Ceres, for example, with her temple on the Aventine, gradually evolved into the tutelary power of the corn-supply which was imported from afar; for the enlarged city with its increased population the cult of this agricultural goddess was no longer a life and death tie with the hinterland of Rome.

Urbanization – an expanding city with increased population and more diverse social structures – was a function of conquest, but did not entail the explicit rejection of the ancient gods. Similarly, the calendar kept its old military rites, it commemorated the distant past when the campaigning season opened in March and closed in October. The ceremonials for these important occasions did not pass away even when armies were obliged to spend whole years abroad, far away from the religious locality which had solemnly authorized their departure. The gods of a past environment persisted into new times though they began to recede as citizens looked to other or newer gods who were more relevant to changed conditions. Many of the new deities, who arrived through the vows made by generals or senate in time of war, had different names and, ostensibly, different functions; but, as they came to Rome in a time of conquest and successful expansion, they all tended to take on the same appearance, the victory-god of a particular campaign.

The gods (though this was not their only role) contributed to the social cohesion of a community faced with the uncertainties of harvest and war, the main dangers. They encouraged the will to succeed. As long as the right ritual was observed, as long as flaws were put right and the procedure re-enacted correctly, the peace of the gods would not be disturbed. We may then ask whether cult of this sort is more than formal ceremony; granted that it helps to increase civic morale, does it also require the citizen-worshipper to be virtuous? The moralists, it is true, are never tired of saying that the gods expect a pious cult, implying that human morality is not a matter of indifference to the divine order. One can reasonably suspect that some of this moralizing is an enlightened habit of using philosophy in order to improve religion, to impose on religion a concern for conduct that was not already present in the foundations. On the other hand a cult like that of Pudicitia, for example, would have had little point if its devotees, the matrons, had been notoriously unchaste. An episode mentioned by Livy describes how a lady was excluded from the rites not because she was unchaste but because though chaste and virtuous she was born and bred a plebeian.[18] The story presupposes that only her social origin was in question and that her virtue was not impugned. Perhaps the right way to view the matter is to suppose that cult demands formal correctness and prefers it to come from a good moral disposition.

At best the gods encouraged virtue, they can hardly be said to have sanctioned it. It is true that certain virtues were obviously useful to the military survival of the people, and so the gods with their sanctions were involved in rituals of war. Jupiter was invoked in the diplomatic ritual of the priestly college called the fetials, who proclaimed that the enemy had refused Rome's peaceful overtures and so ensured that the army would have the sense of fighting in a just cause. Oaths taken in the presence of the gods probably had most effect on the Romans as soldiers. The military oath was a solemn act which bound the soldier to his general and helped to promote discipline.[19] Some of the rituals therefore helped to instil a sense of justice and a code of loyalty. But it remains true to say that the tie between gods and men was formed by results, the success which requires certain practical virtues, not by the attempt or intention to be virtuous. Temples to gods were vowed before or during the battle but they could then only be set up with the proceeds of victory.

The influence or presence of a divine being could be sensed and recognized by a polytheist in many circumstances, even if he could not be sure of the god's identity and so took refuge in the formula already quoted, 'whether you are a god or a goddess.' It was important not to specify the wrong god for that would commit one's community to false religion. The god preceded man's acknowledgement of him in the form of temple or altar. But in public life the usual sign of a god, especially one who was fully accepted by the state, was the temple with its cult-statue set apart in a smaller room (the *cella*); many of the temples in Rome were the centre of political activity as well as of religious worship.

The founding of a city was itself a religious act which illustrates an important technical sense of the Latin word *templum*. It denotes an area which had been marked out by augury, within which the auspices, the essential preliminary to public action, could be taken. Thus the whole of the inner part of a city was itself a *templum* with a sacred boundary. When used to describe a building temple refers strictly to the house of a god the site of which has been inaugurated. The house of Vesta was, in Roman terms, not a temple but an *aedes*; it had been consecrated but not inaugurated, whereas the temples of Jupiter and Saturn were inaugurated. The distinction is important since political business could only be transacted in an inaugurated area; the senate had its own meeting-house, which was itself declared a *templum*, and it could also be convened in a building which we would naturally call a temple, a polytheist's church with one or more cult-statues.[20]

In this kind of organization religious and secular affairs are often handled in the same place even though they are clearly differentiated. The first meeting of the official year was held in the temple of Jupiter on the Capitol, and meetings were also held here when the senate was deliberating whether or not to declare war. Under the Republic the senate would meet outside the sacred boundary in the temple of Bellona, in order to receive a returning general and discuss whether he should be awarded a triumph. The intermingling of the sacred and profane (as we might think of it) is further shown by the other uses to which some temples were put. The temple of Saturn, for example, housed the state treasury and had various public documents fixed to the walls. For a considerable time the temple of Juno Moneta contained not only the goddess but also the mint. Thus a key function of many temples was to serve one or more of the purposes of government and administration.

There are fine imaginative descriptions of this interlocking religious and political activity in Virgil's *Aeneid.*[21] When Aeneas is looking at the pictures of Troy in Juno's temple (Juno here is the protecting, civic deity of Carthage) Dido comes with an armed escort and proceeds to make legal decisions, issue decrees and allocate tasks to those who are building the city. The temple is thought of as the natural place in which Dido's royal power can make its authority known. The temple in which King Latinus acts as host to Aeneas is described in even more significant detail.

> The palace of Laurentine Picus was a majestic building, with its great height supported on a hundred columns, and standing on the highest ground in the city; it was a place of dread, set in clustering trees and surrounded with traditional awe. Here, if he would have a prosperous reign, every king must on his accession receive the sceptre and lift up the rods of office. The palace was a temple, and it was also the hall for their holy feasts, when by custom the elders sacrificed a ram and in unbroken lines took their places at table.

Both the reception of foreign dignitaries and the banquets are attested in the historical temple-practice of the Romans.

Latinus' temple, 'standing on the highest ground in the city', indicates that the location of temples was an important matter. As Vitruvius puts it, 'the sites for those of the gods under whose particular protection the state is thought to rest and for Jupiter, Juno and Minerva, should be on the very highest point commanding a view of the greater part of the city.' At Rome the dominant temple was that of Jupiter on the Capitol, in which his cult-statue was flanked by the allied, though subordinate, figures of Juno and Minerva. This physical eminence corresponded to Jupiter's dominance in the ceremonies of public life. The pattern was repeated in many of the Italian cities which came under Roman sway and sought to emulate and flatter the practice of Rome. Not all the temples could be accommodated in such a splendid position or even in the *fora* which also lay within the sacred boundary or *pomerium.* As Rome developed, especially under the Empire, more room was made by creating new civic spaces, the imperial *fora* with their temples. But some temples were not admitted within the boundary, not just because there was a lack of space but because they were less respectable and failed to win the stamp of official acceptance. A further comment by Vitruvius, though somewhat fanciful in part, shows what the practice could be:

> It is moreover shown by the Etruscan diviners in treatises on their science that the fanes of Venus, Vulcan and Mars should be situated outside the walls, in order that the young men and married women may not become habituated in the city to the temptations incident to the worship of Venus, and that buildings may be free from the terror of fires through the religious rites and sacrifices which call the power of Vulcan beyond the walls. As for Mars, when that divinity is enshrined outside the walls, the citizens will never take up arms against each other, and he will defend the city from its enemies and save it from danger in war.

A temple to Venus Erucina, dedicated in 181 BC, was situated outside the Colline Gate, and has been described as a 'resort of questionable characters.'[22] The temple to Vulcan and most of the temples to Mars were also on the farther side of the boundary. The exclusion did little to prevent fire, a danger to which all ancient buildings were extremely liable, or civil conflict, which was deplored by the ancient moralists but was not an abnormal feature of city-state societies. Vitruvius' reasons are elaborate and too sophisticated, but the substance of his comments points to a valid distinction between the gods within and the gods without the boundary. At Rome, as we saw above, the most eminent was Jupiter, whose temple should be raised on high, as this sky – and hill – god could only be master of what he surveyed, and it was necessary therefore that he should oversee a large part of the city.

The temples of Rome, as buildings, have never failed to make an impression on posterity. Even the layman's eye can be educated by his modern guide, the archaeologist, to set up once more the fallen column and thus see the ruins of the past through the picture-making imagination. We may also reflect that in public life the temples performed a remarkable function, both socially and politically. In an age when politics and religious activity were not put into separate compartments, they were a device which allowed man to combine the sacred and the profane under the same roof.

Both orders of society, the religious and the political, were participants in the introduction of new temples.[23] Under the Republic a temple would usually be vowed by the senate or by a general on campaign in the hope that his army would be successful; in the latter case the senate as a whole often exercised, or tried to exercise, some supervision of the project. The vestiges of senatorial control persisted under the Empire, especially when the issue was whether to grant deification and a temple to a dead emperor. But the actions of the senate were now increasingly affected by adulation of the imperial successor, and the Republican determination to control or discipline a fellow oligarch faded away. Once the building was complete, the ceremony of dedication bestowed a formal welcome on the new god. The ceremony usually required the presence of a priest, a pontifex, who uttered the ritual language appropriate to the occasion, and of a consul or a specially appointed official, who actually carried out the act of foundation. On most occasions, it is true, a priest and an office-holder were both present. But the more important functionary was the office-holder, for the priest did little more than act as prompter to the politician, reminding him of the correct language and procedure. Here (as in other spheres too) religion functioned as the public servant of a benevolent political master. An informative account of Roman practice describes what happened after the temple of Jupiter had been burnt down in the civil war of AD 69. The rebuilding was to mark a memorable day, a new beginning, it was hoped, after the miseries of conflict, and Tacitus takes the opportunity to record the occasion in some detail.[24]

Responsibility for the reconstruction of the Capitol was delegated by the emperor to Lucius Vestinus. Though he belonged to the equestrian order, Vestinus' prestige and reputation had secured him a place among the leading men of Rome. He summoned the diviners, who advised that the rubble of the earlier shrine should be dumped in the marshes and the temple rebuilt on the same foundations, so far as these remained: it was the will of the gods that the ancient plan should be preserved unaltered. The whole area which was to be dedicated as the site of the temple was marked off by a continuous line of fillets and garlands, and on 21 June, under a tranquil sky, it was entered by a procession of soldiers with auspicious names, bearing boughs of olive and laurel and followed by the Vestal Virgins with boy and girl attendants who had both parents alive. All these carefully sprinkled the site with water drawn from springs and rivers. Then the praetor Helvidius Priscus, guided in the ritual by the pontifex Plautius Aelianus, purified the area by the sacrifice of pig, sheep and ox, and offered up the entrails upon a turf altar, praying to Jupiter, Juno and Minerva, as the deities that ruled the Empire, that they would vouchsafe to prosper the labours now begun, and forasmuch as the building of their holy house had been undertaken by the devotion of men, to exalt the same by their divine assistance. Then the praetor laid his hand upon the fillets around the foundation stone, to which ropes were secured. In the same instant, the other officials, the priests, senate, knights and a large proportion of the populace, eagerly and gladly took the strain and hauled the enormous block of stone into place. Everywhere they cast into the foundations offerings of gold and silver – nuggets of unrefined metal in the natural state. The diviners' instructions were that the building should not be desecrated by the use of stone or gold intended for any other purposes. Some addition was made to its height. This, it was felt, was the only change that religious feeling permitted, and the only respect in which the earlier temple had been wanting in splendour.

Erecting a temple needed some financial outlay, an expense which tended to go up as Rome became more prosperous and political rivalry increased. Some temples were paid for by fines, imposed by magistrates such as the aediles. It may seem strange at first that the state should spend money on temples rather than on other buildings such as porticoes which would appear to be more obviously useful; but if it is remembered that temples were often used for purposes of government and administration, we can see that these edifices, being profane as well as sacred, were not just monuments of display. In many cases, certainly under the Republic, the finance was provided by a victorious general who would sometimes endeavour to add the attractions of an entertainment (*ludi*) to the amenity of a temple. Senatorial control tried to make itself felt on the question of expense, an attempt which was about as successful as the repeated efforts to limit expenditure by sumptuary legislation. Thus plunder acquired from a defeated enemy, legitimate wealth won in a 'just war', was the main financial rock on which the temples were founded.

Temples and altars were the subject of precise legislation. Their rites were prescribed through individual 'dedication charters' or they were included in the charter of the whole community. The charter of the altar to Diana on the Aventine[25] was the explicit model for the dedication law of the later altar to Augustus at Narbo in Gaul; the Roman exemplar was relevant here because Narbo was itself a Roman colony in the technical sense and its territory was therefore of the same legal status as the founding city. In the city of Rome the Roman sense of religious legality defined as sacred for all time the area on which a temple was erected. If for any reason rebuilding was necessary it could not take place outside the sacred precinct even if this were an inconvenience to town-planners. But in the provinces where the land was not legally Roman, Roman officials were not hampered by the same punctiliousness and they could determine new limits of the sacred without impropriety: another proof that Romans were most strict and observant about those gods who were housed on Roman terrain.[26]

Individual temples in Rome had their own charters which prescribed certain forms of behaviour and prohibited others. The temple of the Bona Dea,[27] for example, excluded men, myrtle and wine (the last of which could be admitted only if it was renamed milk or honey). The new towns, especially in the western part of the empire, followed the provisions which had been tried and tested in the temples of Rome. Thus several sections of the law concerning the Colonia Genetiva Julia deal with religious matters.[28] Here the members of the local senate, the decurions, and the principal officers, the duovirs, are to decide the dates of sacrifices; they are to be responsible for the election of the priests, pontiffs and augurs, whose privileges are clearly defined. As this is a new colony some care is taken to see that monies collected for religious purposes should not be used to bolster the public funds. Normally, if a collection were declared for the purposes of a public sacrifice, any surplus could be put to other uses. In a new colony such as this the officials might be tempted, unless they were formally debarred, to use such contributions as a way of building up the local exchequer. In general the provisions of this charter and of others show how the religious rules were to be administered by the politicians of the community.

It would be difficult for temples run on these lines to acquire wealth of their own. Revenues, as from sacred groves attached to temples or from individual contributions, were technically profane and could therefore be used for non-religious purposes (with the exception of the new colonies, mentioned above). Most temples could not inherit a legacy, except for a few which had received this privilege 'by a decree of the senate, or by the imperial constitutions'. The property of a Vestal Virgin who died intestate went, not to the temple of Vesta, but to the state.[29] There was an underlying assumption that temples should be prevented from becoming economically independent. Nonetheless, some temples became rich by accident, as they housed the dedications made by pious individuals and by generals who had the wherewithal to be munificent through conquest. The temple of Jupiter, especially, received gold crowns and gold statues from other communities who asked the permission of the senate in order to show their tangible respect and gratitude. In principle such offerings could be transferred and used at the wishes of the state, but in fact this does not seem to have been common practice. Valerius Maximus tells us that by a senatorial decree some treasures were melted down in order to provide pay for the troops. We hear of some incidents in the time of Julius Caesar, including the removal of 3000 pounds of gold from the Capitol. Tacitus complains that 'even the gods' (that is their offerings) became part of the loot needed to supply funds for Nero's building programme at Rome in AD 64. The writers' indignation in these cases is directed against the particular purpose of which they disapprove; Valerius is angered that the money should be needed to pay troops in a civil war, and Tacitus' resentment shows his hostility to the tyrant Nero who in his eyes can do no right.[30] But though the offerings could be used for purposes of a more secular kind, it does not seem that the Romans cared to do this except in emergencies. The conversion of temple offerings to a practical purpose, though legitimate in theory, could easily be represented as unpatriotic and disloyal to the gods. A similar tradition tried to protect the temples of the Greek world, though it did not help much in practice against the greed of individuals like Verres or such pressing requirements as those of the third-century emperor Maximinus.[31]

In the eastern part of the Mediterranean world some of the temples, especially in the Hellenistic period, had enjoyed a considerable financial culture. They functioned as treasuries and safe-deposits and were also active as banks. They were one of the three elements in the banking sector, working alongside the individual entrepreneur and the cities.[32] Apollo's temple at Delos and the temple of Diana at Ephesus were two of the many temples whose economic vigour was useful to the Greek city-states and Hellenistic kings, and was fostered by them. Nothing like this phenomenon seems to have occurred in Rome and Italy. Also, it is noticeable that in the east many temples claimed and often received a right of asylum.[33] The priests of a temple would claim the right to exclude from or receive into their precincts anyone they thought fit; and they would also seek to protect refugees who seemed to deserve assistance from the god. But this political sense of 'holiness and inviolability' was for the most part foreign to Roman practice, even though the authorized version of her origins associated an asylum with the founder Romulus.

I have referred above to the use of Roman temples as places of government and administration. They were also dependencies of god, as there were processions, thanksgivings, triumphs and banquets through which congregational devotion could express itself, even though the temples were not usually open for worship. The congregations were often drawn from *all* social groups; some deities, however, were exclusive and were worshipped by a particular group, such as married women. Cult was regular but was dispersed among many temples and was diffused throughout the year. It had too many focuses in place and time. The sense of belonging to a congregation became most effective when the community felt threatened by danger, and the different orders of society – senators, clients, matrons and freedwomen – addressed their prayers to the diverse gods with the same end in view, the security of all. Congregational regularity, attached to one particular shrine, did not begin to flourish until the oriental religions and Christianity became well established at Rome.

The range of priesthoods – those offices which are held by representatives of the state in its dealings with the divine – comprises the servants of particular gods and the unattached colleges, such as the pontiffs, augurs, and decemvirs in charge of the Sibylline books. The latter groups are of more importance to political history, but the priests of particular gods, though little is known about most of them, can still tell us a good deal about the subordinate position of the religious functionary in Roman political society.

We know of fifteen such priests, called *flamines*, as well as a 'king of the sacred', whose office was a survival from the royal period when the king himself was general-in-chief, political ruler and religious leader as well. The flamens of whom most is known were attached to Jupiter, Mars and Quirinus; all of them were subject to various restrictions and taboos which made it difficult to combine their religious office with a political career. Such priests were theoretically in the service of the gods all day and every day; theirs was, in Roman parlance, a lifetime of holiday from those secular concerns which can most often satisfy ambition. The *flamen Dialis* (the priest of Jupiter) was tied by regulations about a possible absence from the city; technically, he was not allowed to take an oath, with the result that he could not serve as a soldier or hold office. These restrictions, together with the increase in the religious posts which were compatible with office, meant that the flaminates began to seem politically undesirable quite early in the history of the Republic. A patrician lament from a Livian speech gives us an insight into a stage of the struggle between the two political orders; the complaint is that if plebeians have access to the higher offices, the patricians, being fewer, will eventually have to console themselves with the flaminates; they will be able to pray and sacrifice, but not act, on behalf of a state run by plebeian office-holders.[34]

These priesthoods were confined to patricians and remained so, an indication that the plebeians who sought access to the highest political offices were not concerned in the same way about the flaminates. The sense of political impediment was made more acute for the flamens, just because they came from patrician families with a strong tradition of relatives and ancestors who had held the highest magistracies and ruled Rome. It is not surprising that some of the priests tried to break down the restrictions. We hear of two conflicts between the flamen of Quirinus and the pontifex maximus, in which the central issue is whether this flamen (who was not debarred from political office) should be allowed to leave Italy. The pontifex took his stand on the principle that as priest the office-holder must stay in Rome for the rites and sacrifices which he supervised; he should not therefore undertake the government of a province overseas. In one case the thwarted office-holder was so angry at the opposition (perhaps motivated by family and political intrigue) that he tried to give up his flaminate. He was dissuaded from this and compensated by a different office which would require his continued presence in Rome.

The priest most burdened by taboos and restrictions was the *flamen Dialis*. The undesirability of the office is shown by the story that in 207 BC a certain C. Valerius Flaccus was compelled to take it;[35] he was something of a bad lot and it may be that his family wished to prevent him from proving a disgrace in public life. Flaccus, once he was appointed, seems to have changed his spots. He insisted on the right to attend senate meetings, a right which had apparently been allowed to lapse because the flamens before him had been considered unworthy. Later on he became an aedile and overcame the taboo on taking an oath by getting a representative to do so on his behalf. This tale of repentant energy is attractive but may well be untypical of most such priests. The office was not filled for a long period in the first century BC, though it was brought back by Augustus. But the restrictions on the office were still maintained in the early Empire. An attempt in AD 22 to combine the office with a provincial governorship was rejected by the Emperor Tiberius after consultation with the pontiffs of whom he was the chief.[36] It is clear that on the whole these flamens could rarely enjoy a satisfying career in politics or administration. We noticed above that a passage in Livy paints a grim picture of a coming era of austerity for the patricians; the idea is that they will be ousted by usurping plebeians and will find themselves restricted to some inglorious religious posts. It is true that the political offices were the prime target of plebeian aspiration. But though the plebeians did not want to be eligible for the restrictive priesthoods they were not averse to becoming pontiffs and augurs. These posts did not decline but became ornamental adjuncts of the new aristocracy based on high office; a hero who had been both consul and pontiff could surpass a mere consul (other distinctions being equal).

Appointment to the chief colleges, the pontificate and augurate, was therefore highly valued. We should glance briefly at their main functions before considering their political importance. Pontiffs were responsible for the correct ritual in the state cults and, as we saw, supervised the lesser priests who were deemed to be within their college, the flamens and the vestal virgins. They concerned themselves with the provisions in temple charters and with temple etiquette; when the general Marcellus wished to dedicate a single temple to Honos and Virtus they raised objections on the grounds that one room (*cella*) should not house more than one god.[37] They decided what sort of work was permissible on holidays and could determine which places were officially sacred in the eyes of the state and which were 'religious places', privately consecrated by individuals but not binding on the state. They were supposed to be responsible for intercalation of the calendar when required, though their shortcomings here led to confusion in the Republican period and arouse the suspicion that they were corrupt as well as dilatory. Augurs, for their part, were concerned with the observation of signs, with discovering whether or not there was any impediment to action. The signs could be of two kinds, either casual or deliberately sought. Much augural lore (as the etymology suggests) was concerned with interpreting the behaviour and flight of birds. When an augur decided to 'observe the heavens' he would mark out the sky as a *templum*, with notional divisions, a procedure which was also followed when temples were erected. In the course of time these colleges built up a learned tradition, with sacred books. Other groups of priests or priest-like figures also played their part in discovering the will of the gods. The *haruspices* were specialists in a subject borrowed from the Etruscans and could interpret the entrails of sacrificed animals; the Sibylline books were supervised by decemvirs, who might be required to see if they contained a prophecy suited to a particular occasion.

The political importance of the pontificate can be shown in several ways. The plebeians, in the struggle of the orders, sought the right to become pontiffs and finally gained it by the Ogulnian law of 300 BC. Whether pontiffs should be elected or co-opted was a political issue at times in the late Republic; by a law of 103 BC, which was reversed by Sulla only to be restored in 63 BC, the college was required to name candidates, some of whom were then elected by a minority of the tribes voting in the assembly (17 out of 35). The office of pontifex maximus was coveted and filled by great politicians; this honorific tradition was furthered under the Empire and lasted until the office was declined by the Emperor Gratian.

It is not that this office or the post of ordinary pontiff gave political power as such. Such posts were additional distinctions, conferred both on men of promise and on those who had already achieved great success in the world of affairs. The augurate was similar. Cicero, as a man whose family was new to high political office, was delighted when he became a member of the college. The political change from oligarchical Republic to Empire made the religious distinctions even more valuable. The emperor would appoint close relatives as pontiffs, and lesser men too felt that a place in the augural college was a sign of imperial approval. It is noticeable that the two main colleges had gradually increased in size during the Republic. The three pontiffs of earlier times, for example, had become sixteen by the time of Julius Caesar. The oligarchy of the Republic saw some point in allowing the honours to be more widely spread among the ruling families, and the Empire had a like need to offer distinctions to its high dignitaries. The pontifical college had expanded in other ways as well, since it devolved some of its ceremonial activities on the group called *epulones*, who took their name from one of their functions, organizing banquets in honour of Jupiter.

The members of the colleges could only influence the senate or the officers of state in an advisory way. Decisions of the pontiffs were not laws but decrees, effective by force of custom or because they were supported by a senatorial majority. Augural observations were not always acted upon even when reported, as the officials might choose to turn a blind eye, but they would themselves run a grave risk if their course of action turned out to be a failure. Theoretically, as Cicero claimed,[38] augural activity could prevent a meeting or allow it to take place; elections and other political activities were therefore at the mercy of what an augur saw. But the religious order was not independent of the political. It too was composed of senior statesmen and aspirants to high office. The same personnel appeared in both. There was scope for the religious officers to block the actions proposed by politicians (e.g. by indicating a flaw in procedure) but their attempted veto was not always based on respect for religious tradition. Often they acted from a political conviction, in an attempt to move a political dispute on to grounds of religion and so cool an argument about policy by referring to standards that might seem more 'objective', making an appeal to religious custom (a form of persuasion rather than force) instead of using a blunt instrument like the political veto.[39] This device sometimes helped to relax political tensions, but it often failed, mainly because religious tradition was lacking in independent force and because the priests were themselves too much a part of the political order.

I have already pointed out that the system accumulated gods, that although the new deities did not in theory drive out the old the latter in practice tended to fade into the background. Much the same thing could happen to the temples which housed the gods; those which became less significant for the community in its changed circumstances were often less well maintained. Some priesthoods too became the victims of circumstance. The fetials,[40] whose function had been to declare war on other states by casting a spear as a symbolic gesture against enemy territory, were less useful when Rome became involved in wars with distant enemies. Piety sought to add without taking away, but some of the religious past gradually ceased to make sense and could then be shored up only by an act of self-conscious archaism. By comparison with political offices religious posts could not make much institutional impact; they were held for life (except when outrageous misconduct called for dismissal) and they could not be easily organized into a career structure. The yearly tenure of political office made it possible to devise a system in which a career advanced upwards towards the greatest honour, the consulship. It was possible to increase the number of office-holders in two ways, by extending a command (so that the consul, for example, became a proconsul) and by making more posts available, with the result that more aspirants could at least become quaestors or praetors. The priestly colleges were increased in the latter way, for honorific reasons, not because more pontiffs, augurs and so on were urgently needed by the administration. The most prestigious post was that of pontifex maximus, but in general there was some uncertainty about the relative standing of the colleges.

The gods, temples and priests are our main guide to the state of civic polytheism. They show us a society which felt a strong dependence on a sense of the other world but which also sought to control the effects of religious experience on crowd behaviour. Just as the Romans did not allow political assembly without a magistrate, so too they frowned on collective worship that had not been authorized by the priests. The readiness to accept new gods was offset by a conservatism which liked to keep a close link with the past. Here are two themes of the greatest importance in Roman history: the sense that religious expression should be formalized and not be vented immoderately, and the feeling that practices can be justified or included if they fit in with traditional beliefs. Concern for the correct expression of religious feeling and the need to preserve tradition (*mos*) without giving offence are subjects that will recur in the following pages.

## CHAPTER TWO

# *The Late Republic*

From the second Punic War to the civil war between Caesar and Pompey two great changes occurred, one in Rome's position as a world power, the other an internal revolution which led to the overthrow of the aristocracy. Rome in short acquired an empire but was not able to prolong the Republican system under which she had defeated the other great powers. The political direction is clear even if there is disagreement about the reasons for Roman imperialism and about the causes of the internal political revolution. But religious developments, so far as they affected political life, are more obscure; there is no obvious conclusion so clearly absorptive of all the religious past, nothing corresponding to the talent shown by political Augustanism, with its ability to make something new out of the political tradition.

I have chosen here to discuss three aspects of religion in politics in the belief that they are representative of the changes that took place. Firstly it seems that the period as a whole can be characterized as an age of expanding institutions, which gave politicians the means of extending or multiplying the honours available to them. All the phases of Roman civic polytheism (it should be said) exhibit in various degrees the characteristics of concern for tradition, partial neglect of that tradition, and acquisition of new gods and practices. But in this period the novelties and accretions seem particularly important; the new gods and increased offices were an essential part of the aristocratic honour-system; and they should be emphasized if only because they are an obstacle to that uncomplicated view of religion which decries the late Republic as a time of religious decline.

The other topics concern the function of religion in foreign war and in civil disputes. The war against Hannibal shows how religious institutions were adapted or borrowed as the Romans faced the most serious invasion in their history. The civil conflicts, including the civil wars, after 133 BC, provide evidence that the civic gods could be manipulated by both sides and that religion thereby gave some scope for the more moderate expression of disagreements. The theme, in summary form, is that religion helped the war effort and that it later become of use as a weapon of political argument.

Historians have often asserted or implied that this was an age of religious decline. Some have mostly had in mind that increased variety of religious practices which were brought to Rome by the expanding Republic and its successful generals. The anthropomorphic god in his different names and guises is not welcomed by these admirers of the Roman past; they assume that by the late Republic the putative innocence of early Rome had been lost and that the purity of the tribe was sullied by exposure to Hellenization. They may differ about the date of the supposed decline – a case has been made for early in the second Punic War, and another argument prefers a later date – but these differences are immaterial compared with the shared sense that the simple religion of the first Rome was lost or spoiled by imported religion.[1] Some historians have argued that imported ideas were a destructive force in the second century BC, when Greek intellectual influence made its mark at Rome and brought disbelief in its train. For these thinkers decline means either the practice of alien cults, entailing the neglect of true or early Roman religion, or the exposure to sceptical ideas, an education in theories which led to irreligion. The former version portrays the Romans as a people who lost their faith because they had too many gods, and the latter sees them as a people who learned to lose it from their Greek teachers.

These ideas are discussed at various places in the text. In general they are a modern expression of the sense of guilt which was already something of a commonplace among the writers of the first Augustan age. It is part of their modernity that they exhibit the scholar's nostalgia for the thought world of a primitive and supposedly better Rome, untouched by alien ways; they betray too the conviction (which has been popular with many Christians) that any religion is better than none and that every philosophy must have a cold touch. It will however be apparent from the introduction that my approach to civic religion is not concerned with origins. It seems better to insist on a definition of Roman religion that comprises all the cults and practices that became official in the city; to say that Roman was what Roman did. We may then reach a clearer understanding of the relationship between religion and politics in the late Republic and early Empire, clearer than if we measure these later times against an idealized but hardly knowable early Rome. Nor is it the case that the Romans learned nothing but disbelief from Greek philosophy. It is important to remember that much Greek philosophy was theistic and that the Romans could therefore learn from the Greeks a justification of their own cults and practices. Lastly, there is the matter of manipulation. It is always tempting to suppose that manipulation of religion is not compatible with belief; but the fact is that manipulation can co-exist with a wide range of attitudes and is not confined to those who have lost faith completely.

*Expansion*

The period as a whole from the Punic War to the death of Caesar was characterized by conquest and expansion outside Italy. Even hard times like the Hannibalic War saw the annexation of Sicily, and the civil wars of the first century BC were no obstacle to the acquisition of new provinces in the north and east. It is not surprising that the career structure was enlarged, partly because more officials were needed. In much the same way, in order to provide more posts of the ceremonial kind, religious offices had increased by the middle of the first century BC. Games and supplications took up more time, and more space, both inside and outside the boundary, was occupied by temples. The number of the priesthoods grew steadily; the pontificate and augurate especially were increased whereas the earlier priestly institution, the flaminates, continued unchanged. The effect of expansion in these different spheres was not uniform but the same tendency is noticeable throughout: it is a process of adding to religious forms because the politician can make use of them to express his superiority not to the gods but to his would-be peers.

Official games took up more time in the civic calendar, though the increase did not encroach on the time available for legal or political business. Some of the existing games received additional days and entirely new ones were introduced. Thus by the end of the Republic the 'Roman games' were allotted fifteeen days. The extra time allotted for this long-standing entertainment had a like effect on subsequent arrivals. In this expanding system the games for Sulla's victory, like those for Caesar's later on, had to be of fair or moderate length simply to make an impact on the public and to add to the donor's prestige; the former rated seven, the latter fifteen days.

Games were often instituted as a recognition of god's services to man. Gratitude was perhaps most apparent in the case of those games which were votive, intended to be a unique return for granted prayers, but many of the games were so popular that they were repeated every year. In this way the act of commemoration gradually loosened its close attachment to the event which had inspired it. Even if homage directed towards a god initiated the games, it seems that honouring the state officials became more important and rewarding for the electorate than thanking the gods. Older games, such as those in honour of Consus, had been organized by the pontiffs.[2] The expanding games from the second Punic War and later were put on by men with careers to make or finish, the aediles and the urban praetor. The games therefore were a chance to impress the electorate. The political scope of these occasions was increased when it became possible to vow games without earmarking the exact sum. Expenditure had formerly depended on a vote from the senate; but in 200 BC a proposal to vow games without specifying the sum was approved by the pontifical college even though the chief pontiff himself had doubted whether it was sound.[3] It is easy to suppose that his objections were legalistic and political, but political considerations alone probably weighed with his colleagues. It was only prudent for them to remember that as men in public life they had nothing to gain by keeping to the traditional practice; the new scheme might be of advantage to them as ambitious individuals, for they already were, or hoped to be, career politicians as well as pontiffs, and could help their own future by freedom to spend on games.

This outline suggests that it may be right to posit a change of the following kind between the second Punic War and the end of the Republic. At the beginning an office-holder administers an entertainment, financed by the senate, for the war-stricken people of Rome. The function of the event is to express a sense of obligation to the gods and to restore or distract the people. Towards the end of the Republic the office-holder has become more important as he stakes his own future on the success of the event; he has escaped from a financial bondage imposed by the senate and is able to spend his war-profits as he wishes; any military threat to Rome is far more distant than during the Carthaginian occupation of Italy, and the people therefore are less conscious of the need to thank the gods for their relief; they are instead sitting in judgment on politicians. The political implications are clear; the individual has increased his freedom of action, the senatorial hold on the purse-strings has weakened, and politicians are judged more by the amusements they provide. The functions of good games have now shifted; they are both aesthetic (the test is do the games please the people?) and power-orientated (will they further the politician's career?).

This model is only partially helpful. It clarifies the political change and indicates an aristocratic society made unstable through the altered roles of senate, politician and people. It is far less clear about religion. In a sense it implies that the gods have become less important than the politicians who produce and stage this particular form of their cult. As the festivals lengthen, so the particular act that honours the god is diminished; a procession to a god at the start of an eight-day festival marks time for the god less emphatically than when the event is only two or three days. These remarks will satisfy the prejudice of those who describe the late Republic as an age of religion in decline, on the alleged grounds that patriotic Romans lost their grasp of their own Roman religion, or were seduced by scepticism, or treated religion merely as an entertainment with political value. They may be countered by other observations that the religious sense was not wholly lost or reduced. It is true that the politician, as the source of tangible benefit, becomes more and more important, but he is still remembered as the associate of a god and the latter has not been ousted. Also, many of the rites in honour of gods were unchanged, so that Jupiter-banquets remained as the centre-piece of the Roman games in September and the Plebeian games in November. Cult, therefore, when examined from this point of view, shows both the conservatism and flexibility that have to be predicated of this kind of civic polytheism; the god's statue is still present at the games but his human agent has now claimed more of the honour and gratitude. The growing ascendancy of the politician has a religious parallel in the particular honours offered to the goddess Roma and to outstanding individuals; but this was a religious development which at this stage was important only in the provinces, it did not become metropolitan until the Empire.

Games in the sense discussed here consist of stage performance (scenic games) and the circus-shows, with animal and human combats. Scenic games were mostly held in a different venue from the circus-shows. The Megalesian games, first instituted in 204 BC, were celebrated 'in front of the temple'. The goddess was required to watch as the honoured spectator, and the games therefore must be held in her sight.[4] Rome did not have a permanent theatre made of stone until Pompey's theatre, which was built in 55 BC and contained four other shrines, was dedicated as a temple to Venus Victrix. The steps which took the visitor up to the temple were also the seats for the audience as it looked down on the stage. Those who are convinced of Rome's moral decline have all been hostile to Pompey's theatre; they have disapproved of it as a house of lewdness in which idle spectators could amuse themselves with immoral art. These critics draw a contrast with the Romans of an earlier age, who were supposedly ruled by stern censors, officials who prohibited or destroyed theatres. Even in antiquity Pompey was accused of hypocrisy on the grounds that he dare not call a theatre a theatre but had to make it a pretend-temple to Venus. But the charge of hypocrisy does not matter much. The incident shows that there was religious continuity – the god's presence was still needed at the games – which to Pompey and his contemporaries seemed entirely in accord with tradition. The same theatre was dedicated again by the emperor Claudius and enjoyed a long life throughout the Empire.[5] The god survived not just as the politician's subordinate but as the indispensable overseer.

As a ceremony the games are sometimes found in conjunction with supplications. Before the war with Antiochus in 191 BC the senate decreed a preventive supplication and the consul in charge vowed games to be held after victory. Both sets of actions were intended to placate the gods. At the end of a campaign the games and supplications became rituals of thanksgiving instead of pleas and promises to deity. Thanksgiving supplications were affected by the same gigantism that made existing games longer and introduced new ones. By the late Republic supplications too had become more of an honour paid to politicians, less of a service thanking god. Cicero's award to Pompey in 63 BC is sometimes said to have been the first symptom of this particular inflation.[6] In fact the tendency throughout the second century BC was for supplications to be allocated between three and five days. The increase became more pronounced and more extreme in the period of intense civil struggles. Pompey's ten days seem few compared with the twenty offered to Caesar in 52 BC, and this number itself looks small compared with the awards of 43 BC when the going rate had advanced to fifty days.

The political significance of the development is clear. Increase in size, as with the games, tended to direct attention from the god to the politicians and generals. Those whose victories had deserved a supplication, great generals such as Pompey and Caesar, were rivalled or surpassed by pygmies who were determined to make themselves a monument. But the changing function of supplications should not make us suppose that the gods were entirely excluded from a thanksgiving which was now rendered exclusively to politicians. There is of course a marked contrast between the supplications of the Punic War and those in the late Republic. It is tempting to characterize the former war-period as a time when people felt genuine religious emotion and thanked the gods in their temples for their deliverance. The three- or four-day sessions allotted to thanksgiving make up periods which seem more than justified by the events in the Hannibalic war, and the time allowed for expressing public emotion is psychologically feasible. At the later date, by contrast, it seems incredible that the people could genuinely respond for forty or fifty days, to thank the gods for petty events or successes of controversial value. However, it does not follow that in the emotional outbursts of the second Punic War a grateful people thought only of gods whereas later they thought only of politicians. Supplications and games both led to the magnification of politicians but neither the latter nor their followers thought of doing without gods or eventually dispensing with the ascription of godhead to humans. The changes I have described were at work in a society which was always ready to introduce new gods, expressing the acquisitive dynamic of the divine order as Romans conceived it. This is not to say that men were dupes or cynics but that the natural progression was to new gods, not to no gods at all. The political failure of the aristocracy is clear but it was matched by religious developments that are more difficult to understand. Religion and politics were close partners, but this does not mean that their development was alike or that politics grew by choking religion. The fact that politicians could project themselves as the protégés of gods argues that religion was still vital in the public sphere.

From 218 BC onwards there was a steady increase in temple-building. State expenditure on public buildings covered many works including roads, aqueducts and basilicas; the erection of temples and some other amenities (manubial building) was usually financed by generals from their war-booty, with the result that monies from the conquered were used to satisfy both private ambition and public display.[7] An important exception is the temple of Jupiter, destroyed by fire in 83 BC and rebuilt (in part at least) through a sort of public subscription; the implication is that Romans and Italians might be expected to pay something for or towards the chief god, who was bound to be expensive, and that they would naturally expect the temples of other gods to be financed by victories in war.[8] Many such temples were vowed by commanders at a moment of crisis, in the hope of victory. The building itself, usually finished and dedicated a few years later, enabled the victor to pay his obligations and impress the electorate. Temples (the inauguration ceremony often included games) were a politician's monument to himself as well as an offering to the gods. Buildings became more lavish, and marble for a god's residence was not unknown at Rome even before the Augustan age. As a way of keeping a name before the public it may be doubted whether temples did as much for the politician as for the god. It is true that some families maintained their connection with a temple that had been founded by an ancestor; descendants for example were sometimes willing and able to pay for repairs; and one of the Gracchi family put a picture of some men he had liberated in a temple of Libertas which had been built by his father.[9] The founder's statue was often present too as a reminder to the public of a family's achievement. Some temples put the politician on a par with or even in front of the deity – men called the temple of Honos and Virtus the monument of Marius – but it seems that most were named after the gods who dwelt in them and in this sense they were less effective as a device for commemorating men than other buildings were. It was usual, for example, to have a portico named after the founder, as with the portico of Metellus.

We should remember that the Romans of this time were men who often advertised themselves by exhibiting *one* set of games and by building *one* temple. These men, as Julius Caesar might have said, did not know their ABC of politics and religion, if they retired from building with only one temple to their credit. Accumulation of temples by a single individual did not become common till the time of Caesar and Augustus. As a practice it is not in accord with the political values of the Republic. The temples of the Republic lacked the immediacy of games and supplications and were therefore less useful to the self-advertisement of politicians; and in this sphere the gods perhaps managed to stay as the equals of the politicians.[10]

If it is thought that the ambitious did not fully exploit the potentialities of the temple we should look at the matter in a numismatic context. Coins show that Romans were used to acknowledging a tutelary deity; and through coins the association between a family and a god could be made more obvious than with a temple. Some families had private festivals which linked them to a particular god, though perhaps it was a deity who was not very important. Many other families, not just the Cornelii who might be expected to show family pride in Scipio's visits to the Capitol, used coins to claim an association with Jupiter. The moneyer Pomponius Musa put the temple of Hercules and the Muses on a coin not because of a family connection with the founder but because he wished to parade the similarity of name.[11] Coins, it seems, were good visual agents; they made it possible for individual Romans to associate pictorially with important gods like Jupiter and Hercules, gods who were highly regarded by all Romans; whereas some temples were in honour of deities without a Jupiter-reputation, so to speak, they might be no more than minor gods like the Lares Permarini for instance who were installed in 179 BC.

The argument suggests that the gods in their temples were exploited but not eclipsed by the politician-generals. The buildings, with their dedicated objects, were expensive, another sign that senatorial control had weakened and that individuals in the élite could spend as they wished. The greater generals showed their singularity in yet another way, by exploiting a conviction which was shared by many, the conviction that they had a special relationship with a god. The first in time, in some ways the least showy, was Scipio Africanus, who cultivated Jupiter and frequented the Capitol. Three of the later generals were befriended by a deity who did not have the urban importance of Jupiter but still became an increasing part of Rome's early historical legend; in this way the goddess Venus was the protector in turn of Sulla, Pompey and Caesar. There were many advantages in having a deity behind one; it helped to inspire confidence and loyalty and made the beneficiary seem personally auspicious. It is tempting to suppose that the men who gained from the religious sentiment of the masses were more enlightened than their followers, that they took advantage of this irrational attachment while shrugging their shoulders in disbelief. But it is impossible to elicit the generals' private or individual views on their public actions. We may however compare the ways in which the generals continued the traditional practice of making the gods an ornament of Rome. Here the significant change was that they discovered new forms of deity. We might start with the assumption that Scipio represents the norm because of his familiarity with Jupiter, the supreme civic deity. By comparison the later generals may seem eccentric because their choice falls on gods and practices that are less central; Marius and Sulla, for example, were fortunate leaders whose good luck had a religious appeal and was set up with its own apposite deity. This kind of comparison is likely to be more productive than speculation, in the manner of Livy, on whether Scipio could really have believed what he practised.[12] Lastly, we should remember that leaders in civil affairs could inspire the same sort of emotion as leaders in war. The army's enthusiasm for a general has a parallel in the civilian veneration for those cherished politicians, the Gracchi; after their death people offered sacrifice and worshipped their statues as though they were gods. Similarly, the emotion that acclaimed Julius Caesar in his lifetime expressed itself in building an altar after his death.[13]

The richest evidence concerning the relationship between religion and the political order comes from the priesthoods. The flaminates (as we saw earlier) became less important and the political scope of those who held them was restricted. The fact that the office of *flamen Dialis* was not filled for many years after 87 BC should probably not be used as a proof that religion had declined; rather, it shows negatively that men wanted religious posts that could advance a great career or be compatible with it. Julius Caesar tells us as a proof of his enemies' confidence before the battle of Pharsalus that some of them were already arguing about the succession to him as chief pontiff; they were wanting to share out the fruits of victory well before the armies had engaged in battle.[14] The major colleges of priests, the pontiffs and augurs, were increased in number, and a new college, the epulones, was established in 195 BC. The number of decemvirs was also raised, and after Sulla's changes there were fifteen posts available in each of the major colleges, together with the seven epulones. The increase shows that such posts were in demand. But why? What purpose did they serve?

It may be a shock to the modern idea of what constitutes religion to discover that the new college was often concerned with organizing banquets. But these were enjoyable occasions when social harmony was expected in the presence of a god. At a banquet in honour of Jupiter there was a reconciliation between two old enemies, Scipio and Gracchus, and they sealed their new friendship by arranging an inter-family marriage. The importance of such banquets in the religious contexts of antiquity has been aptly described by a French scholar as a 'thanksgiving from the stomach' (*reconnaissance du ventre*).[15] Religious entertainments of this type were not confined to the rich but were common among the less well-off.

Some of the ground-rules for elections to the pontificate and augurate did not change. Usually when vacancies were filled a patrician could only be succeeded by a patrician, and so too with a plebeian vacancy.[16] The practice was essentially an archaism, a reminder of the time when plebeians first won the right to have a share in the priesthoods which had for long been exclusive. It was not usual for two men from the same *gens* to hold posts in the augural college at the same time. The rule was evaded by adoption out of the *gens* so that the law was observed 'in the letter rather than the spirit as was Roman custom'.[17] Similarly it was unusual for one man to be both pontiff and augur. These customs all point in the same direction. They show us an aristocracy eager to create offices that could be shared out and anxious if possible to ensure that no one person or family-group should take too much. The tradition maintained that relations within a college should be harmonious. In theory it was not expected that the members would be forced into close contact with their enemies in the Roman sense; 'no one could even be co-opted as a priest who was the enemy of a member of the college.'[18] This priestly idyll, so unlike the political scene, was missing after 63 BC when the custom of excluding personal enemies was no longer observed. But the tradition of harmony may only mean that there was not the same scope for bitter disagreement in religion that there was in politics.

The competitive energy of politicians had an overflow effect on the quieter offices of pontifex and augur. Symbols of the augurate[19] were put on coins by men who were not themselves members of a college; in this case they were usually showing off the achievement of an augural ancestor. For most of the second century vacancies in the pontifical college were filled by co-option, and only the chief pontiff was appointed by election. But important changes were made in 103, in Sulla's time, and in 63 BC. The purpose of the first and last changes was to substitute a mixed procedure, with election *and* co-option, with the result that in the contests for the office of chief pontiff the electors were gratified by their novel influence and smiled on two advocates of the change, Domitius in 103 and Julius Caesar in 63 BC. The offices therefore began to look like political offices even though they were usually held for life. It is unlikely that the posts were sought because they carried with them certain rights, such as a higher speaking place in the senatorial debating order.[20] They were distinctions which kept a politician in the public eye. In one respect they were extremely curious. In the first part of this period most of the pontiffs, augurs and decemvirs were appointed at a tender age, when they had not yet held higher political office. Again, towards the end of the period, to judge from a list in Cicero, five pontiffs were of consular standing whereas six had not yet reached the rank of praetor.

Our figures are nothing like complete but such as they are they suggest that appointment was made sooner rather than later in a career.[21] Confirmation of this can be found in some of the elections to the position of pontifex maximus. In the 212 election Licinius Crassus, not yet an aedile, defeated two men who had both been consul and censor; he was the first for 120 years to reach the highest religious office with such poor credentials. Similar elections occurred later. Aemilius Lepidus was elected in 180 BC 'even though many great men were competing', and (most famous of all) Caesar (who had entered the college in 74) beat several established politicians in the election of 63. The religious offices tended to be used for political satisfactions but they had an important characteristic which is the reverse of that found in the political offices. In theory it was not possible to hold high political office except at certain stages; advancement there was formalized and the dates in a career were more or less predictable, but the religious offices could be held early in life. Hence the latter allowed younger men scope for a distinction which was denied them elsewhere. The office of pontifex maximus especially could be described as a sort of rogue institution which broke the rules and norms expected of men in aristocratic politics without giving them power to do much harm. It bestowed a certain freedom not allowed in the non-religious political offices, the controlling institutions, but it gave no power to effect changes.

The pontificate and augurate have been described not as honours but as offices that facilitated entry into public life. Young men from great families came to expect co-option or election to these offices quite early in their careers. New politicians would be acclaimed later in life, after their political or military triumphs. But though the new men, the Ciceros of the Roman world, came late to augury, they found it natural to canvass and expect the office for their sons in their early manhood. In assessing the extent to which these religious offices were honours we should always remember that in the political sense they merely helped to move a career somewhat forward, they were not a fixed hurdle in the course. More concretely, all praetors (it may be supposed) were heartbroken if they failed to become consuls, but not all consuls were so bitterly disappointed if they failed to make the grade as pontifex, before or after the consulate.

There were some obvious political advantages to the position of pontifex maximus. The consuls of 131 BC for instance were in dispute over which of them should make war on the pretender Aristonicus.[22] One of them was chief pontiff and was therefore able to insist that his consular colleague, a mere flamen of Mars, should not leave his rites unattended. There were not many occasions when the pontificate was so directly useful to a politician's ambitions of the moment. A particular form of pontifical intervention shows how far the holder of the office could expect to go. On several occasions the chief pontiff, as a way of stopping action he considered undesirable, imposed a fine on the supposed offender. The offender would then appeal to the people to have the fine cancelled. The usual result of the appeal was support for the pontiff's policy and at the same time remission of the fine. Thus in the cases known to us one magistrate who also holds priestly office attempts to control or discipline another politician, as the holder of a lesser priestly office. His success is partial and there are limits to the political punishment he seeks to inflict. A pontiff-consul could therefore expect to outmanoeuvre a consul who was not a pontiff; his inverventions were usually supported by the assembly to which they were referred, but he got his way without his opponent suffering too great a penalty.

Most of the expansion described here was of more political than religious significance. In the games and supplications the politician became more prominent than the god; and the increase in the number of priesthoods gave the ambitious a taste of office before their political acme was due. The new temples did not make the same impact on politics; their gods were often less central than Jupiter and the existing temples would have been sufficient for senate meetings and other business. But to interpret these developments correctly we have to think of the élite as men who were bent on modifying religion not on destroying it. By expanding the forms of religious expression the politician made it possible for himself and for his followers to accept what Toynbee has called 'man-worship', a phase when man makes himself at home among the gods.

### *The Second Punic War*

Most historians have felt justified in assuming that the final years of the third century BC were a critical period in Roman history. Their argument is in the end based on Hannibal's occupation of Italy, from 217 to 204 BC, and on the heavy losses sustained by Rome in the great battles of the second Punic War. The early years of the war especially brought casualties and defeats on a huge scale, the more overwhelming as they had not been expected. The military setbacks were accompanied by political humiliations, the secession of Rome's friends and allies, many of whom were confident that Carthage would eventually win. Though it may be an exaggeration to say that there was also a religious crisis, it is certainly true that morale at Rome showed a noticeable edginess, and religious practices were quite naturally made to contribute to the war-effort. The impact of the war on religion should be considered in the broader context, to allow for the period immediately after Hannibal's defeat as well as the war years themselves.

We might expect to find that civic religion of the Roman type would express its anxiety by acquiring new gods to help the state in its hour of need, so that the early Roman defeats of the Trebia, Lake Trasimene and Cannae would then be countered by an optimism rooted in new cults. The initial setbacks spurred the Romans on to set right some religious omissions. Thus a temple to Concord had been vowed in 220 BC; the contract for building it had still not been let in 217 BC and as Hannibal's victories seemed to be convincing evidence of the divine anger officials were appointed to get the work done quickly.[23] Temples to Venus Erucina and Mens were vowed in 217 BC and were finished by 215. The importance of these buildings is shown by their position – they were sited on the Capitol – and by the fact that they were put up with some haste. Religious activity of this sort was a useful means of persuading everybody that the right steps were being taken, a point made by the great Fabius Cunctator when he commented that the defeat at Trasimene had been caused by the Roman general's failure to observe religious protocol. Many years passed before the Romans saw Hannibal leave Italy, but this emphasis on religious correctness at an early stage was meant to raise and sustain morale.

Temples were also vowed at later stages in the war. A temple of Virtus was promised in 208 (as an addition to the existing temple of Honos); in 207 Iuventas was vowed a temple, shortly before the battle of the Metaurus which denied Hannibal his reinforcing army; and in 204 a temple was vowed to Fortuna, and another god was imported from overseas, the stone which was held to represent the Great Mother, Cybele.[24] These last temples were not in fact dedicated till several years after the end of the war.

The political significance of some of this building is not wholly clear. There are question marks, for example, against the acquisition of Venus Erucina in 215 and of Cybele. Is it possible that the temple to Venus represents an attempt by Rome to emphasize the connection between Rome, Sicily and Aeneas by showing courtesy to the famous shrine on Mt Eryx?[25] Similarly one might wonder whether the Roman invitation to the stone of Pessinus was part of a diplomatic encirclement of Hannibal's ally Macedon.[26] The temple to Mens (it has been argued) may have been an integral part of a religious policy directed against the dominant good fortune of Hannibal.[27] Such details of the immediate political context are uncertain and are likely to remain the subject of speculation. But the siting of these temples, their central position, shows how important they were thought to be, as the dwellings of gods who were the guarantors of ultimate victory. The men who vowed or dedicated them were agents of the senate's collective will, being more concerned to represent a victorious state than to dominate the élite themselves from within. If the norm of the second century is set by the generals who offer a temple to be built out of easy money, their predecessors, the generals of the second Punic War, faced greater difficulties; their enemy was more elusive (for a while he must have seemed invincible) and, except for the plunder of Syracuse, the victories of Rome brought little reward until the final defeat of Carthage.

At this stage in their history the Romans were not sure of themselves as full peninsular beings, let alone as the advancing rulers of an empire which might require long absences from the city. Their armies were made up of citizen-soldiers, and departures from Rome were solemnized by their commanders' appearance before Jupiter on the Capitol. The troops of this era were therefore quite different from the imperial soldiers who still owed some allegiance to Jupiter but who were also tied to the gods of their unit and sometimes to the gods of the provinces in which they were stationed. It is not a difference between belief and scepticism but between qualities of cult attached to various objects. By the time of this Punic War, the Romans had come to know forms of Hellenization by contact with the Greek staging-posts in Italy. They had not yet become familiar with the Greek homeland of the anthropomorphic god, there were in Rome relatively few easterners with their gods, and so the emotional geography[28] of the Romans in religion was still localized in Rome. Citizens and wives were devoted to the deities which had helped to thrust Hellenization on to the city from relatively close at hand. Some forms of this Hellenization were multiplied by the war with Hannibal as we shall now explain.

Some of the ceremonies and practices, which were introduced in the course of the Hannibalic war, functioned (in part at least) as entertainment. The people could not sustain a war effort on this scale without a degree of relaxation from the more obvious religious anxieties about unnatural portents and signs. At this date (217–216 BC) the Saturnalia was still a country festival, and the god Saturn, in spite of having a long-established temple in the forum, did not have the standing of the greater civic gods. By the reform of 217 the festival was turned into an annual ceremony and became a great urban occasion, a kind of unity through entertainment. This is not to say that the well-known features of the Saturnalia as it was celebrated in later Rome were installed at a stroke by a single decree. Features of the Saturnalia – exchanges of presents, dining and a sense of holiday – were tokens of civilized living in the eyes of the Romans of the Empire except for the moralist who complained that the December holiday, which used to be no more than a month, had later come to usurp the whole year.[29] Very little is known in detail of the change introduced in 217 but it is safe to say that the intention was to provide some limited relaxation for the whole people. There would not have been time to spare for the lengthier Saturnalia that only developed in Rome once the city had survived the threats of defeat and occupation. It was far-sighted to make this sort of festivity an institution; carnival needed active encouragement in a society which had suffered greatly and which even had to curb the length of time allowed for the public expression of mourning.

Similar functions can be attributed to the new sets of games and to the great and imposing entertainment of gods, the *lectisternium* of 217 BC. The sum of money allocated to the Roman games was increased, and in 212 games for Apollo were decreed; at first these were voted on a yearly basis, and they were fitted into the calendar when the timing seemed right. Their popularity is shown by the fact that after four years they were made permanent and were given a regular date in the calendar. They show that the process of Hellenization could take several forms at once. There was a consultation of the Sibylline books, sacrifice was made in the Greek not the Roman manner, and the god thus honoured was clearly Greek. Games were also held to celebrate the arrival of Cybele in 204 BC. The function of the games was entertainment and something more; they gave the people a feeling of coherence and of participation in a rite which (so Livy put it) was concerned with winning the war. The people were dependent on the gods whom they honoured by a collection or (in the case of Cybele) by a special offering. The great gods' feast (*lectisternium*) of 217 was not in itself a novelty, for the first such occasion had been celebrated many years before, in 399 BC. The innovation of the Punic War consisted in the greater number of gods, twelve altogether, who were paired on six couches. By these means the gods' presence was exhibited in the intimacy of a ceremonial meal, and the people therefore were given the opportunity to meet for reassurance as well as for the obvious convivial purpose.[30]

The Rome of this time was able to find in religion great resources that made military defeats and the stresses of war more tolerable. Commitment to the struggle against Hannibal was expressed, also in 217, by the promise of a sacred spring.[31] The Romans vowed that if the state were to survive the next five years the god Jupiter would be honoured with the offering of the animal produce of the spring in a given year. Nothing else shows quite so clearly the majestic importance of Jupiter, who was thus honoured by the promise of the whole people. The vow was not finally settled until the years 195 and 194 BC. A reason for the delay is that although the prayer named a five-year period it also expected that full term would only come with the end of warfare against Gauls as well as Carthaginians, and a major defeat was not inflicted on the Gauls until 196 BC. Only then was it possible to give the god his due, though the political context in which Jupiter received his reward is extremely baffling. But on the other hand the purpose of the original vow is unmistakable; it committed the whole people to their chief god, it made an extravagant promise (a form of *potlatch*) which in the end did not apparently cost the farmers very much, and it secured the people by trusted formulae against the fear of sacrificing something at the wrong time by accident. The Romans were adepts in these byways of piety.

There can be little doubt, even if we discount many of the portents mentioned by Livy, that the war was a time when emotion naturally found a religious outlet. The Sibylline books prescribed the burial alive of two Gauls and two Greeks, a rite, if not a sacrifice, which has always been a great embarrassment to the friends of Rome's claim to be a civilized power.[32] Vestal Virgins were harshly punished for their alleged transgressions. Most supplications were of the preventive type and during them the temples were thronged with believers who had suffered or feared bereavement. On one occasion the incidence of mourning among the families of Rome was so widespread that it interrupted the celebration of an annual rite in honour of Ceres. Although Ceres was an old Roman deity, with games of her own, the process of assimilating her to Demeter had begun and at a date in the late third century a new rite of a Hellenized kind had been introduced. This was the rite which could not be completed when the news of their defeat at Cannae made the Romans realize that nearly every family was polluted by death. In order to make it possible for religious activity to continue the senate limited the period of mourning to thirty days.[33]

The above sketch shows some of the many ways in which religion functioned as part of the Roman resistance to Hannibal. But I doubt whether it is legitimate to speak of a religious crisis at this time, though it is tempting to posit a religious equivalent to the political and military setbacks experienced by Rome. The search for new deities continued a tendency that had long been at work; the Hellenization of religion was not new; and the increase in gods and the expansion of games were essential to civic polytheism of the Roman kind.

Some of the new gods may well have seemed to Romans of the time to represent a bold step into the supernatural and the unknown. But they do not make this impression on the historian who should consider the theme of acquiring gods in relation to Roman history as a whole. The gods of this period were brought in to help victory come near and so to raise morale among the people. It seems more apt to speak of religion at this time as the pliable and industrious servant of the military state in its hour of need. In affairs of state religion enjoyed a priority which proved of great value. It was authorized by the senatorial élite and so organized as to give the people a sense of full participation. We may infer from one or two passages in Livy that there was something of a division between town and country, but Livy also indicates that sharing in religion was a means of bringing the two groups together.[34]

The available evidence is not sufficient to enable us to judge how the ruling élite or the army were affected in their religious behaviour. But, surprisingly perhaps, there are more indications about that important, but less martial, group, the respectable married ladies and mothers of families. The matrons of the city played a key role in preventive supplications. During Hannibal's march on Rome in 211 BC, the matrons showed their alarm by public demonstrations at the temples and altars of the gods. They tried to affect the course of events by their prayers and their offering to Juno on the Aventine. In 207 BC they joined the young girls of the community in approaches to the gods and goddesses of the state; the girls were to go in procession, chanting a song composed by Livius Andronicus, while the matrons contributed some of their dowries to make an offering and then carried images made in cypress wood to present to Juno Regina.[35]

The conduct of matrons in events like these is, we might say, the historical basis of more familiar imaginative treatments in poetry. In the sack of Troy as described in the *Aeneid*[36] a crowd of women is portrayed round Priam's altar, and in another war scene, from the fighting in Italy, the women go with offerings to the temple and citadel of Pallas Athene. At critical moments such as these there is nothing for women to do but pray and attend to the gods whereas the males of the society have two other functions which are ostensibly prior to prayer: argument and fighting. Two passages in Livy very neatly (but not wholly intentionally) illustrate this division of function. Before the Romans hear that they have won the battle of the Metaurus the various groups are full of anxious anticipation; the senators are in constant attendance upon the officers of state, the non-combatant males are 'busy' waiting in the forum, and the ladies 'because there is no other resource in them' express themselves in prayer and frequent the temples. Contrast this form of preventive supplication with the jubilant scene which follows the news of victory; a thanksgiving supplication, three days in length, was attended by men and women together. The point is that once the danger is felt to be over men are liberated from what they suppose to be the near-dangerous or at least prestigious tasks of debating and waiting on events, so that they can now join the matrons of the state in expressing their thanks to gods. At this stage in events the senate orders the opening of the temples for all good citizens to attend.[37]

The women of Rome, it should be noted, although they came from a more advanced civilization and a relatively settled way of life, had much in common with their nomadic German sisters. The matrons of Rome were expected to put forth all their energies in prayer when the city was threatened; and similarly the stern ladies of the north would use prayer to exhort their menfolk in battle and were sometimes treated with religious veneration.[38] In both societies married women with children were among the most reliable and habitual devotees of the gods.

These incidents reveal something which was true of Roman society not only in the Punic War but also for many years after. Religion, that is, as a spiritual value, can be more readily predicated of women's life than of men's. The Turia obituary commemorates the lady as one who was 'religious but not superstitious'. If she is commended for sensitivity to her religious duties, the obituaries of men are apt to dwell on more tangible things, such as wealth and high office. When religion is mentioned it is often because of an association with office, the post of chief pontiff, for example, or because of acquaintance with pontifical law. Men are praised (in general) for having filled high positions, for having fine sons to survive them, for their victories in war, and so on.[39] The Romans had no difficulty in admiring the Scipio who defeated Hannibal for his generalship and political achievement, but they found his apparent religiosity at the temple of Jupiter a complicated phenomenon.

Perhaps we should say that the difference is between women's religion as a frequent activity and masculine religion as an activity on special occasions. Cicero says that 'his wife has worshipped the gods with purity and that he himself has been complaisant to the wishes of men', and the younger Cato is made to say by Sallust that the 'gods' help is not secured by prayers nor by women's supplications.' Remarks like these might lead us to suppose that religion is here disparaged as fit only for women. It would be better to say (though the difference has many shades) that religion is valued as the feminine complement of masculine action or debate, though stories from the Punic War show that it is proper for men to join in thanksgiving. An imaginative expression of the harsher male attitude comes in the *Aeneid* when Turnus tells the supernatural figure Allecto, who comes in the disguise of a crone, that she should stick to religion, leaving politics to men. Allecto, in reply, is incensed because he has failed to pierce the disguise in which she has appeared; but she does not quarrel with his idea about women's religious role. Religion (we might suggest) is the last rather than the habitual resort of the harassed male; Cicero's final act before leaving for exile was to dedicate a statue of Minerva on the Capitol.[40]

Control of religion throughout the Punic War and for some time after was safely in the hands of the senate. The conventional wisdom[41] of some modern scholars has tended to portray senatorial control as a force of repression, denying true spiritual fare to a people who were thus given stones instead of bread. The implied model here is on the one hand a power-hungry aristocracy based on tenure of office and on the other hand a god-hungry populace deprived of religious comfort. This interpretation may well be inspired by a modern regard for personal spirituality as a value and it has some support in events. In 212 BC it was noticed that foreign rites were being practised in public and a praetor was instructed to make himself available for the handing-over of prophetic works and manuals of sacrifice; sacrificing in a novel or alien manner was forbidden in a public place. In this case the senate's attitude was dictated in part by the laudable desire to stop quacks from imposing on gullible refugees from the country.[42] Clearly, too, the senate was determined to set itself up as the guardian of correct form in public worship. The charge of senatorial repressiveness seems better founded in the cases of the Cybele cult and of the Bacchanalian conspiracy. The goddess Cybele, as we have seen, was invited to Rome primarily as an emblem of a victory to come. The importation of Cybele was prompted by the senate after consultation with Delphi, and the goddess was officially welcomed by worthy citizens. But the cult was orgiastic and Roman citizens were forbidden to serve as priests. Even more serious (so the argument runs) was the suppression of the so-called Bacchanalian conspiracy in 186 BC and after. The cult of Bacchus or Dionysus had become widespread in Greek Italy; it was reported to the senate as an objectionable nuisance on the grounds that the worshippers formed secret societies and committed acts of sexual licence in mixed congregations of men and women. The senate's policing of this affair was intended to prevent large assemblies but it also allowed the cult to be observed by groups of not more than five, if the members could show that the worship was traditional.[43]

There are, it should be said, many puzzling features about the Dionysiac investigation of 186 BC. The Romans had a roughly equivalent god called Liber and there was nothing to stop the Dionysiac cult from enjoying full civic status, as was the case at Tarentum. It is easy to forget that Dionysiacism was not just an emotional religion, that it was capable of living up to the orthodoxies of the civic gods. But a solution of this kind, to invite the god to full membership of the Roman state, to introduce him through assimilation, was not acceptable to the authorities. They disapproved of Dionysiacism in its non-civic form, as a protest cult of an ecstatic type, popular with outsiders and with less respectable members of society.[44] For this reason alone it does not seem right to make the unqualified assertion that this form of Dionysiac worship was a means of spiritual liberation which was checked by the senate; if it was liberation it was giving spiritual release to a different group of women from that which had (not unwillingly) borne the hardships of the Punic War. An earlier incident, in which the censorious Cato argued in effect for sumptuary curbs, suggests that great Roman ladies had learnt like Roman men to crave display and wanted to impress the public by travelling in style. It is perhaps likely that they would have put the gratification of open esteem above (or at least on a level with) the secret and dangerous ecstasies of an unauthorized god. The official attack on the Dionysiac cult proscribed it in the short term as a public worship, but by allowing the cult to continue as a private religion it merely postponed the time when it would be strong enough to plead for inclusion among the gods of the state.

But the case against the senate as an upper-class body with no understanding of the people's spiritual needs is poor. Throughout the Punic War the senate's religious role, as far as one can judge, was managerial and on the whole non-coercive. It authorized ceremonies and rites which were acceptable to citizens and their wives. The matrons of Rome found that supplications and processions were adequate as means for expressing emotion of a religious type. The story as told by Livy suggests that rulers and the people alike were satisfied that the civic cults and the natural-seeming expansions of them were able to satisfy their wants.[45]

Why, then, has there been a marked tendency to decry Rome's civic religion in the Punic War and to criticize the senate for its alleged censoriousness? I suggest that the main reason is a failure to look at the evidence coupled with a lack of sympathy for civic polytheism. Modern scholars have usually been ready to interpret this kind of religion as manipulative and political in the bad sense, without recognizing that we may have to admit a compatibility between manipulation of religion and belief in religion. This distrust of the state's role in religion has been reinforced by other factors. Firstly, the antiquarian – and at times aesthetic, or even folksy – regard for an earlier, more truly Roman, religion has persuaded scholars to put a high value on the earlier religious practices of the countryside and of the traditional Roman family home. In the second place some interpreters have, understandably, been impressed (at a distance) by the orgiastic cults as a source of religious excitement or inspiration. In contrast with these cults from home and abroad, the civic ceremonies, casting a spell on all the citizens, can easily seem too coldly political a religion. Nostalgia for an earlier and a rural Rome, a Rome projected with such skill by Walter Pater in *Marius the Epicurean*, and an anthropological hankering after the ecstatic cults are two of the prejudices which have made it difficult for us to grasp this phase of Roman civic polytheism under siege and in battle.[46]

### *The Civil Conflicts*

It is often said that the late Republic was a period of religious decline from a state of original belief, a decline shown by the abuse of religious institutions for political purposes and by the loss of faith attributed to the dominant political class. This approach may be misleading for various reasons, including those which are in part the theme of the introduction and of the earlier part of this chapter. In the first place civic polytheism has the defect corresponding to its appetite for expansion; it has specialized gods and suffers, when it does, from *specific* neglect, and the result is that a particular cult may be long- or short-lived without impairing the vitality of the system as a whole. Secondly it is naive to suppose that Rome evolved or declined from a state of religion without manipulation to the disturbed conditions of the late Republic. It is probably better to make one's starting-point the maxim that there is no religion without manipulation, and that manipulation does not as such give proof of decline. Both neglect and manipulation are usually local rather than thorough and complete. The purpose of this section is to show how manipulation worked and to point out the different attitudes to religion within the élite; and secondly to set against the evidence of decline through neglect the increase in the cult of great individuals.

Religious manipulation is to be put against the background of the political struggles which affected religious institutions such as the priesthoods and the temples. We have already seen how the office of chief pontiff was politicized even more, by making the other pontificates the object of popular election. Temples were put to different uses from those which normally obtained at the time of foreign war. In civil conflicts, accompanied by urban fighting with all kinds of improvisation, it was to be expected that temples would become available as strong points. They were used for military purposes, mustering troops or for lying in ambush. During the Gracchan troubles Opimius, acting as the senatorial leader, occupied the temple of the Dioscuri, and the Gracchans took possession of Diana's temple on the Aventine. There were also attempts, understandable but usually pointless, to make use of temples as a refuge. In a later incident the supporters of the tribune Apuleius looked first of all for safety in the Capitoline temple; later they were moved to the senate house, also a temple, but the mob tore off the roof and stoned them to death. In the proscriptions ordered by Sulla men were put to death wherever they were found, 'in private houses, in the streets and in temples.' A plea to Marius for mercy while he was sacrificing on the Capitol brought immediate execution of the suppliant as its reward. Civil war made men look to the temples for an asylum which they were not likely to find there.[47]

These developments were, of course, occasional, but some of them had a deep effect both on contemporary and on later opinion. Men felt affronted that the *locus* of religion appeared to have little practical effect on enraged patriots even though they shared the same rites as the fellow citizens who pleaded for their lives. The fact is that many temples were often the scene of activities which could properly be called secular, and public sacrifices were performed by men on behalf of the state's good. Neither temple nor sacrifice was sufficiently set apart from ordinary civic purposes; it could even be said that the bloodshed of civil war was a more brutal continuation of the meeting within the temple.

The explanation does nothing to remove the sense of outrage, though it shows very clearly that religious institutions were lacking in independent authority. A possible exception is the temple of Vesta, perhaps because it was the official hearth of the state and was revered as the home of the Vestals who had some powers of protection and intercession. It is therefore understandable that an official tried to reach the temple of Vesta for refuge and that his pursuers were determined to head him off. Later writers often expressed their indignation that temples had been so misused. Ovid, for instance, in describing the death of Julius Caesar, explicitly refers to the fact that the assassination was made in the senate house, a *templum*. The term as he uses it is rhetorically most effective and momentarily shocks the reader. But, clearly, the religious associations of the locale had no effect in putting the conspirators off the attempt. For them, after all, he was a tyrant in a meeting, not a god-to-be in a shrine. Nor were temples of much use as refuges in war or civil war, as Augustine pointed out with some relish. It would seem that when men bemoaned the use of temples for violent actions they were deploring something there was no sanction to stop.[48]

We saw above how temples might be exploited to advertise a victory or to raise morale within the state against the enemy abroad. In civil conflicts they were sometimes linked with a particular internal policy. Two incidents, not in themselves of eye-catching importance in politics or religion, illustrate this feature very clearly. After the senatorial opposition had defeated and killed Caius Gracchus it instructed its leader Opimius to rebuild the temple of Concord. This attempt to suggest that harmony had been restored was unsuccessful, for many ordinary people still demonstrated their political and religious allegiance through cult of the dead Gracchi; Opimius' Concord was felt to be a sham, an unwanted imposition. The temple of Concord outlasted its unpopularity in the Gracchan period and had a distinguished history.[49] More ephemeral, though also indicative of an attempt to forge a link between temples and policy, was the shrine of

Libertas, dedicated by Clodius in 58 BC on property which had been confiscated from the exiled Cicero.[50] It was an attempt to make sure that the exile would not be able to recover the land on which his house had stood and to proclaim that a temple of freedom had been raised, commemorating the defeat of the man who had put citizens to death without trial. But Cicero, on his return, was able to recover his property by showing that the forms of consecration had not been observed.

It is perhaps too generous or too abstruse to speak in these cases of temples linked with a policy. Proclamation would be nearer the mark, giving a religious dimension through accepted values to a set of political events, in one case the return of civic harmony, in the other the achievement of freedom. In neither case did the proclamation succeed, mainly because of personal frailty: Opimius had too bad a name, Clodius was too violent to pass as a man of freedom within the law. The guarantor could only carry with him a minority following. The basic idea, however, was entirely sound, to validate a state of affairs by means of a temple. To be persuasive a good cause needed an honest broker and an undivided people. In an earlier age both factors had been present when the great general Camillus had first vowed and then built the temple of Concord, since he recommended what was agreeable to all. Advancing a cause by means of a temple was therefore nothing new. In fact it was to prove one of the principal resources of Augustanism, when the founder of the Empire turned out to have both character and time on his side. This model is perhaps insufficiently detailed to help us decide whether Julius Caesar sought deification himself or whether he was merely passive, an instrument in the hands of political rivals who tried to make him unpopular. If Caesar had a deliberate policy of seeking self-deification in his lifetime, he showed a lack of political grasp by not making it clear to the mass of his contemporaries what his intentions were. On the other hand he may have had no religious policy and there may have been no popular demand for him to be a god; if so, his opponents were offering him honours (religious and political) to which he was indifferent, but they made the offer in the hope that popular opinion would be alienated from him. Caesar would therefore become objectionable as a man who scorned the conventions prized by the pious. The question could only be decided by more evidence. The point of the comparison is only negative; on either theory Caesar seems to be surprisingly deficient in the political will to exploit temples in his own interest, unrepresentative of the generals whom in other respects he typifies.[51]

In the cases of Opimius and Clodius (to generalize) religion is exploited by politicians but only moderately; the temple seems apt for a given political end but it still gives the appearance of being in the service of gods as well as at the disposal of men. In some other manipulations the independent element in the act of religion is obscured by its political function and in such cases the religious form apparently holds nothing but a political content. The activities of Bibulus, consul in 59 BC, and Ateius in 55 BC, are relevant here. Bibulus sought to prevent Caesar's proposed legislation by serving notice on him that he intended 'to watch the sky', and Ateius tried to prevent Crassus' departure against Parthia by uttering curses against him. Both actions can be assimilated to the use of the political veto. Thus Bibulus had recourse to religious obstruction after other measures had failed to stop Caesar, and Ateius made two attempts to stop Crassus, first by 'watching the sky' and later on by cursing him as he left Rome. Similarly, the veto was at times used as a second resort.[52]

It is very tempting to see these incidents as symptomatic of a manipulated religion *in extremis*: to say of Bibulus that he used religion without believing it against Caesar who certainly earned a reputation for flouting religious convention; and to make similar charges against Ateius and Crassus. No one can deny that these are prime specimens of a politicized religion and that they show its weakness; at critical moments it is no use to have nothing but the gods to put against the might of others with massed swords and votes behind them. But other forms of civic polytheism were still observed by the opponents of Bibulus and Ateius when it was convenient to do so. For all politicians of the day conforming to religion was usually an advantage, departing from it was likely to make some enemies without bringing positive gain. The rules about this kind of religious obstructionism had been drawn up in the Aelian and Fufian laws of the mid second century BC.[53] They specified which officers of state could publicly announce that they were going to 'watch the heavens' (which might lead to the procedure known as *obnuntiatio*). The measures were not intended, one may suppose, to stop an objectionable proposal for all time but to allow a political breathing-space. They were not meant to operate in a house so divided against itself as the Roman aristocracy in the dying Republic. It is for this reason that the comparison with the tribunes' veto seems apt. Both the veto and this form of religious obstructionism were useless when political rivalry was so intense. The conclusion should be that religion was powerless to heal internal political divisions (we should contrast its success at confirming a pre-existent unity against the outside enemy, like Hannibal). There was little point in tinkering with the Aelian and Fufian rules as Clodius did, by restricting the right of obstruction to augurs and tribunes. We should perhaps withstand the temptation to speak of a religious decline, unless we remember two things: one, that religion here is an assortment of incoherent practices, it does not constitute a unity which suffers as a whole when a part is afflicted; secondly, that religious decline is in this case a consequence of political decline and is not yet entitled to a memorial service of its own.

Manipulation, in general, gave considerable scope to those politicians who wished to make political capital out of the formalities of religion. A surprising feature of Roman political life (to a modern way of thinking) is that the private interest was allowed or even encouraged to make or define the public interest. There would have been advantages if some of the religious controls could have been turned into administrative arrangements instead of leaving them at the mercy and whim of politicians. The calendar was the responsibility of the pontifical college, but the issues were seldom put out of bounds to political argument. Politicians argued for and against intercalation simply because it suited their own purpose, without reference to the public interest.[54] When the intrepid Clodius was caught in the act of committing male trespass at the rites of the Bona Dea, the religious ceremony was started all over again (quite correctly) but there were lengthy debates in the senate before it was decided to prosecute the offender.

The over-interpretation of manipulation treats it as though it were all of a piece, a certificate of decline. But there was a dividing-line between the acceptable and the ultra, a line that is sometimes very difficult for the later outsider to follow. The structure of civic polytheism admitted the idea that the state religion could be deployed as an instrument of cohesion, but religion could not itself impose unity or reconcile factions. It is, furthermore, a mistake to suppose that society was as bad as its most offensive manipulation. Members of the senatorial élite and their immediate hangers-on had the most varied interests in the divine. The manipulating class was neither solid nor uniform and responses to the religious apparatus varied widely. A glance at a few biographies will show that religious curiosity (in however peculiar a form) flourished during this period of alleged decay. In a manipulatory system, the archaic or traditional can be praised or blamed according to one's position, and it is especially useful to consider attitudes to the archaic.

Several people took their religion (or parts of it) very seriously. Appius Claudius Pulcher, the brother of Clodius, was an augur and wrote on augural law. He took his duties and the subject so earnestly that he was known as the Pisidian, getting his nickname from an eastern area that was a byword for outlandish provincialism in religion. He was said to have been the first augur for many years who did not just chant the formulae but studied the subject as a true science. He was also interested in necromancy and consulted the oracle of Delphi shortly before the battle of Pharsalus. He was obviously something of a joke to other Romans, but it is important to note that his religion helped to define his political attitudes. He told Cicero (in 63 BC) that a grim civil war was in prospect, on the evidence of augury. As censor he applied the official stigma of disapproval to Ateius for making up the bad omens with which he had tried to frighten Crassus. He showed his interest in religion in his dealings with the provinces; he started to build propylaea for the goddesses at Eleusis and he probably gave material help to the shrine of Amphiaraus at Oropus.[55]

Other traditionalists were Nigidius Figulus and Aulus Caecina. The former, admired as one of the learned men of his age, wrote on private augury and on the study of entrails. He was supposed to have advised Cicero during his consulship, but as a senator and politician he was unimportant and remained so. Caecina became an expert on divination from lightning. He was led to specialize on the Etruscan side because his family came from that part of the country. He apparently made use of his expertise to prophesy to Cicero that he would soon be restored from exile in 57 BC.[56]

Such interests seem faintly ludicrous and they only deserve a mention so that we can put religious conservatives and religious moderates into some sort of perspective. These men were not typical of their class; Appius was tormented by Marcellus and others on the subject of augury, and Caecina was told by Cicero (writing in 46 BC) that forecasts based on political experience were worth far more than those based on Etruscan divination.[57] But they were representative in a somewhat eccentric way of a more or less general will to preserve the religious traditions. If their views and ideas seem quaint or pedantic it is not because religious traditions were forgotten but because the victory eventually went to a more moderate conservatism. The historical or pseudo-historical facts gathered by Varro proved more acceptable and more influential than the theories which were advanced by Appius, Nigidius and Caecina.

It is a mistake to expect consistency from these polytheists. Even Appius apparently incorporated part of the shrine of Tellus into his house,[58] and he took from provincials valuable objects which they had dedicated. This does not mean he was as bad as the plunderer Verres, but it shows that there was common ground even among men who were in general at opposite ends of the religious spectrum. Offences of this type, as well as acts of manipulation if they gave offence, were not usually remembered against their instigators for very long. Most Romans in politics were amused by Appius, but they themselves, in a less demonstrative way, wanted to keep religion as a going concern. Even Cicero's scepticism, for example, had two layers: there was the theoretical doubter, who denied religion its foundation, and the uncertain traditionalist, who did not want to see old customs die. Perhaps the main difference was, to develop this particular example, that an Appius thought of augury as both true and useful, whereas the moderates would defend it only on the grounds of use or expediency. Sentiment of an antiquarian kind was a powerful influence wherever it was found, among the cranks and those who thought themselves normal.

Manipulation did not entail decline whereas antiquarianism was a force for conservation. This is not to say that there was no decline, for it would not be in keeping with the character of polytheism for that to be true. Decline should be regarded as specific and for the most part as independent of manipulation. Some omissions were symptoms of a declining population; three towns near Rome (so Cicero says) were now so unimportant that they could hardly scrape together enough people to take the meat which was their due at the Latin festival. Similarly, population decline was seen as the reason for the decline at Delphi, and it may also have been the reason why the temple at Eryx in Sicily was not so well frequented.[59] Expansion of the Empire was another factor which caused practices to lapse. It seems that declaring war through the fetials was not practised after 171 BC; this is not because the Romans no longer needed 'a means of self-reassurance' which fetial rites had formerly obtained, but the procedure seemed too cumbrous when wars were fought at increasing distances from Rome.[60] Of the religious offices the post of *flamen Dialis* was not filled after the death of Cornelius Merula; the honorific and political value of the pontificates and augurates had far outstripped posts like these so that they had become unattractive even to the patrician families for whom they were reserved. The objection here was not to religion as such but to religion without a political capacity.[61]

Some of the decline was no doubt accidental, which was probably the case when Appius incorporated part of the shrine of Tellus into his house. It could also be simple economic inadequacy; ancient temples were vulnerable to fires and lightning, and they needed considerable outlay from time to time for maintenance or repairs. The private sector may have suffered more than the public sector. Political auspices were still an essential form for the conduct of state business, but auspices for private occasions had almost entirely disappeared.[62] The rites and ceremonies peculiar to certain families were losing adherents, not gaining them. And in some cases private shrines were (quite lawfully) ignored by new occupants of property.

The shrinking of the private sector illustrates an important distinction in law between what is sacred and what is religious. In the Roman system only the sacred is binding on the community and the citizens. For a shrine to be sacred it is essential for a state official to be present, whereas individuals are free, for example, to set up a shrine to a dead person on their land; but they cannot make the arrangement binding on others or on posterity. Some interesting consequences flow from this. To ignore a private shrine (to put it once more to ordinary human use) is not like desecrating a temple, it does not involve sacrilege.[63] Secondly we see that Romans had private religion of a kind, though not highly developed or varied. Thirdly the decline within the private sector probably helped to dispose people to an interest in eastern cults. This was the sociological ground on which they and Christianity were to develop; we should not look solely at the psychological explanation which is often put forward, the theory that public polytheism had ceased to offer (or never had offered) the emotional satisfaction provided by the new cults.

Even though for various reasons there was some neglect of existing cult and disregard of inherited temples, new deities continued to appear in Italy and the eastern part of the Empire. Most of these can be classified as forms of political cult but we should not for that reason dismiss the religious content as trivial or simply as quasi-religious. Religions which are other-worldly have naturally been ready to look down on the sort of religion which is orientated towards success in the here and now.

New gods were still imported as the monument to a successful general or politician. Lutatius Catulus vowed and dedicated a temple to Fortuna Huiusce Diei, to commemorate his success at the battle of Vercellae; Marius put up a temple to Honos and Virtus, taking care that it should not be too high a building and thereby saving it from the charge of interfering with the state auspices; Pompey built a temple or theatre-temple to Venus Victrix.[64] The temple-monument of the individual victory had long been a part of the Roman tradition. In the most austere version of Republican religion (we might say) the temple was the official expression of the relationship between the community and any one of the gods; the dedicator was an obedient instrument of general policy. The dedicators of most temples in the late Republic (this was not a novelty but they were especially numerous after 200 BC) gradually modified this relationship, in order to enhance the glory of an individual aristocrat. In the past the great man had stood, though not modestly, in the shadow of the state. But before Caesar or Augustus no one seems to have realized to the full the resources of associating with several gods and enjoying several religious offices at once.

The imported deities kept their devotee's name alive but they were not in any way a challenge to the supreme civic god, Jupiter. The success of Rome's armies made the city itself the diplomatic centre of the world, and it was not good manners to send ambassadors without an offering for the god. It is therefore not surprising that from the second century BC onwards the cities of Italy and of the east embarked on an emulation of Rome. Cities wanted to have their own capitols with a temple of Jupiter, and in the east the cult of Zeus Capetolios was popular. The spread of these cults cannot be traced in detail. The process as a whole is of interest because it continued to show honour to the gods in a traditional way at the same time that a new cult, the cult of Roma, was becoming widespread. An inscription from Faesulae tells of a dedication to Jupiter, Juno and Minerva on account of the restoration of the Capitol; a reminder that historical events in this case confirm what was ordained in Etruscan theory, that a city could not be properly constituted unless it had temples to the Capitoline triad.[65]

The goddess Roma, a remarkable innovation of the early second century BC, became a cult-object in many Greek cities, especially those in Asia Minor. The cult began at Smyrna in 195 BC when this Greek city, feeling itself outbid by other Greek cities which could boast a tie with Rome, invented a connection, 'the deification of the city of Rome'. The full sequence in the history of this cult in a given locality might be as follows: first, a temple of Roma on its own; next, a cult of Roma and a Roman benefactor; then, a temple to Roma and Julius Caesar; and finally a cult of Roma and Augustus. These stages are all attested for Ephesus, where the original Roman benefactor is Servilius Isauricus. Thus in the late Republic we can observe the Roma-cult at an intermediate stage. A Greek city was willing to show its admiration for Roma and to link it with a great man of the Republic; the individual is here expected to offer in return a measure of protection, for without an intermediary the hope of influencing the great city was far less certain. The cult of Roma was in one respect extremely curious. The goddess concerned was not at this stage a deity acknowledged by Rome itself, and did not become so until the time of the Emperor Hadrian. Rome usually imported the gods of other places but in this case she was apparently the unconscious means of imposing a god on others. In fact the long view shows us that we again have after all the expected characteristic of civic polytheism. The goddess was eventually absorbed into the acquisitive Roman system, but only after it had flourished in the Republic and early Empire as an outsiders' cult. The great Romans who were put in as benefactor-figures derived some political advantage from this narrow congregation-base, through clientship, but the link with Roma became most effective when combined with an ascendancy that was supra-local.[66]

In these remarks we have necessarily looked at this particular cult from the point of view of the Roman man of affairs. To many Romans, especially to those who were commemorated, the cult was just a symbol of Greek inferiority, a religious equivalent of Greek political and military weakness. The cult, that is, might be decried as no more than the subservient adulation of a defeated people. Naturally the cult was seen as nothing but far-off servility when viewed through a Roman glass. But it would be surprising if the defeated peoples only devised such forms of worship with the purpose of humbling themselves yet again before the victor. The cult, with its festivals, was not only a submissive affair; from the natives' point of view it was a means of allowing some cheerfulness to break in and so helping them to make the best of their distress at defeat in war and political inferiority. The cult, then, was well able to fulfil different functions for the two peoples.

The most important change was in the cult of individuals within the city of Rome. The developments were such that in the end a new form of political religion was created, in which an outstanding individual was conjoined with the gods of tradition, with Jupiter and with the seemingly artificial Roma. Cult of a religious kind, directed at one or more great individuals, became more prevalent and developed into emperor-worship. The chief ingredients without which this sort of personality cult was doomed to a short life, not having a secure niche in the public imagination, are as follows: an esteemed politician, a devoted following (civilian or military), involvement of the senatorial élite, a hallowed place, and the political will to make the most of the popular enthusiasm. We can see how these factors worked both early in the period and late, by contrasting the cult of the Gracchi with that of Julius Caesar.

The cult of the Gracchi, on the obvious interpretation, was a spontaneous honouring of the dead men's memory. If it began soon after Caius' death in 121 BC, it was a heartfelt popular outburst, a match to the equally popular hatred for the temple of Concord as restored by Opimius. It had heroes, a considerable following ('many sacrificed ... everyday, as though coming to the temples of the gods'), and a sacred place, the grove of the Furies where Caius was killed. But the cult was not supported by the senate and there was at that time no outstanding politician powerful enough to exploit and guide the mass emotion.

On the other hand the movement may not have arisen until later if it is the case that the politician Saturninus (in 101–100 BC) hoped to strengthen his cause by disseminating the Gracchi cult in Rome among and through their admirers. The twenty-year delay in itself may well seem enough to make this version improbable. But the really remarkable feature of the theory is that it tacitly introduces a missing element, the determined political will of Saturninus. Thus to suggest a much later date for the cult would in effect be tantamount to making it a cult of a different kind.[67]

Probably the Gracchan cult died out because it found no leader who was ready to orchestrate the emotion. By contrast the cult of Caesar after his assassination has the missing elements: senatorial participation (not entirely willing) and the strong political will of his successors, Antony and

Augustus, to keep the feeling of loss alive. The cult therefore has all the requisites: popular regard for the lost leader, shown by the attempt to erect an altar where the pyre had burned; senatorial assent to the programmes of deification; and the determination (though with many differences of opinion between Antony and Augustus) to exploit the occasion and to hallow the great man's memory in the appropriate place, the temple of Divus Julius.[68]

I am not saying that Gracchan cult is at one extreme, a sort of improverished Caesarism, and that Caesar cult is at another; or that the latter exhibits a political and religious maturity which was impossible at the earlier date. The point is that Romans became familiarized with the features of this kind of cult which in the end ensured that it would neither shock too much nor be ephemeral. It found an entry and a Roman home through ancestor-worship as a source of the reverence which moved men at the death-place of Gracchus or the tomb of Catiline. Events showed that at Rome it was essential for a cult to be closely linked with a particular family, as Augustus was with Julius Caesar. Veneration of the living also contributed to the growing sense that a man could become a god. The Greeks had coupled important Romans with Roma; and in Italy esteem for the living great was noticeable when men poured libations to the general, Marius, as the conqueror of the northern tribes, or to the popular politician, Gratidianus.[69] This gratitude, though comparable to the affection which was lavished on Augustus, was dispersed into many family and domestic cults and did not have one focus in a particular place.

It is too easy to dismiss this sort of religion and put it aside in the special category of religious pretence, like some of the stories told by Livy and by Valerius Maximus. The story of religion in the late Republic is not a tale of cold rulers imposing on the gullible or naive; it is more a case of devotion and calculation finding a common ground for all groups in leader cult. The religion we have been describing was not factitious but needed a leader who knew how to respond to popular emotion and how to make it enduring.

### *Some Contemporary Views*

In the earlier studies in this chapter I have tried to show how Roman polytheism operated in the wars and civil wars of the late Republic. The city acknowledged new gods many of whom were imported to satisfy or advertise the claims made by aristocratic generals, and at the same time it became less attentive to some of the older deities whose rites now seemed obsolete. Polytheism of this type was not static, it was a set of impromptu acquisitions and imperceptible losses. It is perhaps a slight exaggeration to describe the system as merely a coming and going of gods, but at any rate it was entirely normal for polytheism to be working in both directions at once. However, many writers and thinkers in this period did not see their civic religion in so objective or detached a manner. They were understandably more sensitive to the loss of the religious past, inclined to suppose that political failures might need to be explained as failures in religion. Their theoretical interests in the field of religion and politics touch on three main questions: the value of religion to the state; the nature of the difference between the religion officially authorized by the Roman state and its difference from the religions of other peoples; and thirdly the feasibility of constructing a philosophical defence of religion. In most of this account I shall refer to the ideas of Varro, Cicero and Lucretius, though I have not hesitated to allude to other writers where there seems to be evidence of persisting attitudes, common to the Republic and the Empire alike.

In Greek and Roman discussions about the value of religion, the problem of its use to a community is seldom far removed from assertions or doubts about its truth or falsehood. Various solutions were put forward by Greek theorists. At one extreme Plato advances the view that religion is both true and necessary, that there are such beings as gods who cannot be seduced by promises of fine temples or herds of animals for sacrifice. At the other extreme is Rome's admirer Polybius, who singles out Rome for her use of religion even though 'if it were possible to make a community of wise men, this sort of thing would not be necessary. But since every gathering of people is unstable and full of lawless desires ... the only resource is to control the multitudes by fear of the unseen and suchlike imposing spectacles.' On this theory some religion is better than none not because it is certainly true but because it offers a sure means of social control. Men are irrational and can be frightened into better behaviour by means of threats derived from religion. The broad difference is between a theory which sees religion as both true and necessary and a theory which admits it is necessary while expressing doubts about, or indifference to, its truth.[70]

In the Rome of the first century BC Varro and Cicero are perhaps to be considered as midway between Platonic certainty and Polybian manipulation. They are certain that the gods exist and care for men but they are unsure of the proofs; on the other hand they believe in the value of religion as a social control. Varro, for instance, like Scaevola before him, made use of a distinction, probably Stoic, between three theologies, the gods of the poets, the gods of philosophy and the civic deities recognized by the state. The trouble with poetic theology is that it consists of myth, much of which is plainly untrue and clearly offensive since it shows us the gods committing immoral acts; god as described by philosophy is a moral being but too difficult for the mass of people to comprehend; by elimination, therefore, the only possibility left is civic theology, the gods not as they really are or might be imagined, but as they have in practice been found useful by the state. Varro's book, the *Antiquities*, dealt first with the non-religious institutions of Rome before going on to discuss the gods and their *Roman* properties; even then he put priesthoods first and gods later: a sign that he was resigned (quite properly in his own view) to describing not the gods in themselves but the gods as the Romans had paid them cult. Cicero's position in the *Laws*, however, is in theory closer to a Platonic model, and he inculcates the idea that religion is both true and necessary; citizens who believe in gods will in effect be admitting that the universe is orderly and they will behave better through respect for the deities who are invoked in oaths. Yet it is fair to add that Cicero's religion here is not political philosophy but his own version of the religion of Numa; it is therefore civic religion with a cosmetic taken from philosophy.[71]

Varro's attitude, his self-imposed limitation, is clearly illustrated in his remarks on the representation of god. According to him the earliest Romans were ignorant of the cult-statue in its anthropomorphic form. Those who introduced this form of worship 'brought in error but made people less afraid.' He means that in the absolute sense it would be better to do as the Jews do, to worship god without an image; but even so there are said to be advantages to this public misconception, the most obvious being that the anthropomorphic cult-statue makes the deity a familiar thing and lessens man's fear of the unknown power without leading him astray into contempt for it. Representing god in the form of a statue is a particular case of the more general question whether the deity itself can be housed within the boundaries of city-states. Both the statue and the temple, that is, are improper or unnatural limitations of god; they are forms of reverence which have no foundation in truth or nature, since god is more than human and, as a being above cities, he is everywhere. But, as Cicero points out, god is in the eye of the beholder, not just in the mind's eye. Even though god is not by nature a 'political animal', for it is not the case that he needs a city in order to lead the full life, there are still advantages in making god a visible civic entity; the practice of setting up cult-statues in temples does not impair the divine nature and it gives material help to human nature from which god is otherwise hidden.[72]

These remarks show why Varro supposed that statues and temples, gods like humans in dwellings with some resemblance to houses, were necessary. Although the anthropomorphic statue was not coeval with Rome (the Varronian history of civic god put his first statue *after* the key date of all chronology, the year of Rome's foundation) Varro thought it important to maintain or revive knowledge of the gods in their Roman form. Some of them had become little more than names, and some rites had lost their meaning except for a few adepts. The polymath did not want Romans to be like foreigners in their own city.

This antiquarianism, like that of the emperor Augustus, had its roots in patriotic feeling for Rome. Many aristocrats, of course, took such things as the maintenance and upkeep of temples as a matter of course, a tradition to be followed even without a theory. Varro's significance is that he offered a theory which would explain his storehouse of religious facts. The statue hints at an answer to the question why religion is valuable to the state: if men need statues of gods (though reality has none) civic religion is valuable because it ministers to the ignorant, those who might be described as neither philosophical nor Jewish. Varro therefore is making allowances for the majority of men; he is a gentler Polybius, supposing that conventional religion is good for man's irrationality. Yet it is not clear from Varro exactly how the political morality of the masses is improved by having before them the evidence of god in statue-form. Perhaps it can be inferred that the condition of Rome would be even worse if the gods' statues were to topple and the temples were to decay.

In Varro's theory civic religion seems to be of most value to the élite. It is advantageous for states (he says) that brave men should believe they are of divine ancestry, for the belief (even if it is false) will give them the confidence to carry out heroic deeds. In this case the theory apparently does justice to some of the ways of contemporary politics, the claims made by Roman nobles like Caesar which linked their family tree with the gods. It would have been easy for Varro to go one stage further and advance the view that great men can themselves expect to become gods as a result of their services to (Roman) mankind. The idea that the gods, some or all of them, are deified humans had been put forward by Euhemerus and had been Latinized at Rome by the poet Ennius. It was made even more magnificent by Cicero's *Dream of Scipio*. But neither Scaevola nor Varro was willing for a city-state community to think that gods such as Hercules and Aesculapius were ex-men, promoted from the ranks.[73]

Euhemerism could have explained some of the contemporary political phenomena, such as the association of great Romans with the goddess Roma and the cult of Julius Caesar as a god both before and after his death. It was a theory of some practical consequence in other matters as well. The tax-farmers of Rome had argued that the revenues of Amphiaraus at Oropus should not be treated as sacred, since Amphiaraus (in their view), having been mortal, could not possibly have the title of a god.[74] But the ruling went against them and the god's revenue was declared sacred. The doctrine that the gods are former men can be expressed as a value in various ways. If the emphasis falls on the discovery that there are no gods as such, that gods are nothing but men, we have a reductive theory which might lead men to disparage gods on the grounds that reality does not consist of gods and men but only of glorified humans. If, on the other hand, the theory makes the point that men too can become gods it encourages what is best in man to strive towards the divine nature. The former might be called negative euhemerism, the latter positive. Conventional men reject what they think of as negative euhemerism because they are firm believers in keeping gods and men apart, as distinct beings in separate worlds, and are afraid that the heavens may fall if the doctrine becomes widely known. Cicero, for example, treats the subject in this way when he attacks Antony for being the priest of Julius Caesar; it is not possible, he thinks, for dead men to have priests, since priests (flamines) are allocated not to the dead but to gods.[75]

Neither Varro nor Cicero discussed the political value of religion with a thorough grasp of the important contemporary issues. Their reverence for the Roman past does most credit to their sense of tradition, and the general tendency of their thought was antiquarian and conservative. They might be described as adjacent to the school of thought which asserts that religion is both true and necessary; in their case however the doctrine is that religion is probable and necessary. At the other extreme is the theory of Epicurus, expressed in its Latin form by Lucretius, which asserts that religion is both untrue and unnecessary. Untrue, because many of the ideas usually found under the shelter of religion are intellectually indefensible; events in the Lucretian universe, for instance, should be explained as the properties or accidents of atoms, not as the consequences of gods' anger with or partiality for man. Unnecessary, in the second place, because men are said to behave worse not better as a result of believing that gods can be affected by prayer: the Agamemnon who sacrificed his daughter as the price of obtaining a fair wind for his journey to Troy was a believer and practitioner, not an atheist. The consequences of religious doctrines are in Lucretius' view pernicious; men who fear punishment in the after-life certainly behave badly when they fear dying, and it is in Lucretian terms immoral to disturb oneself in the here and now under the mistaken idea that the soul can survive and suffer after death.

In so describing Lucretius I am bound to disagree with the interpretation of Lucretius which exempts Roman religion from his attack, the argument that because Lucretius does not mention the Roman gods as such Roman civic religion is not implicated in his account of man's early bullying by priests and the gods they served. The theory under review supposes that the poet is therefore attacking Greek and barbarian religion but not Roman. However, Lucretius' points are philosophical and general. We have to ask what difference it makes if we read the line 'Such wickedness did religion persuade men to commit', as a comment *solely* on the objectionable act performed by Agamemnon without also supposing that it must describe *all* such religious acts performed by religious men. The difference is considerable. Even though Lucretius is no more than a philosopher at secondhand, it would be strange if he were making tacit exemptions, so that every time a general attack is made the reader has to make the proviso, 'not true of the Roman gods'.[76] The fact is that Lucretius works through Greek examples not as a way of excluding Rome but of subsuming it in the dominant literary culture.

These remarks of Cicero, Varro and Lucretius do little to illuminate the contemporary setting of the subject. But Roman accounts of religion and superstition are in closer touch with the realities of the age.

Polytheistic religion was mostly cult, consisting of such acts as processions, supplications or sacrifice. The obvious and natural Latin expression for religion is cult of the gods, the expression used by Cicero when he credits the Romans with supremacy in this sphere. His justification for this is that Rome and the Romans have in fact allowed and encouraged the most reasonable expression of *religio*, man's basic sense that gods are present or have claims upon him. Cult is the formal expression of man's religious sense; in discussing Roman ideas about the underlying religious emotion I shall use 'religion' to stand for the Latin term *religio* and 'superstition' for the term *superstitio*. In what follows I am therefore discussing Roman theories about the experience which gives rise to religion and superstition in a common modern sense, where the former stands for a belief deemed orthodox and superstition stands for eccentric belief or practice.[77]

In some passages there appears to be a hard and fast distinction between the two. Cicero says:

> Religion has been distinguished from 'superstition' not only by philosophers but also by our ancestors. Persons who spent whole days in prayer and sacrifice to ensure that their children should outlive them were termed 'superstitious' (from the word for a survivor) ... On the other hand those who carefully reviewed ... the lore of ritual were called 'religious' (from the word for retracing or rereading).

And at the conclusion of Cicero's dialogue on divination 'religion' is again differentiated from 'superstition'; the former is said to be associated with the study of nature and should be preserved whereas the latter is to be expelled. In the first comment above Cicero is reflecting the fear of the practical politician that 'religion', unless it is controlled, will inhibit the conduct of everyday affairs; and in the second he is criticizing 'superstition' on the grounds that it is inimical to understanding nature as the work of reason. But there was in fact no hard and fast distinction between the two terms. It would ease the task of modern interpreters if 'religion' as here were always commended and if 'superstition' always denoted a wrong belief and a harmful practice. This rigour does not seem to be found until Christian writers use 'religion' to describe their own belief in a single God and to designate the worship of the pagan Romans by the ignoble term 'superstition'. In classical Latin usage is confused. When Caesar describes the Gauls as a people who are addicted to 'religion' he is not paying them a compliment; he might instead have written of their 'superstition'. When Cicero says that the whole province of Sicily is affected with 'religion' and 'superstition' he is referring to the islanders' religious anxiety, their fear that the gods, whose statues have been filched by the criminal Verres, will no longer be present to provide for their interests; and it is obviously thought to be right and proper to feel pain at such loss, just as it is wrong and improper to be the cause of religious deprivation in other men.[78]

The usage is variable but these terms are recurrent in Roman theorizing about two subjects of great importance to the state, the attitude of Rome to the religions of other peoples and cultures, and the distinction between public and private religion. The constant in the argument is the sense that 'religion' should be allowed some scope but ought not to go unchecked.

The Roman perspective on the religious practices of other peoples was usually short and ethnocentric; it tended to notice either an anxiety of its own, the fear of immoderate religiosity, or to discover grounds for self-reassurance based on the idea that the gods of other peoples were identical with some of those at Rome. The first preoccupation led to an even greater confidence in Rome's superiority. It enabled some Romans to see Jews, for example, as the practitioners of outlandish rites without the cult-statues that were held to be normal among the city-states of the Greek and Roman world.[79] To take another instance, a senatorial decree abolished human sacrifice in 97 BC, some years after a scandal in which the populace and its gods were placated by burying alive two Gauls and two Greeks in the forum. This was an advance in religious civilization in the view of a later writer who shared the confidence in Rome's superiority that had been voiced earlier by Cicero.

Magic certainly found a home in two Gallic provinces, within living memory. The principate of Tiberius did away with the Druids and this horde of seers and medicine men ... It is beyond calculating how great is the debt owed to the Romans who swept away the monstrous rites in which to kill a man was the highest religious duty and for him to be eaten was a passport to good health.

Thus the Jews and the Druids could readily be seen as practising forms of cult which to most Romans would be alien and immoderate. They could be used as evidence of Rome's superiority in religion. The attitude was tersely put by an imperial lawyer: 'if people do anything whereby the unstable minds of citizens are afflicted with fear [''superstition''] of god, Marcus Aurelius decreed that such offenders should be exiled to an island.' As this emperor admitted some foreign practices it is likely that his measure was intended to reject those alien rites which were likely to remain unassimilable.[80]

But the gods of foreigners were far from being wholly remote. The Romans found similarities as well as the differences mentioned earlier which made them sure of being a society in control of its own advance. Caesar asserted that the Gauls were addicted to religiosity, but he also found that some of their deities could be equated with those at Rome. The habit of identification was as widespread among the Romans as it was among their Greek predecessors and contemporaries. It had been most understandable and apposite when Rome was engaged in warfare against the nearby towns of Latium and discovered the namesakes of her own civic deities in societies that were roughly alike. This habit of thought made it natural to see likenesses among deities even when the Roman armies came to fight against peoples with their own, non-Italian, *mores*. The supposed religious similarity was a source of comfort to men who might be told that they already had at Rome a god like that worshipped by the enemy, or that their general would invite to Rome the civic deity on the other side. The gods of foreigners were therefore treated like the defeated populations; they were sometimes despised, if they were the centre of rites unacceptable at Rome, or allowed to become half – or even full – citizens of Rome. In order to explain these processes theory ascribed to Rome (in general) a controlled form of cult, a moderate 'religion' which it did not always ascribe to the gods of foreign communities, even if they appeared to be like those in the city.

The theory behind Roman assessments of foreign cults was accurate about the Roman fear of excess; it was however less than fair about the Roman acquisitiveness of other gods. Similar preoccupations with 'religion' and so on affected what might be called the theory of internal religion. Cicero makes it a rule that his ideal citizens should not have separate gods or new deities except those with a public licence; private cult is permitted if it is directed to traditional gods, handed down in the family.

The idea is echoed in Festus' remark that a citizen with due and proper regard for religion will only pay cult to the gods acknowledged by the state.[81] Individual religion on this showing would be confined probably to forms of ancestor – or relative – cult. It would be permissible for others to observe but would not be binding on other people as an inheritance; after the death of his daughter Cicero thought of erecting a shrine to her memory but was naturally concerned about securing the monument against later invasions consequent on buying and selling.[82]

But if theory seems to be so restrictive of individual or private worship it may be misleading. On this subject some interesting details are recorded by Suetonius; although he is writing of a later period and his subjects are emperors, who might not be so easily denied as lesser men, he may be a guide of sorts to earlier practice. Nero, for example, became greatly attached to the model of a little girl, a gift from a plebeian which acquired great religious significance for Nero when a conspiracy against the emperor was exposed. Similarly Domitian showed great reverence for Minerva. In these cases cult by an individual was either impossible for other Romans (only Nero and his circle would be able to make the three daily sacrifices which were paid to the toy deity) or on a scale that others would find odd or unusual. Devotions of this type may therefore suggest that the practice of religion in a more individual way was not only to be sought or gratified (as is sometimes suggested) through the pursuit of the Oriental religions. Even if theory and general practice frowned on emotional individualism of the Neronian kind, it was difficult to stop such a natural development.[83]

There is much in the observation that pagan religion was mostly taken up with public activity, and that it was backward in the ways of private spirituality. It is a variant of the idea that the religious sense among the city-states was orientated towards honour and glory. The great ceremonies of state measured the god's esteem and gave standing to those who were the main officiants. But, clearly, there were other ways in which cult was performed and which admitted a great variety of experience, whether or not the deity concerned was also an official god.

The third subject of theoretical interest in the Ciceronian age was the question whether religion can be defended through philosophy. At this time the question was the more important as Cicero set himself the task of showing that Greek thought could be adequately rendered in Latin. The literary dimension does not concern us for the present. The argument as Cicero saw it was whether philosophy could be expected to confirm the idea that there is such a thing as divine providence, whether it might provide the theoretical grounds for such practices as divination. In the treatises on the *Nature of the Gods* and *Divination* Cicero or his spokesman argues with the voice of Academic doubt against Epicurean denials of providence and against the over-confident assertions made by Stoicism. The great objection to the latter theory is that it proves too much. It purports to show that some present events, such as dreams or auspices taken from the flight of birds, are necessarily connected with later events, and that there is a discoverable method of explanation.[84] Stoicism therefore makes a promise of rationality but Cicero for one does not accept that there can be a scientific account of dreams or auspices as pre-determined signs of the future. In his view religious Romans who are also serious Stoics are bound to be 'superstitious' in the sense mentioned above; their piety will be trammelled by a set of theories about the universe which are untrue. Thus their cult of the gods will be made useless by an association with false theory.

The implication of this argument is that religious Romans who are not Stoics have sufficient justification for their piety in that it is the custom or tradition they were born into. Ciceronian doubt is aimed at philosophies which claim too little or too much for the gods, but it is not as such anti-religious. It leaves religion without a philosophical leg to stand on but with more than sufficient support from custom. The history of Rome gives a political justification for certain practices for which there is no justification at all in nature.

We are, it seems, back with religion as untrue or doubtful but necessary as a social control. There is, however, a slight difference. The view of custom which is found in the *Divination* shows that there is a difficulty in interpreting the far-off Roman past. If we have to give some account of why Romulus, for instance, introduced augury in those first days of Rome, there are two possible approaches. On the one hand the friends of divination and philosophy suppose that Romulus acted as he did from conviction, on the grounds that antiquity, being simple and primitive, could not knowingly have imposed religion as a fraud. The implication is that men at first believed without knowing why and that the reasons were discovered only later by (Stoic) philosophy even though some of the practices have fallen into neglect. On the other hand Cicero himself considers that Romulus, like others of the ancients in many matters, was simply wrong-headed, that his ideas are rightly doubted now even though his religious inventions are known to be politically useful. These versions of early Rome, as the seat of a venerable tradition, are irreconcilable; either Romulus is good and has been proved right or he is good but wrong. As the latter is more likely, then custom has to rely on itself for its own defence, it is pragmatic only and the Romulean beginning was an act of ignorance set in an age of darkness; custom therefore has a weakness at the centre which is bound to detract from its supposed grip on the freely given allegiance of a distant posterity.

The religious conservatism found in Cicero was designed as a patriotic protest against the invasion of an alien philosophy. It lasted as the centrepiece of many appeals in support of Roman religion; it is present in the pagan's apologia in the *Octavius* of Minucius Felix in the second century AD and recurs much later still, when Maximus the grammarian writes to Augustine and tries to defend the traditional approach to urban gods.[85] But acquiescence in custom with scant regard for Stoic philosophy was in part a Ciceronian expedient, natural enough in a writer whose mind was much attracted by philosophy as a stylistic challenge. Different arguments were put forward by the younger Seneca. As a Stoic thinker he tried to reconcile the common-sense Roman regard for traditional practices and custom with a respect for Stoic theory. The early Etruscan account of thunderbolts is not literally true, according to Seneca, but it can be brought up to date and accepted into a framework of Stoic explanation. Similarly (he thinks) when the ancients said that Jupiter hurls thunderbolts at the wicked, they did not actually mean what they said. They must have been aware that his aim was erratic, that the divine marksman often hit his own temples instead of the dwellings of the unjust. But this doctrine is said not to prove that the ancients were simpletons, good men but wrong-headed; it is to be taken allegorically, as a sign that the masses must be given a god to instil fear in them. To say that thunderbolts are from Jupiter is thus made compatible with the Stoic idea that nothing comes to pass without Jupiter (where Jupiter is a name for the supreme Stoic god).[86]

In the late Republic Cicero and Varro especially tried to make sense of the political value of religion as shown in Roman public life. Their respect for tradition was far more influential than their competence in offering a theory of religion. They put most emphasis on religion as a form of social control, useful for managing people who might otherwise be ungovernable. In so doing they probably failed to do justice to other uses of religion, as a mode of independent solace or regeneration, for example. Their defence of religion as a thing of custom lasted as long as imperial paganism, but a weakness of the theory was that it denied religion the intellectual support of philosophy.

CHAPTER THREE

# *Augustanism*

It is not really a paradox to say that the Republic had ended in the very year (27 BC) when it was officially restored by Augustus as the victor over Cleopatra and Antony. The essence of Republican politics was conflict and co-operation pitched between aristocrats of roughly equal status, with limited tenure of office. There had been many degrees of inequality within the élite, most notably the difference between families with consular ancestors and those without, but there had as yet been nothing like the gap which gradually opened between the emperor and the other members of his class. Although many forms of Republicanism were maintained, the year 27 began the process of exalting the ruler, and the change towards an autocracy of the Diocletianic type was always pronounced even though the gradient varied from one emperor to another.

The year of the 'restored Republic' is no more than a convenient symbol. A case could also be made for placing the end in the years immediately before the assassination of Julius Caesar. But there are better reasons for starting with Caesar's heir rather than with Julius Caesar himself. The latter's aims, both in politics and religion, have to be inferred from a confusing number of measures passed or rejected in a short space of time, and it is not surprising that political and religious Julianism (as one might call it) has not been given an agreed form by its many interpreters. If the question whether Caesar deliberately sought and encouraged self-deification could be settled once and for all, it would be a great advance. But as things stand, to pass from Caesar to Augustus is to go from doubt to certainty, and the historian can now venture to interpret the basic facts instead of trying to determine what they are or whether they are facts at all. Also, Augustanism can be observed over a longer period, as it was a good forty years in the unfolding, apart from the years of prefatory struggle between Caesar's death and the battle of Actium.

The broad question is whether there was on the religious side anything parallel to the political change I have indicated. We have to decide how far the emergent autocracy, which made use of the conventions of the Republic, also borrowed the inherited forms of religion; and to decide whether a similar blend of conservatism and originality prevailed in religion as it did in politics. The object of this preamble is to discuss in outline the main questions that are bound to arise in an account of religious Augustanism. Politically, 'Augustanism' can be interpreted as shorthand for an absolute rule that hides its autocracy under a pious regard for traditional offices; there is (in part at least) a parallel in Augustan religiosity, with its concern to preserve what is felt as truly Roman, something inherited from the past before the age of religions from abroad.

A consensus version of Roman history portrays the Augustan age as a period of revival in religion. The expression is perhaps somewhat doubtful, especially if it is taken to imply that comparisons can usefully be made between a return to the temples and a return to the churches in the modern world; the congregational functions of the buildings were different, as we saw above. More important, however, are the reasons why this view has come to dominate accounts of the period. It is partly that religion in the Augustan age took on a different role from religion in the late Republic, and it is easy to assume that the difference should be quantified, to suppose that the Augustan age was more religious than its predecessor because the field of enquiry is dominated and even enlarged by great monuments to religion. The more peaceful ceremonies of Augustanism, the Secular Games and the scenes on the Ara Pacis, are apt to strike the modern as being closer to his understanding of religion than, say, the disturbed and violent manipulations in late-Republican politics. In coming to this judgment historians have been led not only by the evidence but also by the received idea that wars (both foreign and civil) compel men back towards the beliefs they have abandoned or destroyed.[1]

Historians have also been too ready to accept the verdict of the Augustan writers on the late Republic as an age of religious decline. It is easy to select facts which will seem to support this view, such as the continuing failure to appoint a *flamen Dialis* or the abuse of religion out of political self-interest. Some of the charges thus brought against the late Republic are certainly true, but they are no more than symptoms of a neglect which was as essential to civic polytheism as the active increase in gods or the multiplication of religious posts with a political bearing. Augustan creativity in religion is better interpreted in the light of assumptions which define civic polytheism as subject to unstable increase and decrease at one and the same time. A useful way to interpret polytheism is to see it as a bulge-and-squeeze religion, not as a religion which either expands all over or declines in the same way. There may indeed be less 'decline' in the Augustan period, but it will be obvious that there was some; for instance the coming out of fashionable Augustan gods meant the relative retreat of other deities.

But the term revival does nevertheless point to a significant concern of Augustanism, the cult of the antique, the rediscovery of the religious past. Even though partial neglect is a necessary part of the system, it is also true that citizens and others will not experience it evenly, they will notice or perceive neglect far more at certain times. The sense of a culpable neglect seems to have been prevalent in the Augustan age and it meant that government interest in the past would never be merely an imposed revival; government here was responding to a definite mood among the people, but this is not to say that all the Augustan attempts to bring back the religious past were equally successful.

Religious Augustanism includes within its diverseness a sentimental nostalgia for the antique. In this it has some resemblance to political Augustanism, in its readiness to bring back the forms which (it was thought) had made the Republic great. But it also included other features of which one at least was relatively new at Rome, the ruler-cult which had spread over the Hellenistic world. The acquisition of this new form of cult was a gradual process which Augustus and many of his successors did not wish to advance too hastily.

Many historians have been prone to praise Augustanism for attempting to bring religion back and yet to blame it for not doing more to stimulate a religious impulse that might be independent of political satisfactions. One critic admits that 'there was a genuine core of religion in the Augustan revival' but goes on to say that 'it failed to satisfy the growing demand for a personal religion.'[2] Such a view seems to be commending Augustus for restoring religion (supposedly on the grounds that more of any religion is better than none) and at the same time to be criticizing Augustanism for not helping individual religion. Thus Augustanism could be fitted into a useful limbo, between a wholly unacceptable civic polytheism, which was blatantly party-political or directed at personal ends, and Christianity with its capacity for helping to develop individuals' spirituality outside the civic framework as well as within it. We would be hard pressed to find a more temperate encomium of Augustanism than this:

> Rational religion is the wider conscious reaction of men to the universe in which they find themselves. In its last stages in the Western World we find the religion of the Roman Empire, in which the widest possible view of the social structure is adopted. The cult of the Empire was the sort of religion which might be constructed to-day by the Law School of a University, laudably impressed by the notion that mere penal repression is not the way to avert a crime wave. Indeed, if we study the mentality of the Emperor Augustus and of the men who surrounded him, this is not far from the true description of its final step in evolution.[3]

These comments on Augustanism are not untypical. I do not quote them in order to deny or assert that personal religion is superior to group religion. The object of the study is to further our analysis of the phases of civic polytheism and so to understand why it was replaced by Christianity; we shall do this better if we remember that civic polytheism dealt in the group requirements of citizens – matrons, aristocrats with their own cults, soldiers in the army, and so on. It is difficult enough to compare group objectives and group satisfactions without complicating the subject still more by supposing that personal religion was then (in the age of Augustus) or later (in the period of Constantine) as urgent or common a need as it has been at times in the modern world. Some of the cheer-leader ceremonies devised by Augustanism certainly look gregarious and shallow, but along with games and festivals they contributed something to the play side of the social order as well as to its sense of solemnity. The deities were not just formal solitaries in their own temples; they were in part available to marshal crowds for pleasure.

Religion (it is undeniable) was important to Augustus and his advisers, perhaps more so than might be suggested by the short treatment it gets in Maecenas' fictitious speech of advice to his leader. It is difficult, however, to be exact about the nature of Augustan interest in religion. An older view was confident that religion was merely being used to help the people forget the liberties they had lost; but the implied division of interest between gullible throng and unbelieving politicians has little warrant in the sources. Some of Augustus' tics and habits, as described by Suetonius, are superstitions of a kind that probably made him one of the many.[4] The Empire, one begins to feel, might have lasted forever if there had been enough rulers like him, men who could treat rare and remote matters sometimes with awe and at other times with the slight irreverence of an urbane joke. Another possibility is that imperial statesmen turned to religion as an authority which would legitimize their power. It has been said of Augustus that 'to be considered the son of a god would tend to legitimize his authority since the claiming of divine parentage was a practice sufficiently common among the Hellenistic rulers.'[5] There are of course many reasons for seeing Julius Caesar, Augustus and the Romans as part of a Hellenistic world, but they do not entitle us to say that the Romans themselves saw things in this way or that they saw themselves as Hellenistic in quite the same style and degree as their Greek neighbours. There is a similar assumption in Professor Taylor's remark that dedicating a temple to Venus Genetrix served as a legitimization of Julius Caesar's rule.[6] But it seems unlikely that Julius Caesar or Augustus could have thought of religion as a source of legitimization. They were men assured of powers that had been legally bestowed. To speak of legitimization in this context is to ascribe to civic polytheism a power of sanctifying which is alien to it. Religion was certainly indispensable to the ruler, not as a sanction but as the means of accumulating more posts and offices of a quasi-political kind. There was in effect no one particular religious rite without which Augustus and his moderate successors would not have been true emperors. There was no religious coronation to mark the accession of the new ruler. What religion did was contribute features to a structure that had been home-made by the first Augustus. Both the additions and the framework were important to one another, but there was no absolute completion, it was determined and then modified by individual emperors as they required.

In the rest of this chapter we shall see how exactly religion in the Augustan age was related to religion in the Republican period and how it began to function in the new Empire. Political Augustanism cannot be expressed in a succinct phrase. There are however some important political characteristics which have their effect in religion as well. Augustanism is a shorthand for the citizen autocracy of an imperial state, at a late stage in its history, with a sense of a duty to conserve the past as well as a mission to expand. The ruler projects himself as a benevolent despot and as far as possible dissuades subjects from thinking of him as a usurping tyrant; the first Roman Augustus was perhaps more successful in this respect than some at least of those who have also earned or received the name.[7] Augustan culture is secondary and derivative, but its makers of literature, like the rulers of men, are inspired by the idea that the new is not to be condemned merely as the posterior of the old model. Two of the main themes of Augustanism are Roman patriotism and moderation on the part of the ruler; in religion as in politics they enabled ruler and subjects to adjust to the present by appealing to the past. They perhaps seemed more durable qualities than they turned out to be at a later stage in the Empire. Even in the age of Augustus himself the ruler's moderation in politics (making use of Republican offices to describe his authority) was more of a piece with itself than his moderation in religion, for here there were great differences between parts of the Empire, especially between Rome and the provinces.

## *Augustus and the Republican Tradition*

The Emperor Augustus enjoyed a given name, awarded him in 27 BC. It had religious associations with augury and auspices, conveying the suggestion that all was well with the state, for the tradition spoke of Rome as founded by augury. The religious name (as we might call it) did not as such validate his rule, but it was sure to be a form of recommending the ruler as the author of changes both religious and political.

Augustus as general and statesman was in significant ways the heir of the great Republican conquerors, from Camillus to Julius Caesar. Like many of them he vowed and built temples from the spoils of war and his inheritance from Julius Caesar. Some of these buildings were clearly victory-temples. In 36 BC he consecrated land of his on the Palatine to Apollo after it had been struck by lightning. The choice of deity seemed especially appropriate after the victory at Actium where the promontory boasted a temple of Apollo. Since Apollo had watched Augustus conquer, the local temple was enlarged and a new temple in Rome was finally dedicated on October 9 of 28 BC. As Sulla had been the favourite of Aphrodite, so Augustus had now declared himself a man who was aided by Apollo. Being the protégé of a god he resembled some of his Republican predecessors, but he went beyond them in various ways; he erected more temples than they had and he eventually made the Palatine into a new Roman hearth.[8]

But he did not try to revolutionize the manubial temple-practices, which had become a tradition, by concentrating on Apollo alone and so making him a god to overtop the others. Apollo had an esteemed place and he was at times promoted, but he was not Augustus' only god. Another type of the victory-god was Jupiter Tonans to whom Augustus vowed a temple in Spain in 26 BC and dedicated the finished building four years later on. The fact that this temple was vowed and dedicated as enough to show that Augustus' Apollo was not meant to drive out the established gods with their variant labels. Different campaigns, different gods; this was part of the Republican orthodoxy about gods that Augustus could practise and respect. But his Jupiter was never as popular as the Apollo; indeed Augustus dreamed that the new Jupiter, the Thunderer, was something of an affront to the greatest Jupiter of the state cult.[9]

With these two gods, however differently, Augustus was following the well-worn path of the victory religions. But his relationship to two other gods introduced a completely new dimension into Roman politics. Julius Caesar was deified and vowed a temple, though it was not dedicated till 29 BC; the original vow was made by Augustus, Lepidus and Antony, but by the year of the dedication only the first was able to come forward as the satisfied votary. Secondly, in 42 BC, before the battle of Philippi, Augustus vowed a temple to Mars Ultor. To all appearances this was yet another victory-temple, vowed by a general on the eve of battle. It was however a special case since Mars the Avenger was here invoked as the guardian of the murdered Caesar. In the event two temples of this name may have been built: a temple was decreed in 20 BC, apparently to receive the standards returned by the Parthians, and much later the temple of 2 BC was erected to satisfy the vow made forty years earlier and was a significant monument in the new Forum of Augustus.[10]

The temples to Divus Julius and to Mars Ultor were striking innovations. They connected Augustus with his deified father and paid a tribute to the emotion felt by many ordinary people at Caesar's death; and, further, they both showed that the living man was able to demonstrate his piety and honour towards a folk-hero within living memory. Honouring a man-god, not just a deity with merely literary, genealogical or Trojan connections, forged strong links for Augustus with recent historical events. They made for a more authentic sense of connection with the gods than had previously been the custom. Before this time men had only been able to boast of an association with the gods by the anaemic stemmas of genealogy, as when Julius Caesar himself had traced his descent from Venus and the kings of Rome.[11] Augustus, however, was a genuine novelty within the true line of the generals' tradition. He had victories of his own, with their own gods and their separate temples, and he combined these with other temples which proved his loyalty to the immediate past. Roman pride in history was expanded by the accidents of Caesar's deification, and there were also religious overtones to Caesar's murder and the posthumous comet. The popular enthusiasm and Augustus' own ability to respond gave Rome the sense that she had recently acquired a god she deserved. Rome was going through the common experience of Hellenistic states which prostrated themselves before their rulers, the sense that other gods are remote and that the god of the here and now is the current ruler. Julius dead offered the advantages of a genealogy that was still fresh in the mind of the living.

Augustus did not challenge the dominance of Jupiter Optimus Maximus but in various ways his new temples shifted the territorial centre of religion and rehoused some of the old functions. When he became chief pontiff in 12 BC he naturally wished to stay in his own residence on the Palatine instead of moving to the pontiff's house near to the temple of Vesta. To maintain the tradition Augustus declared part of the Palatine public property and built there a small shrine of Vesta. Thus the hearth and home of the state religion was localized on imperial land.[12] The temple to Mars Ultor of 2 BC identified the régime with functions which had previously been dispersed in several temples. It was here that boys performed the transitional rite that symbolized their arrival at man's estate. It was here that those appointed to posts abroad took official leave of the city. Also the senate met in Mars Ultor when discussing the award of triumphs and triumphal insignia.

Augustus might have found it difficult to refute the charge that he was, as far as new temples were concerned, exceeding what had been the custom among his Republican predecessors. The aggrandizement of the imperial family was displayed in the favourable colours of patriotism and magnificence. The Augustan building programme, spread over many years, was intended to make Rome a city of marble instead of brick; it was also meant to make an imposing distinction between Rome, a city in which state temples dominated the urban whole, and those more chaotic towns of the Greek east, where the positioning of the temples was ill-designed and not commensurate with their civic role.[13] The first emperor had inherited a city that was of poor quality (hence the complaint about brick) and Greek or casual in its layout. Such improvements could be called the work of patriotism; religious appearances were changed by the greater use of marble on the outside of temples and by spatial innovation within. Artistic spoils brought from abroad made the temples even more imposing, though their function as museums was not incompatible with their function as the palaces of gods. The grandiosity of these building measures was offset to an extent by the well-advertised Augustan claim of moderation. Gold and silver statues of Augustus were melted down and the proceeds were offered to Apollo.[14] The gifts were made in the name of Augustus and of those who had paid for and set up the statues. Other men were encouraged to undertake the rebuilding or repair of temples and were given credit for their achievement. The temple of Diana on the Aventine became known as the Diana of Cornificius, a public sign that rebuilding was no Augustan monopoly, and an indication that lesser men could be honoured in this way because they were not a political threat to the ruler. Towards the end of Augustus' rule associating a person other than the ruler with the rebuilding of a temple fulfilled a different function. Tiberius was made responsible for the temple of Concord; he began the work after his triumph in 7 BC and when he finally dedicated it in AD 10 he was designated as the successor by this imperial favour along with other honours. Thus temples built or repaired in the names of others were not feared as the rivals of Augustus' temples, they were welcome as supports; and at a late stage in the reign they were used to mark out the successor.[15]

Augustus, as Ovid expressed it, was not merely the designer of new temples, he repaired and restored the old. The reputation of a great restorer is claimed in Augustus' own version of his achievement. 'In my sixth consulship [28 BC] I repaired eighty-two temples in the city, overlooking not a single one of those that needed to be rebuilt at that time.'[16] The year was as significant as the fact of the restorations; it was an advertisement that the civil wars were now finished, that there was a victory over Cleopatra to celebrate, and that years of Republican neglect were going to be put right. In this area Augustus perhaps exaggerated the extent to which temples had been allowed to fall into disrepair; or perhaps he did not object to people confusing the neglect endemic in polytheism with the thought that the late Republic had been notoriously careless or even wicked. The fact is that all temples were extremely vulnerable to fire caused by lightning and to the damage caused by floods.[17] It is instructive to note that flooding from the Tiber, as well as fires, was a serious nuisance throughout Augustus' own rule, and in some cases the repair work lasted over years. The Augustan repair of eighty-two temples should not perhaps be taken quite at the face-value of the virtuous announcement. The huge number makes it more than likely that some of the repairs were minor works, and we should not be too harsh on the Republic for a neglect that sounds alarming. It is arguable that after 28 BC there was no great alacrity to restore or repair buildings which were not of prime importance to the régime.

Conservation of this sort was in part a serious government adaptation to the popular feeling that a temple in disrepair was an offence to the gods. A repair therefore was equivalent to the process of correcting a ritual that had gone wrong or had been interrupted. Rome, because of these repairs, was shown to be returning to normal. But the preservation was probably more in the nature of a hasty patchwork, without the impulse or the taste that at other times and periods has improved the past with an archaizing style founded on simulation as well as on knowledge. Architectural energy, at any rate, and statesmen's wealth were put into the new buildings. Augustus was scrupulous in his regard for existing sites, but, though he did not commit acts of trespass, he was still an improver and the new monuments together with the restorations enabled the panegyrists to apply the term 'magnificent' to the Augustan city; and to coin the expression 'golden temples' as the Augustan cliché par excellence. The temples were in fact only a part of the great building works devised by Augustus, Agrippa and others – they should not be allowed to count for so much more than the ordinary civic utilities, the great porticoes, roads and aqueducts – but they were the showpiece of the new city. The new temples, like the restored, were regarded as the dutiful achievement of a leader in the Republican tradition, commemorating his own glory and preserving that of the past.[18]

Restoration of buildings, important though it was, was a particular expression of the archaizing mood, the nostalgia for an earlier Rome. Some obsolete rituals were also revived. War against Cleopatra was solemnly declared at the temple of Bellona by the fetial rite. In 29 BC the temple of Janus was closed, to symbolize the return of Peace; and the augury of *salus* was performed: 'a kind of augury, which is in the nature of an inquiry whether the god permits them to ask for prosperity for the people, as if it were unholy even to ask for it until permission is granted.' It had lapsed because Roman armies had been engaged in incessant warfare, both foreign and civil, and so the formal requirements for taking the augury had not been present. The three rituals just mentioned were closely connected with events before and after Actium. The fetial declaration added to the war against Cleopatra a sense of religious endeavour, and the closing of Janus was a proof that pious Italy had been rewarded by the coming of peace.[19] The taste for archaism did not die out but was put to good use at later times in Augustus' rule. Augustus appointed a flamen of Jupiter, a post which had been left empty for many years, and he increased the privileges of the Vestal Virgins.[20]

None of these archaic rituals called for much participating on the part of ordinary people. Some, even though they were important in the Augustan scheme, were limited to a small group within the governing class, such as the re-creation of the Arval Brethren. The most successful of the revivals was undoubtedly the Secular Games held in 17 BC.[21] Augustus was the chief celebrant though he made the point that he was only acting as the authorized representative of the college of quindecemvirs, who were ultimately responsible in theory for transmitting the decrees of the Sibylline books. The main events took place over three days and nights, consisting of games in the Campus Martius and of sacrifices to different gods and goddesses, culminating with a hymn, specially composed, and a sacrifice to Apollo. The purpose of the rite was to celebrate a form of purification (the people were given fumigants at the ruler's expense), to give thanks for recent prosperity, and to utter prayers for Rome's happiness to continue. All free citizens were encouraged to attend partly on the grounds that (on Augustan calculations, at least) one lifetime could not hope to see the Games a second time, but partly too 'because as many people as possible should witness them, for the sake of religion.' Thus the rite was meant to attract a large congregation which would see the sacrifices performed, some in honour of established gods like Jupiter Optimus Maximus, and some in honour of gods who, like Apollo, had become prominent through their association with Augustus; the latter stood out as a man of restraint, both as messiah and as chief.

The monuments and rituals, in varying degrees, were spread out over the long period of Augustus' rule. Building and restoration never stopped (at the time of Augustus' death four temples were being repaired) even if the grand scale of 28 BC was never quite reached again. The temples perhaps did not offer much more than spectacle for a people that might wish to express its religious sense by congregational acts, though one should not underestimate the role of thanksgiving supplications. But the senate showed it could speak for popular emotion by erecting monuments that were more than a testimonial to the aristocratic sense of grandeur. In 19 BC it dedicated an altar to Fortuna Redux, in honour of Augustus' return from Syria, and later, in 13 BC, his return from the provinces of Gaul and Spain was celebrated by an altar to the Augustan Peace.[22] The monument, dedicated in 9 BC, showed scenes of Augustus, members of his family, and senators, all engaged in sacrifice. The régime became famous for its altars as well as its temples. Some of them were offered by Augustus himself; thus in 9 BC the god Vulcan was honoured by an altar which was financed out of the new year's gifts brought to the emperor by the people. A single theme is apparent in both types of altar, those which were offered by the senate and those which were put up by Augustus himself. With the former Augustus makes the point that he is declining other honours and accepting only that which brings more honour to the gods or deified abstractions than to himself. With the latter he refuses the gift earned by his popularity and success, and neutralizes the dangerous element in the gift by handing it over to the god or gods. In both cases there is as a result a sense of moderation expressed in a traditional religious form, the setting up of an altar. But by the end of the reign a tour of the city would have convinced a traveller that the particular acts of moderation added up to rather more than the sum of the individual altars. Temples, rituals and altars were more than items of self-effacement and in the end they helped to interchange the relative positions of god and man.

For good reasons I have discussed at some length the religious monuments of the Augustan period, as a matter of concern to government and governed. Nor did Augustus neglect the great priestly offices for which his predecessors in the Republic had competed. But his actions show that he treated the priesthoods differently from such important offices of state as the proconsulship and the tribunate. Here the tendency was to take power (such as proconsular power) separated from the office with which it had normally been associated. Augustus had tribunician power but was not a tribune. But the priesthoods were not susceptible of a similar distinction between power and office. There was on the religious side nothing equivalent to the *imperium*, nothing which could be set up without the office; a man could not practise the business of a pontifex unless he was a member of the pontifical college. The priestly offices therefore were less sophisticated than the political. But they were (in Bagehot's terms) among the dignified parts of the constitution and Augustus could not afford to overlook any of them. If he were pontifex, for example, and not an augur, or if he were both these yet not a quindecemvir, the upshot would have been that the offices he did not hold would have declined in prestige, and part of the traditional apparatus of the Republic would have been undermined.

Thus, in order to be a good Republican in one sense, to save the tradition, he accumulated religious posts and offices in a way that would have offended Republican sentiment. It was not in the Republican manner for one man to combine all these religious posts; but Augustus might reply to this charge that there were still plenty of other religious posts to be filled, and that his presence in a college conferred even more dignity on it and them. Yet the accumulation of posts by one man, beginning with the office of pontifex which was given him in 47 BC, marked a significant break with the traditions of the Republic. Augustus indeed, as with other honours, spoke of his moderation in waiting for the death of Lepidus in 13 BC before he claimed his rightful post as chief pontiff, the head of the state religion. The posts kept their appeal as ornaments of a sort but they had lost some of their lustre. It is noticeable that the religious posts continued to operate in the Republican way, as honours in advance, for the heir-apparent. Tiberius, for example, acquired a number of these offices after his adoption by Augustus in AD 4. Other aristocrats, some of them helped by Augustus' support for patricians, were glad to be associated with the ruler by membership of the same college – a process more clearly illustrated under the Empire.

At this stage of the account there may be some advantage in coming to a more general estimate of the part played by revivals of the archaic in religious Augustanism. The archaic (as I have described it here) comprises a mixture of religious activities and rituals, and includes restoration of temples and the filling of traditional offices. This recovery of the past was an important, though not the dominant, aspect of religion in the period; it has to be put by the side of Augustus as the man who continued the Republican tradition made by the great generals, the custom of setting up one's own battle-gods. Thus Augustus's temples to Apollo and Mars Ultor can well appear to be a legitimate and meaningful development, building a religious monument to events of great contemporary significance. By contrast some at least of the revived archaisms had no contemporary value or very little. We are, it seems, faced with the task of evaluating Augustanism as composed of discrepant parts; the vital on the one hand, linked with the modern world, and on the other the pathetic attempt to revitalize a doomed institution like the post of the *flamen Dialis*. Why, then, with a supply of living material, attempt to incorporate dead tissue?

The contrast, when expressed in this way, does not do justice to the whole range of the archaizing movement. It has to be admitted that some of the revivals, temples as well as priesthoods, look fairly empty of value for the contemporary world. But the same cannot be said of the Secular Games; here, if anywhere, is a successful revival of an old ritual, adapted in part to the latest gods and accompanied by games and sacrifices that could be enjoyed or watched by many.[23] The archaic is not confined to outmoded formalities and rites, but covers activities which people can feel have been applicable before as well as in the present. An archaizing movement has a home for the ceremony that can still make itself felt as an occasion of substance, as well as for those other ceremonies that are apparently no more than hollow pageants.

Even the emptier archaisms (I mean by this empty of immediate contemporary relevance) had much to contribute to the growth of religious Augustanism. People were able to see the ceremonies of the past again, not just from curiosity but to confirm their sense that a period of disorder and conflict had come to an end. The classic archaisms, those which are apparently without point for the present, have in fact the function of helping to unite the people, to provide opportunities for observing cherished rituals from the age before the fall. Society in Augustan Rome was greatly helped by the fact that Augustus ruled as long as he did, and distributed the work of restoring the past over many years.

In this version I am laying stress on the idea that archaism had social and political functions which harmonized with the individual monuments of religion, such as buildings which drew attention to Augustus as the modern conqueror, whether we think of his gods in Rome or of temples to the imperial cult in the provinces. Though not directly useful, they gave an illusion of the past and a perspective in which to view the novel anthropolatry of the Augustan age. Open gradualism not stealth was the mark of religious Augustanism. It follows that on this view of events both the emperor (with his immediate circle) and the public were willing partners in the Augustan revival. Because the political climate was now less disturbed, the old practices were no longer the source of division that they had been in the late Republic. The archaizing attempt cannot be dismissed on the grounds that it was imposed by a ruler on a sceptical élite and a 'mongrel city populace, [that] had long been accustomed to scoff at the old deities ...'[24] The archaism of Augustus would not have worked as well as it did had it merely been a civic duty imposed on the recalcitrant. It has been said that 'the archaist is condemned ... to be ever trying to reconcile past and present, and the incompatibility of their competing claims is the weakness of archaism as a way of life.'[25] But Augustan archaism, it seems, was not open to this charge; it worked in such a way as to make the changing present into part of a continuing history.

Augustan Rome has so far been the dominant subject of this analysis. Before we consider religious Augustanism throughout the Empire it is necessary to describe developments within the city which were the religious expression of a civic reorganization. In the Republican past Rome had been divided into separate districts, each with its own cult of deities at the centre, the Lares Compitales; here the pagan sense of the protective deity was multiplied again and again within the same broad locality. When the districts had been remodelled (between 12 and 7 BC) they reappeared with a cult of the Lares Augusti and the Genius of the ruler himself.[26] It had clearly been the custom for some time already to make a libation to the Genius of Augustus as to the power in him which symbolized the begetting of family and prosperity. Here again was restoration of a sort which brought the past into the present by substituting the Lares of Augustus for the district Lares of the past. It was a development which was meant to appeal to the sense of locality and to offer some scope for religious honours to the freedmen, who formed the group from which the supervisors of the cult were selected. Freedmen therefore in Rome had their own priestly honours and celebration of the cult gained in stature because the correct offering to the Genius was upgraded to a bull. In Italy, too, there developed similar honours for freedmen in those towns, increasing in number, which had a cult of Augustus. The cult was managed by six freedmen, appointed every year, who were admitted into the order called Augustales after their office had expired. They were expected to give money for the material comforts of the citizens and received public acknowledgement. It is tempting to suppose that politically and socially Augustanism here was on a different tack from the religious programme; we might say that Augustanism was a system of defining and preserving the lines between the political and social classes but that there was no objection to free men of whatever kind having a share in the loyalty-cult of the ruler. But there is in reality more likeness than difference between the programmes; free citizens and citizens who were freedmen were alike able to pay their respects to the ruler's Genius, but provision was made for ambitions commensurate with status. The citizen who had been established for generations had various social and political goals available; consequently expressing his ambition in religious terms was less important, and indeed in the eyes of an autocrat with pretensions to be treated as a citizen it was even desirable that a libation to his Genius should be enough to satisfy civic enthusiasms. On the other hand first-generation citizens such as freedmen had less to go for in the social and political sense, and it follows that religion (through the cult of the Genius and the Lares of Augustus) could be used to offer them a form of aspiration.

Outside Rome, in the provinces of east and west, the pattern for the imperial cult was set by another Republican tradition, the custom of honouring great Romans with temples. Augustus, like many of his Republican predecessors, associated Roma with his own name, and so made a religious focus for leagues and federations of towns. Each province had its assembly, with a temple to Roma and Augustus and a priest who supervised the sacrifices. The priests became men of importance to be rewarded with honorific statues and a seat in the local senate. Arrangements of this type had long been familiar in the Greek east, as an understandable device for ensuring the patronage of leading Romans. They had not been known in the provinces of the west in Gaul and Spain, which were new to urban culture. In this case, it seems, we have clear evidence that the Romans took a Greek religious invention and re-exported it. What had grown up in the Greek world, through familiarity with Hellenistic rulers, was imposed by the Roman government on the peoples of the west. On the whole it met with a good response. Sometimes the temple was preceded by an altar. The altar at Lugdunum had its dedication day on the 1st of August, the day of the festival of the Celtic god Lug.[27] The new province in Germany had an altar at Cologne, *oppidum Ubiorum*. In peaceful times the altar or temple was a symbol of loyalty; but it was double-edged, for it could easily become a symbol of revolt as when the priest at Cologne tore his headbands and set off to join a rebellion.

Augustus was made the son of a god but did not advance to full godhead until the apotheosis after his death. His religious achievement was extremely complex. He made use of the living traditions of the late Republic – he was Augustus the great general, in receipt of nearly divine honours from Greek cities – and he combined these with revivals from the Roman past, some of which were far more than quaint archaisms. Religion, as we have seen, was made by Augustus to affect the actual lives of different people in many ways, as spectacle (by games), as recurring ceremony, and as celebration of great events, on the leader's return from abroad or on his recovery of the Parthian standards. It provided a new status for some and an additional ornament for others. The most influential element was, without doubt, the glorious tradition, as one might name the Republican habit of building temples out of spoil. The great man Augustus came to be the dominant religious factor in the cities of the Empire, especially in Rome itself.

In spite of the taste for archaism (it was a taste that could be visually enjoyed even by the illiterate many who were unable to venerate the written authority of a Varro) the gradualism of Augustus invaded many parts of religious life. He superseded the great proconsuls of the past and present; their successors and contemporaries were his inferiors and were eventually deprived of those temples to Roma and themselves which would have been their due in an unexpired Republic. The temples were restored, often in the names of their founders, but it was not uncommon for their original birthdays to be replaced by great and auspicious moments taken from the life of Augustus; his own birthday (September 23rd) was a day that had to be solemnized and was made the new birthday of several temples.[28] As a last instance of the spread of Augustanism, calendars of smaller communities developed their key-dates around the theme of events in Augustus' life: August 19th, the first day of his first consulship, was the start of the year at Cumae, and other days of significance in his life, such as January 16th, when he was called Augustus, were also commemorated by official sacrifice or supplication. Augustus had prepared the way for the godhead which was not conferred until after his death. Augustanism on the religious side seems far more complex than the Republic which it succeeded. This is, however, something of an illusion, comparable to the habit of treating the earliest days of the Republic as the time of a simple and purer religion. Augustanism is a continuation of certain habits which had become marked during the latter part of the Republic (I mean the individual monopoly of temples and priestly offices), with a spice of archaism that could be relished after the Republic was over.

Augustanism has been defended and attacked by modern exponents. On one interpretation it succeeded as a form of religion which put right the neglect of the generation before, and so, both formally and aesthetically (with its splendid temples), did justice to the Roman sense of civic deity. On another view Augustanism can be criticized for its failure to take account of the more imaginative or philosophical glosses that can be put on the need for religion. Perhaps the former version pays too much attention to Augustus the antiquarian whereas the latter assumes that spirituality outside politics is more to be commended than the crowd ceremonies of a nearly totalitarian government. Sympathy with the second point of view should not prevent one from trying to judge Augustanism as a complex operation. Its relationship with politics was not simple but was based on a world made up of different phases. The Greek east was experienced in the habits of divine monarchy; Italy and Rome itself had long been used to victors who were almost gods when they celebrated triumphs but who were also exposed to aristocratic carping and military invective, coarse but not ill-humoured; and there was the different world of the Latin west, as we call it, with Gaul and Spain mostly pre-urban except for their littorals. The merit of Augustanism, politically, was that it devised or accepted loyalty formulae that with the usual blurring of a polytheistic age satisfied a great part of the collective impulse.[29]

In the late Republic old-fashioned rituals and prayers had been used to hold up changes of law and new personal appointments; they had been means of expressing disagreement about reform, and had been regarded as tolerable or not according to the sense of interest. With the Augustan age, however, archaism became a means of healing, it was no longer another symptom of disease: between Rome as a city and other towns the difference was one of scale; Augustan archaism was the common link that connected a minor tourist attraction in the provinces with the monumental grandeur of the city itself. A way of understanding the change is to remember that the civic polytheist always suffered from an irritability of the religious temper (he needed reassurance that he had enough good gods and had done the rituals correctly), and that religion was constantly pushed and pulled by politics. Consequently the Republican discontent and the Augustan satisfaction with religious archaism can both be read (in part, if not entirely) as displaced expressions of disapproving or approving of the political order.

CHAPTER FOUR

# *The Later Augustanism*

The history of religion under the Empire, especially that part of it which concerns the interaction with politics, shows that civic polytheism became even more complex. The pantheon was increased by the apotheosized emperors and by the deities imported from the Greek east; the two classes of gods were not exactly like one another, and the eastern gods often had to overcome a Roman will to persecute to which the deified rulers were naturally not exposed. The multiplication of gods is itself a source of confusion and makes it difficult to find a clear meaning in the varied evidence from coins, monuments, inscriptions and literature. A history therefore has to be large enough to accommodate the imperial cult, the surviving traditional cults and the public acceptance of eastern religions. There is here a broad difference between first-order loyalty cults, in which devotion to a man-god coexisted harmoniously with the respect paid to Jupiter or Mars, and secondary cults which were at first feared as outsiders. They were in the end able to enter the dimension of civic loyalty, but they often began their Roman life as the marginal cults of individuals or small groups. This distinction is only made for convenience, and it should be remembered that the next two chapters are complementary, that their subjects were not so easily put asunder in real life.

The later Augustanism was a medley of practices which modified the religious topography of Rome by adding a man-god to the civic cults. The man-god of this period was always of local and international significance, whereas the existing deities might have had either of these characters or both. The deified emperors were revered as such throughout the whole Mediterranean area as well as in the favoured peninsula. Thus any account of the fortune of Augustanism has to take in the provinces in addition to the temples of Rome. It includes the city and those other towns which to a Roman imagination were so many less perfect copies of the one true city.[1]

Augustanism was an elaborate arrangement of the novel and traditional composed in the lifetime of the first emperor and one of its appeals was through its moderation; the ruler advertised this virtue that made him look more like a citizen than an autocrat, without the grandiose touch expected of aristocrats and kings. In politics Augustanism promised to keep up a Republican tradition, and in religion it advertised ties with the past that would satisfy conservative sentiment. But it is undeniable that in the three hundred years between Augustus and Diocletian the Empire became more autocratic and that the new autocracy was expressed in religious as well as in political terms. At the end of this development the would-be citizenly bearing of the first Augustus had become the 'sacred countenance' of a ruler who was approached like a god apart, through the rituals of adoration and ceremonial silence. Diocletian and his co-emperor were described as 'born of gods and creators of gods', a form of religious honour that would have astonished Augustus.[2]

The purpose of this chapter is to show what the emperors gained from the forms of the imperial cult and other more traditional forms of devotion; and to consider why political religion shifted away from the moderate Augustanism with which the Empire was initiated by Augustus and Tiberius. The rulers of course were the apex of a layered pyramid; they were, at their best, admired and sustained partly by the religious acts of certain broad groups, such as upper-class politicians, various guilds and the army. It would be best if we could see how these different elements in society altered, if at all, with the emperors. But as it is impossible to consider the developments in detail I have tried instead to show how men conformed through cult when they were able to observe its practice and enact its rituals in the fullest possible way. Thus the emperors of this chapter are portrayed as the beneficiaries of cults performed by various groups which are assumed for the sake of argument to be in their most flourishing condition, when men are willing and able to pay for what the cult requires. We need an insight into that optimum state of religion (the combination may be imaginary rather than historical) when emperors, whether moderate or autocratic, were surrounded by so many perfect polytheistic servants. Through this contrast we may then be able to put forward a hypothesis to account for the defeat of civic polytheism by Christianity.

### *Imperial Cult*

The first Augustus received cult in various degrees during his lifetime but full divinity was not conferred until after his death. This pattern of apotheosis was usually followed in Rome itself as long as the Empire lasted. The new deity was sooner or later housed in a temple which could be shared with other members of the same family, and cult was performed by a special company of religious officers, usually at first important relatives of the deceased.

Cult of this sort was first and foremost an honour paid to the meritorious dead. It might have been regarded as a prime duty for the living to perform, especially for the successor, even if he were to gain nothing of political or religious value for himself from the deification. Mass gratitude expressed by the senate, people or the army, was often more important as a constructive force than the calculation of personal advantage as it might be worked out by the next emperor. The city gradually acquired new temples to house these deities, rather as less equivocal gods had been or still were installed in Rome. The temple to Augustus was started by Tiberius, dedicated by Caligula, and restored later on, possibly by Domitian, and then by Antoninus Pius. Claudius the god did not acquire a secure home until Vespasian made up for Nero's slight to his predecessor's memory. Domitian housed his father and brother in a temple peculiar to the Flavian family, and most of the second-century rulers were rewarded with their own temples. There was also, apparently, a general temple for all these gods (*divi*) built in the second century AD, and later still the Emperor Tacitus ordered a temple for the 'good rulers', to be filled with the statues of the edifying dead. The cult of the deified emperors has its roots in ancestor-cult. In the late Republic it was not easy to ensure that a memorial to a relative would be binding on others outside the family. But it was now possible to claim that land on which an emperor had been born should be treated as public religious property, and to have the claim accepted.[3]

One purpose of the ritual of apotheosis, with its attendant ceremony of releasing an eagle to soar upwards, was to acclaim the good emperors and to distinguish them from the bad. Not to be deified was always a form of condemnation, the first and most decisive step in posthumous unpopularity. The tributes paid to the first Augustus show a wide variety of honours.

> At the time they declared Augustus immortal, assigned to him priests and sacred rites, and made Livia ... his priestess ... A shrine voted by the senate and built by Livia and Tiberius was erected to the dead emperor in Rome, as were others in many different places, some of the communities voluntarily building them and others unwillingly ... While his shrine was being erected in Rome, they placed a golden image of him on a couch in the temple of Mars, and to this they paid all the honours that they were afterwards to give to his statue.

Probably no later emperor accumulated so many tokens of divinity.[4]

The temples of the good and the dead greatly enhanced the reputation of the living. Although the senate did the formal conferring, the proposal came from the successor; 'nominally by the senate, actually by Tiberius and Livia', in the case of Augustus. The political advantage for the next ruler was considerable, especially if he could deify his immediate predecessor. He could take pride in demonstrating his piety. For Augustus this was a way of emphasizing his connection with the dead Julius who had adopted him. Tiberius met the demands of piety and religion on entering the senate after the death of Augustus in a way that seemed somewhat eccentric: 'He offered sacrifice after the example of Minos with incense and wine but without a flute player, as Minos had done in ancient times on the death of his son.' The newly appointed Claudius, 'turning to the duties of piety', made it his most binding oath to swear by the divine Augustus; he had to go back that far in order to avoid being contaminated by the intervening reigns of the undeified Tiberius and Caligula. The first Antoninus was named Pious early in his reign though his historian is unable to choose between several reasons for the title: his support for his father-in-law, his sparing the lives of senators condemned by Hadrian, or his ready support for the deification of Hadrian.[5]

Piety was one of several virtues which the emperors liked to associate with their rule; there was a tradition of four bequeathed by Augustus, consisting of piety, courage, clemency and justice. Piety could be defined as a form of paying what was due to others, a definition which resembles that of justice. Cicero defines piety (and sanctity) as that which settles the gods and makes them benign towards mankind. It would seem that for much of the Empire the successor's piety was his way of announcing a quasi-filial obligation to a revered ancestor. Filial piety was always a significant Roman value, and a ruler could certainly not dispense with it if he were the successor of a popular ruler who had been deified. Even the semblance of piety was desirable. Macrinus rose against his emperor Caracalla and had him killed, but took care to have him deified as well. It was a virtue which could be used to advertise the harmony supposed to preside over the relations between close members of the imperial family.[6]

Since the family concerned provided the ruler of the Empire, the virtue was no longer of domestic import only but acquired wider political significance. The sense of what was owing to one's family became linked with the will to maintain a dynasty or to fabricate links of ancestry which would initiate one. The great dynasties of the Empire were the Julio-Claudian, the Flavian, the Antonine, the Constantinian and the Theodosian. The pattern of dynastic relationships is shown in Nero's titulary which draws attention to his descent from Claudius the god and from the deified Augustus; it includes forebears who were not deified, not all of whom were creditable, but it can boast a genealogy with at least two names of which any pious successor could be proud.[7] This is not to say that the deified ancestor gave the successor a title to rule, a legitimation, but he forged a connection with an era of undisputed goodness by means of a respected virtue. Piety was itself a way of consolidating a dynasty. The emperor Philip showed that he knew the first letters of the imperial alphabet when he had his own father deified. The senate took what must have seemed a convincing course of action when it asked Severus Alexander to accept the title Antoninus, a revered name in spite of the fact that it had been disgraced by Commodus and Elagabalus. It was natural enough for the senate to make this proposal, but Severus rejected it. He is reported (it is probably an interesting invention) as saying that all emperors succeed to the name of the first Augustus 'either by some form of adoption or by hereditary claim.' But even so his titulary gives him an affiliation with recent *divi*, Caracalla and Septimius Severus. Piety, it should be remembered, had an entrenched value and was therefore of wider use than as the political instrument of rulers in search of recent affiliation. At a late date, in the fourth century AD, the Emperor Julian sacrificed to the divine Gordian merely because his movements in the near east took him past his remote and undistinguished predecessor's tomb. Julian's tribute was an act of free piety without any obvious link with his own political advantage or dynastic gain.[8]

The imperial way of life imposed some religious duties. Piety or the assertion of that virtue enabled the living ruler to associate himself dynastically with a celebrated god. He was also expected to build temples (without being extravagant) and to maintain or repair them. Augustus' own temple, we might say, to anticipate a little, outlived its own dynasty and was repaired by emperors who lived in a different world from the one he had prepared. As a descendant of the deified and as builder-restorer, the ideal emperor was an Augustan moderate. He had a duty to make an appearance on certain religious occasions of state and to offer sacrifice as the son of a deified emperor or as chief pontiff. For an emperor to appear at a sacrifice was to make an act of submission before the gods; the act was necessary but it made the rulers vulnerable to would-be assassins. Tiberius in fact insisted that only knives of lead should be used at sacrifices when he was present, and Hadrian decreed that armed men should be excluded. An emperor would be guilty of neglect if he were to make himself known as one who paid no attention to sinister key dates – (it was not etiquette to disregard the religious calendar in this way, partly because of understandable fear, partly because a break with custom was resented) – but he would not get much credit as a religious man merely by appearing as a chief celebrant on great occasions. The likelihood is that the emperors' observance of public religious occasions was not greeted with much comment; what men noticed was the flouting of conservative tradition or the suggestion of undue indifference to religion. Augustus, Tiberius and

Nero were all correct on state occasions, but in a less public sphere they varied considerably: Augustus was a man with some habits of a superstitious kind that were acceptable to the man in the street (he liked for example to put his shoes on in a certain order) but the other two were indifferent to a marked degree. Tiberius was an adept of astrology and Nero is said to have spurned all cults except that of the Syrian goddess. As Marcus Aurelius said of his father, the ideal was to show respect in a conventional way without being superstitious.[9]

The manufactured gods of the Empire were in many respects like the gods offered by polytheistic tradition. Augustus the god and Hadrian the god had much, if not everything, in common with the civic deities whether or not these had found an equivalent in Olympus. They often had their own shrines, the Augusteia, a name which suggests the grandeur of colosseums and aqueducts even though the actual religious edifices were humbler. They received cult as individuals or as names within a group, and they had been consecrated by means of official decrees. Their legality was not in dispute, any more than their standing as benefactors; like the gods of the past who had been invoked before or after battle they had shown their value to society by their services. Successors were expected to applaud their deified predecessors; rather similarly, ordinary citizens as they died sometimes thanked the other gods that the existing emperor had not yet been called away to the heavens but was still on terrestrial duty.[10] It was only prudent to assume that one's current ruler would eventually be deified, whatever his deserts. More negatively, the new man-gods were subject to the vagaries of fashion and could well expect to see their fortunes retreat after a period of dominance, like some of the deities from the Republic.

The likenesses seemed even more acceptable in a culture that had learned to explain its inherited gods through the doctrines of euhemerism. It was certain that the man-gods had once had a human history, that Claudius or Trajan had been rulers on earth before they flowered as gods; and, similarly, it became at least probable by analogy with euhemerism that the earlier gods too had had life on earth. No one would have said that a god could be no greater than the kingdom he had once ruled, but most would have expected that the two achievements should be commensurate. But there were also substantial points of difference between the imperial gods and the inherited civic gods. Some of the man-gods (or, rather, their nearest and dearest) could have their names struck off the register. Similarly, a temple could be transferred, and so Faustina gave way to Elagabalus. As the Empire went on some of the new deities did not receive cult as individuals, as gods in their own temple, but collectively. They did not have the vitality of the older gods, the ability to attract to themselves that wide range of cult-epithets which bewilders the student of Jupiter, Hercules or Silvanus, to name only three. We hear of Jupiter Augustus, not of Augustus Jupiter; but Augustus, it is fair to add, enjoyed some variety of titles, as Soter or Eleutherios. The emperor-gods multiplied not as individuals but through the generic form of the name Augustus; the great qualities and achievements – peace, victory and health, for example – could all be described as 'Augustan', with the understanding that the claim would be referred to a recent particular emperor, not solely to the first Augustus. The man-gods were regarded with piety by their heirs and successors, but they were never quite on easy terms with the other gods. A possible reason is that during their lives they had been thought of as in the care of the standard deities – men prayed to Mars, for instance, as the guardian of 'our master Gordian' – and so it might be difficult for these new gods to rise above or equal Mars, even when they had passed over into godhead. Their accomplishments as gods were on the whole confined to the political enhancement of family interests.[11]

As Lucian indicates, some forms of deity were no longer as satisfied as they were supposed to have been in the past, a past that could be evoked by poetic tradition and sentimental history. If a god was mainly kept going by sacrifice then the deities at Olympia would have a four-year interval between decent meals except for the snacks provided by the shrinking population of the locality.[12] The satire is meant (quite rightly) to draw attention to the importance of the link between the gods and their worshippers; a god who eats can only be as operant as the sacrifice and is perhaps the inferior of a deity who can be consumed symbolically. This kind of starvation was spared the new gods of the Empire. They had immortality of a sort, for even many years after their apotheosis they might have their temple repaired or receive prayers collectively. But on the whole they had the secret not of immortality but of longevity. Their effectiveness as originators or transmitters of piety flourished and lasted as long as the dynasty to which they belonged. Augustus as a god mattered far less after the death of Nero, for this marked the end of the Julio-Claudian family. Similarly the Antonines counted for little as gods after the death of Severus Alexander, and the Constantinian tree of gods, which started with Claudius Gothicus, ended with Julian. Thus for brief periods the civic sky looked Augustan or Flavian or mostly Antonine, and so the political gods invented for the protection and welfare of the Empire were essentially dynastic. They survived of course in invocations and prayers after the dynasty had come to a stop, but it is still true to say that the collapse of the dynasty made some of the gods less relevant. Modern historians of the cult have usually been embarrassed by the very idea that politicians or rulers could be the recipients of worship, whether during or after life. The real trouble with the arrangement was that the dynasties afflicted the state with the ills of their own terminability. Dynasties could die from various causes, such as lack of heirs or unsuitable conduct on a ruler's part; the ultimate rejection came when a new ruler did not even want to be regarded as the adoptive successor. It would have been better if all the emperors one after the other, as Severus Alexander implied, had been able to maintain or parade a connection with the first god, the divine Augustus. The *divi* of an earlier dynasty might be included in oaths but the gods who mattered most were those of the immediate past. In this assessment I am attempting no more than a general estimate of a man-god's later potency as a political friend to emperors. Some forms of benefactor-cult lasted a long time but we should make due allowance for mere courtesy to the past. To take an example, at Gytheum near Sparta the general Flamininus was still remembered some two hundred years after his liberation of Greece, but there can be little doubt that in the celebrations the recent and living benefactors mentioned in the inscription, Augustus, now deified, and Tiberius, counted for more.[13]

So far the main theme of this account has been the political effect of the cult on the living emperors at Rome in helping to create a form of dynastic piety that would be most apparent on great occasions in the city, such as sacrifices or meetings in the senate. Outside Rome, in Italy and the provinces, the cult was extended and developed, though not, it seems, in a systematic manner. The practice began (as we saw earlier) as a genuine demonstration in the Greek east, where the living emperor became the main recipient of a cult to Roma and Augustus. The Greeks, accustomed to the ways of Hellenistic cult, set the pace, whereas in parts of the west at least it seems that imperial policy made the running. There were altars to Roma and Augustus set up during the lifetime of the first Augustus; given that the three Gauls at this stage were years behind the east in political development, it is likely that the main initiative was imperial though this need not rule out an enthusiastic native response. It is certain, for instance, that in Spain a native Iberian and Celtic custom of acting as a group loyal to a victorious war-leader was readily adapted to certain forms of Roman rule, such as clientship and imperial cult. Similarly in Africa the native regard for a ruler like Masinissa was naturally transferred to a Roman object.[14]

The cult was practised at different levels in towns and in whole regions, in municipalities and in provinces. One of the objectives was to create a provincial assembly which represented a wide area and held its meetings at larger centres, as at Narbo or Lugdunum. The cults were not, however, instituted at a single Augustan stroke. The provincial cults in proconsular Africa, in Narbonese Gaul and in Baetica, for example, do not seem to have been introduced until the time of Vespasian. The system, such as it was, grew slowly, and though there were two partners, the province and the emperor, the initiative did not always lie with the government. In some parts, as in Moesia and Dalmatia, little seems to be known about the starting-date.[15]

The provincial cult with its meetings had several functions of a social and political kind. It gave an outlet for glory-seekers at a higher level than that of the small town, since priests of the cult were men of considerable influence and wealth. It assisted the Roman authorities by introducing a form of Romanization that was palatable to the inhabitants of a province. This was probably most successful in those areas which had been effectively subdued, as in the three Gauls, where feelings of loyalty were already established and could be fostered by a loyalty-centre. The cult was probably introduced as a matter of urgency into less Romanized areas, but it was at times markedly less effective in parts where the degree of the conquest had been overestimated. At Cologne, for example, in the year of the great rebellion, the German priest discarded the insignia of his office and was quick to join the disaffected. Tacitus refers to the temple of Claudius in Britain as a stronghold of undying tyranny; this is rhetoric, of course, but it is rhetoric of a kind that amplifies the truth, not of the kind that tells outright lies. The Romans put altars up but the Germans looked upon them as the hostile tokens of an invader who should be dispossessed. The signs are that the altars and temples of the cult helped to confirm the presence of Rome. They were part of an urban package that came with the conquest but might inflame opposition if the timing were premature.[16]

Provincial assemblies were concerned with more than paying tribute in the form of cult to a living or departed emperor. Its members were in a sense representatives of communities within the province and could initiate legal proceedings against unsatisfactory governors. They also had the power of reward as they could decide whether ex-governors should be set up forever in congratulatory marble. A deputation from the assembly to an emperor might have several matters to raise at court, but complaints about governors' conduct could well be among the more serious items. The assemblies therefore had the right and duty to worship coupled with a right to open the procedure for legal redress.

But it is difficult to decide which of the two activities was more important, whether (to put the question in a traditional form) the religious function of the assembly was prior to its quasi-judicial role. Both views have had their advocates. It may be more instructive, however, to compare the religious activity of the assembly with other religious activity, and to compare the administrative role of the assembly with other forms of administration. The key fact is that the assemblies did not meet more than once a year. It follows that neither their religion nor their administration could be regarded as a full-time concern. Within the Roman world as a whole cultic religion was often of the once-a-year variety, but administration was different; though no one would pretend that a Roman governor was over-worked, his activities were spread over a greater part of the year. This might suggest the conclusion that religion in the provinces was just as occasional as in Rome itself, whereas the assembly's political or judicial capacity was (however important to the locals) highly marginal compared with the full-time administrative roles of emperors and their subordinates, such as governors or prefects. The hypothesis might thus confirm the theory that the provincial assemblies' political role was in effect an 'afterthought', posterior to its cultic function. But the comparisons adduced here are of course extremely crude. It is worth remembering that quantitatively a complaint about a governor might have counted for a great deal, that there could have been a lot of politicking within the province before the day when the decision was finally made to approach the emperor on a given issue.[17]

For nearly all of the imperial period provincial cult differed from the urban cult at Rome in one apparently significant respect. It was cult of the living emperor not of a deceased ruler with whom the living could claim dynastic links by descent or adoption. The distinction seemed important especially to those who were convinced that the emperor ought to keep up an appearance of Republican moderation and piety towards an ancestor. But the distinction may well seem too fine to matter much, especially if we take a broad view of the ways in which religion affected public life. The imperial cult, for all the differences between Rome and the provinces, was the celebration of a dynastic leader who was either god already or a god-to-be proceeding from the deified.

It is important to avoid making the obvious assumption that Rome provided the colonizing power and that the provincials were the colonized. The idea, if it were to be applied at all, could only be relevant to Roman religious development of the western territories, not of the east. It seems plausible at first in view of the fact that the migratory movement of religions and cults was in general from east to west across the Mediterranean. We may therefore be tempted to think of Rome as colonizing the west with a particular brand of political religion in the shape of the imperial cult. But the meeting between Rome on the one hand and the Spains and the Gauls on the other was not of the kind in which the defeated succumb resentfully or sullenly before the gods of the missionary victors. Both sides were alike in that they were polytheists prepared and able to recognize their own gods in the deities of others. In Spain too there were particular factors which helped to make the whole region a consenting territory on which the imperial cult did not have to be imposed.[18]

The cult should be set against its background of polytheistic assimilation. It was never expected to supplant the existing or traditional gods but to co-exist. The emperor-gods did not have the sort of countenance in which the practised onlooker could see other deities; they would not absorb other gods and they did not have the mobility of a Roman or a Gallic god, but they were good, or at least adequate, neighbours. Admiration for Rome (together with a voracious appetite for more forms of god) led the native peoples to give Roman names or cult-titles to their own divinities. The polytheistic way was to blend and combine gods without expelling them. The general tendency of the religious culture was to be all-inclusive, a tendency which was reinforced as provincials started to emulate Rome, and Romans and Italians accepted local ways by effectively settling as businessmen or soldiers.

When the first Augustus visited Alexandria he made scornful remarks about the Ptolemies but showed respect for the memory of Alexander the Great. He was taking no account of the fact that pre-Roman ruler-cult in Egypt had deified both the Ptolemies and Alexander, establishing in the harmony of one dynastic cult founder-figures who were not separable except in the prejudiced mind of the Roman invader. Egypt and Rome may legitimately be compared as having variants of ruler-cult. The Roman system was looser than the Ptolemaic; it did not create so many priesthoods for the ruling family and it lacked the dynastic continuity of the Ptolemies. Whereas the Roman version in the main was merely adjacent to the major civic cult of Jupiter, the Ptolemies proclaimed a special link with Dionysus, because the god's genealogy showed him as their ancestor and his alleged travels made him into a proto-Alexander. In speaking of the greater looseness of the Roman imperial cult no criticism is intended; for one thing the greater size of the Roman Empire would not have made it possible for the emperors to practise a supervision with Ptolemaic strictness. As far as we can judge there may well have been a considerable degree of voluntariness in the provincial expression of the Roman imperial cult, and there are too the visible signs of a ready co-operation with central government through the provincial assemblies. The possible effects of the religious organization and the failure of the assemblies to mature as political agents will be discussed later.[19]

### *Emperors and Subjects*

The imperial cult did not displace the traditional cults but reinforced them by adding new deities and new forms of religious office. Deification had an autocratic potential to which individual emperors adopted varying attitudes. The extremes among these attitudes can be depicted with some sureness of touch, and it may become clear whether the drift away from Augustan moderation was mostly affected by deviant individual rulers or by more general factors.

The first Augustus had portrayed himself as a religious traditionalist pitted against the strange gods of Egypt on the side of Antony and Cleopatra. He stood out in this way as the subordinate of Neptune, Venus and Minerva or as the adept of Apollo, whereas Antony on many occasions appeared as Dionysus himself. The relevant difference is between regarding oneself as a minister of the gods and appearing in the guise of a deity. Most of the emperors can be considered either as Augustans (moderates) in religion or as Antonians (extremists). An outline of their characteristics may help to fix their types.[20]

The model Augustan ought to give the impression of being a reluctant ruler. He refuses honorific titles such as *pater patriae*, even though they are sincerely offered by a grateful senate and people. Probus for example was made to wear a purple robe taken from a statue in a temple, but he is said to have shown a becoming resistance to this form of accession; if it was taken from the statue of a god the soldiers were presumably indifferent to uncovering a god in order to dress an emperor, but the latter was more coy. It was important for an Augustan to show modesty about his own religious claims while being punctilious in securing divine honours for his own family or close relatives. He acts in a citizenlike manner by not allowing state events like Jupiter's games to be interrupted because of a death in the royal family; he will not have his own name inscribed on temples that have been repaired during his reign, but restores the founder's name. Above all he makes it plain that he has a high regard for venerated Roman tradition. He attends official sacrifices and may even know the arcane formulae without having to be prompted by an expert. He makes his vows on the Capitol or undertakes a purification of the city before an important campaign. He allows the pontiffs and other priests some scope in sacrifices which he has (rightly) made as chief pontiff, and he makes offerings in temples on a royal scale. His deportment in matters connected with religion shows his modesty, his respect for and knowledge of the tradition, his willingness to let the gods come first and put himself second. Many of these traits have good precedents from Republican history or from the career of the Emperor Augustus.[21]

The Antonian on the other hand (to adopt the name as a convenient metaphor) appears as a god in public, like Caligula standing between his brother-gods Castor and Pollux, or like Commodus dressing up as Hercules.

He arranges for sacrifice on too extravagant a scale, with animal victims that are not authorized by tradition; or he accepts for his own Genius a sacrifice that an Augustan would properly offer to Jupiter. He flouts the religious order in various ways: by celebrating games when the wish takes him instead of following the calendar; by entering temples when he has just taken citizens' lives; by not going to the Capitol when he should or by making a visit there for merely personal ends, like Nero rejoicing after his mother's death; by destroying religious buildings or not having them repaired; by compelling the pontiffs to meet in an imperial residence instead of in their usual place and getting them to pass a barbarous decision.[22]

A good way of distinguishing the two extremes is by discovering an emperor's attitude to statues of himself in precious metals, gold and silver. Augustus himself had defined the ideal when he had silver statues of himself taken down and replaced them with offerings of gold in the temple of Apollo. Maecenas is said to have spoken against silver images and to have urged his leader to make his true memorial in his subject's hearts. But the tradition was in fact somewhat more indulgent to sculpture as good emperors were allowed to be set up in bronze. Trajan has one or two statues of himself in the entrance-hall of Jupiter's temple, whereas in an earlier reign all the approaches to the temple were 'polluted' with gold and silver idols of Domitian. The reason for the distinction is that gold and silver were the traditional material for likenesses of gods. Humans, even emperors, should not usurp divine property or let their statues be put up among the images of gods – they may however appear among the temple ornaments. Provincial statues of emperors were not always controlled as strictly; thus Baetica produced a gold Augustus and in AD 104 Ephesus was adorned with silver statues of Trajan and Plotina.[23]

These characters are composite or Theophrastan. No one emperor was ever quite as pure or impure as the above catalogue might suggest. It is also important not to exaggerate the role of religion as an influential factor in imperial history. A moderate and a modest attitude to religion would help a candidate for the Empire in time of civil war, as it was used to commend Vespasian. But wrong religion does not appear among the complaints made against Nero by a rebellious officer, nor does it feature among the causes of bad imperial conduct discussed in an important passage in the *Augustan History*. The values expressed in the above catalogue of qualities and defects are, broadly speaking, senatorial and old-fashioned. But even so, with these various provisos, they may well indicate what many men, not only senators, expected of their emperors' religion.[24]

It would be difficult to get complete agreement on a list of Antonians, but it would certainly include, for one reason or another, Caligula, Nero,

Domitian, Commodus, Caracalla and Elagabalus. The tradition accuses nearly all of them of religious presumption, in claiming identity with a god. But we should not therefore suppose that all we have to do is to invoke a simple theory of outrage on the supposition that a believing or credulous populace was shocked by a ruler suffering from delusions of grandeur. Probably many people *were* shocked, but what they objected to was the flouting of tradition through what seemed a misplaced parody; they were wounded in their sense of decorum as well as in their convictions. A temple had religious, administrative and aesthetic functions. The emperor who identified himself with a god was therefore trespassing on the domain of the gods by appearing as a live person among the images. This intrusion into the temple ornaments can aptly be described as an aesthetic incongruity, the false impression made by a strange mixture of the live and the inanimate.

The antics of Caligula, or of Commodus masquerading as Hercules, had little long-term effect. The emperors who identified wholly or in part with a god cannot be said to have caused the breakdown of religious Augustanism, to have brought the day nearer when the emperor would no longer be merely the first citizen in religion. The distinction between Augustan moderates and Antonian extremists is legitimate but it was of more importance to contemporaries than it is to historians. Some of the resented emperors, like Nero and Domitian, could for much of their rule be interpreted as Augustans in religion. Domitian for example was nothing but correct in his filial piety for the Flavian temple; he fostered traditional cults like those of Jupiter Optimus Maximus, Jupiter Custos and Minerva, but he became infamous because of his title 'master and god', which suggested that he was absolute both as human and as deity.[25]

Even under moderate emperors there were at work extreme tendencies in religion. Tiberius, for example, was moderate but ineffective in that he did not receive apotheosis after death. Clearly, as far as he could he set himself to follow an Augustan model. He allowed the province of Asia to erect a temple to himself, his mother and the senate, but shortly after disallowed a request from Spain to put up a temple for himself, and his mother. He objected to the idea that the emperor should be worshipped as a deity through all the provinces, though the latter, of course, could be more audacious than the metropolis. In general, however, Tiberius ended by receiving the titles he had at first refused. Moderation was, somewhat paradoxically, a virtue for display rather than use and it did not have much effect on holding back the widespread tendencies to absolutism.[26]

The first great moderate left his successor one of the thorniest problems of all. It concerned the asylum-rights of the statues or portraits of the deified Augustus. If the new god were really an absolute deity his effigy might be thought to confer impunity, so that it could become a legal refuge for those who chose to insult the upper classes, secure in the knowledge that they would be protected by the inanimate power of Augustus. Asylum would therefore be granted to the impudent, and the social order might be endangered by fraudulent appeals to the god's majesty. But Tiberius made it clear that taking a self-appointed refugee by force from a statue or image of the deified Augustus would not as such constitute a treasonable offence against the god. Asylum-right, which had been conferred earlier on a temple of Divus Julius, was an attribute of the deified but it did not have much effect on social and political life. The codes show that the imperial statue was empowered (in theory) to function as a refuge for a slave who complained of maltreatment, but not for those who merely wished to vilify others.[27]

On a natural interpretation Tiberius' words to a request from Gytheum – 'I am content with more moderate honours' (than those offered to Augustus) – suggests an attempt to be moderate, with the living emperor put discreetly in the shadow of the acknowledged god.[28] But whatever interpretation is put on this episode, it seems to be undeniable that the emperor's religious position was affected by processes to which the individual merits or demerits of particular rulers were irrelevant. Two illustrations will clarify the general trend. The Republic had known the custom of making prayers for the welfare of the whole state; in the late Republic this practice was modified, as when prayers were made for Pompey's recovery and for the Consul Hirtius. Though Cicero sneered at this as so much Greek flattery, the Romans showed they had little or nothing to learn in this respect. With the arrival of the Empire the state had now become so much identified with one individual that prayers for 'the emperor's safety' and similar forms were the up-to-date equivalent of the early Republican prayer for the 'safety of the state'. A similar development occurred with supplications, for here too the practice became closely associated with the royal family. The provinces could make a supplication to the 'godhead of Augustus', and calendars show that the rite was required on important days in the emperor's life. It is natural to suppose that the supplications to the first Augustus, fifty-five in all, were an expression of genuine devotion, but that, by contrast, in the much shorter reign of Nero, the honour of ten supplications, still a relatively high number, was not given with the same enthusiasm. However, the Empire is not merely to be studied as an oscillation between subjects' sincerity and hypocrisy. Supplications had followed much the same track as prayers. They had started as a rite to a god or gods on behalf of the state, they developed into a form of rivalry between leading men, and ended as an honour (not without religious feeling) for one man; even though in the supplications of the Empire the ruler does not have a complete monopoly.[29]

The general interpretation of religion in the Empire should allow that the emperor himself became the principal or even the exclusive object of the religious ceremony which had developed in the Republic and had been dispersed among the aristocrats of the late Republic. The change to a near-monopoly is the instructive theme, not the speculative question whether genuine religious feeling faded away. Religion was still relatively undeveloped compared with the political operations of the Empire, even if we suppose that divine election,[30] the notion that emperors are appointed by god, became accepted doctrine and practice as time went on. The later Empire has much in common with the earlier; its religious activity, though multifarious, is still secondary and dependent on political functioning; the difference is that the later emperor is now surrounded by more of the ceremonial attaching to religion, he is still thought of as a human being but one who is more protected by the apparatus of godhead. In the end the whole tendency was to make the emperor feel even more powerful and still more able to command religion to assume the postures he required.

But the emperors themselves did not advance this policy by deliberate intent. They absorbed deity and godliness, they did not set out to diminish the gods. Their appetite for religious ceremony was assisted by the adulation of the upper classes in the senate. The emperors were often in the paradoxical position of having to refuse what was offered, and senators would find themselves offering exaggerated honours which they would rather have withheld even in their simple form. In the Augustan, early phase of his reign, Nero found himself having to refuse the senate's wish to honour him with gold or silver statues, and rejecting their decision to make the official year begin with his birth-month instead of in January. The flattery, which was difficult to avoid given the nature of the relationship between emperor and senate, made it difficult even for emperors who were vigilant in the cause of moderation to refuse what was offered. In other words moderation became an artificiality with no roots at all in the attitudes of senate or army, where inflation and hyperbole of language became the order of history.[31]

Another reason for the changes in the Empire lay in the archaism which was originally a creative part of Augustanism. For the first Augustus archaism was a revival of lost or dim traditions and it achieved a notable success in the Secular Games. These were repeated during the Empire. But archaism was not always the same source of strength to later emperors. The historian Tacitus noticed several instances of archaism that had become a means of concealing political innovations of an autocratic kind. In a certain trial Urgulania, a protégée of the great Livia, ought to have given evidence openly, on oath, but she was allowed to give it in private, ostensibly because of respect for her position as a Vestal Virgin. This was (in Tacitus' opinion) merely a camouflage for the crucial fact, her relationship with the empress Livia, by which she hoped to keep out of the public eye. Again, Tiberius criticized Germanicus for attending funerals on the grounds that he was an augur, but his real reason, according to the historian, was fear of Germanicus as a general. Domitian, not dissimilarly, abused the archaic by having a Vestal Virgin sentenced to a form of death that was traditional but now seemed cruel. The archaic therefore could be made into a pretext for arbitrary action. It was, too, objectionable as a way of distracting citizens from their lost freedom. Tacitus, for example, refers to several discussions of ceremonial minutiae, with the implication that the senate was given nothing more important to talk about.[32] But though such occasions all support Tacitus' idea of the Empire as a tyranny, there was another form of archaism that could be used by an emperor to work against the aggrandizement of the royal family. A senator proposed that the official priests who were appointed to conduct games in honour of Livia should include the fetials in their number; his intention was no doubt to add more distinction to the event by increasing the number of religious officials. But Tiberius was more than a match for the sycophant; he showed with pedantic thoroughness that fetials had never had this privilege and so should not have it in modern times. Archaism here was used by the emperor as an argument against over-extending honours of a religious kind. It combats the flattery offered by the citizen. The event exhibits a curious and not untypical tension; adulation of the ruler by the subject tended to widen the gap between the two, and archaism could be an instrument used by the emperor against making the royal position more autocratic and in defence of civic moderation. Religious archaism, then, might be put to the service of intensifying the autocracy or taking away from it. In both cases it becomes clear that archaism was not just a piece of simple healing, acclaimed by all as a reverent tribute to the past, but could be a political device with a potential for causing friction and disunity.[33]

In earlier Rome, even in the city of the late Republic, the social and physical expression of religion was often a bond between citizens. The latter would in the natural way of things hold meetings in temples, see games celebrated before the gods' residences or visit the temples for acts of supplication. The imperial system continued to express religious feeling in a search for a way of showing allegiance to the emperor and through the religious interdependence of the provinces. The new world needed institutions and practices that were viable away from Rome as well as those which were locally Roman. Loyalty to the system was given something of a religious expression by the upper classes, by freedmen, and in the various guilds and army units. The following account is meant as a static depiction of certain practices assumed to be in their optimum condition, with no attempt to consider whether or not there was change.

It might be difficult to find a more exemplary senator than the younger Pliny. Like his own Republican model Cicero he was proud to be made an augur. In this he would be able to take pride in the fact that the emperor's commendation of him played a part, and Pliny says it is important to obey the emperor in small matters as well as great. The religious office is valued as a visible piece of the Republic, not waved away as it might be. Also it is clearly an honour for which Pliny has been competing over several years; he has been nominated many times before but has only just been appointed.

There are some similarities with the system of the late Republic, a like enjoyment of religious office not for any power it confers but for its ceremonial adornment. In the late Republic politicians from families that had often held this office would expect to acquire religious posts early in their careers, before they made their own political impact. Their closest cousins or successors under the Empire are those near to the reigning emperors who were given such priestly titles early in their lives and in great profusion. Not only were they pontiffs and augurs, they were also priests in the fraternity devoted to the deified emperors. On the other hand the less great had their rewards later. Pliny therefore, who makes much of his rather factitious rivalry with Cicero, is, like Cicero, to be placed in the less important of the two camps; his augurate is a confirmatory reward, it is not and cannot be the sort of preparatory honour that marks out one who is the royal heir or a relative of the first rank through natural ties or adoption.[34]

The Plinies of the Roman world received honours like these from the emperor, and were also expected to give in return. Pliny, who had inherited some statues of various emperors, decided to bring them all together and have them housed in a temple, built at his own expense, in his own town of Comum. He asks Trajan's permission (which is granted with suitable imperial modesty) to add to the collection a statue of Trajan himself. There was more than one purpose to this act of generosity by one of the new aristocracy of merit. It was partly munificence – the town Comum would itself be beautified and would be able to visualize the *princeps* in his own temple-museum – partly piety, for Pliny's bounty would be a proof of his pious duty to his emperor rather as his emperor showed piety towards the deceased and deified Nerva. The small-town temple is to the greater exhibits in Rome as Pliny's piety is to his master's piety. The imperial statues would not be merely museum pieces; one of them, at any rate, would be tangible proof of the emperor's magic presence. The loyal functioning of men in Pliny's class would be tested in part by the gifts they received from on high and by the offerings they made in their turn.[35]

The priesthoods (except for those which were conferred on closely related royals) lost what political bite they had had in the Republic. Even in those days the pontiffs or augurs could not make much political advantage out of their office. Under the Empire they were consulted, if at all, as something of a charade, to give authority to an imperial whim. Thus the pontiffs were approached to see if there were any obstacle to Claudius' marriage with his niece Agrippina. Their freedom of manoeuvre was very little and their office was easily made to look like an archaism, covering up an arbitrary action in the present. On the other hand they held their position for life and its value was probably increased slightly because the number of ex office-holders willing to be honoured in this way was greater than the number of posts.[36]

In a world full of secondary persons, in which the activities of the political office-holder were so dependent upon the emperor, augurates and other priesthoods gave their holders another form of ceremonial power. In the early Empire at any rate the titles of religious office gave a lifetime tenure of something very like that which a man had held only briefly as consul or as praetor. In much the same way ceremonial power of this type can be observed among the well-off provincials who serviced the imperial cult in the provincial assemblies, and among the freedmen Augustales who held a like office in the towns. Only provincials who had filled 'all the offices in their own community' were selected as provincial priests, and only freedmen of means were chosen as Augustales. To say of senatorial augurs, provincial priests and municipal Augustales, that they held ceremonial power is only a small (though important) part of the truth. Their positions were more obviously quasi-magistratual, especially in the case of the Augustales. All groups were alike in that society expected benefits from them, amenities like baths or temples, in return for honorific statues and, perhaps, a profitable influence in business affairs. If imperial cult was benefactor cult, it associated with the source of all benefits, the emperor himself, a multitude of lesser benefactors, who provided as a rule for their localities what the emperors might do for Rome or for special places like disaster areas. This form of religion was used to improve the material quality of life; it is unlikely that it functioned as a refinement of manners, unlikely that the offices described were felt to be a moral or a spiritual challenge. The provincial priesthood has analogies with the Roman flaminate, but the borrowed archaism was in the externals and was probably not matched by awe of the ceremony; and the only realistic description, by Petronius, shows us an Augustalis whose self-importance has been increased and made even more gross through his religious office.[37]

Traditional goods provided through religious institutions consisted of sacrifices, banquets and games. These were made available in many forms. The different towns in Roman society had an amazing variety of guilds, colleges or corporations, some of them being unions of craftsmen, others being formed by wealthier groups such as merchants and traders. A college in the Roman sense was itself a small version of the city, it had to acknowledge a patron deity and might also pay cult to other deities. The members might hold their meetings in a public temple, like the college of Aesculapius and Hygia which met in the temple of divus Titus, or the smiths who met in the temple of Neptune at Ravenna. Alternatively it might meet on its own premises in a *schola*; whatever the name (it could also be called a temple), the building was dedicated to a god. The main religious activities were concerned with celebrating the god's birthday, with holding special dinners and making special distributions of presents or food, and sometimes with acting as funeral clubs, ensuring that provident members would have a decent burial. Some colleges or guilds had originated in a benefaction and one of the functions of the club was to hold a yearly sacrifice in memory of the donor. Some guilds were explicitly loyal – they might pay cult to the Augustan family or celebrate the current ruler's accession day; some were the appendage of traditional gods; and others were formed by the cult groups of newish, eastern deities that had become respectable and had earned their entrance-ticket into Roman culture. The link with the emperor was real enough even if he were honoured only indirectly.[38]

Another large group to be considered is the army, with its numerous divisions into legions and cohorts. The army was the Roman people in its full military expression. Thus the army too would naturally seek the protection of certain gods, and in its camps, as in the temples of Rome, 'secular and religious affairs were indivisibly mixed'. It showed particular regard for its own standards and eagles (Valerius Maximus, by a plausible rhetorical touch, imagines the eagles of a legion punishing a lustful centurion for his homosexual appetites) as well as for the emperor's Genius. A legion therefore showed its loyalty in religion. But it also offered cult to a great variety of deities. The clerks for example would have a special cult of their appropriate power, Minerva. The whole legion would naturally have regard for the Genius of the place where it was stationed, and for the local gods, the *dii campestres*. When Trajan and Julian in their campaigns honoured gods they happened to pass near they were only performing temporary cult on the move rather as an encamped legion would have offered cult in a more permanent form. Apart from the special legionary deities, officers and men acknowledged many gods, some of them the gods they had known in Rome or Italy, some of them gods discovered in the provinces. The familiar gods brought from Italy and the more obscure gods of the lands of service were the cult-objects of private or off-duty worship.[39]

The army calendar shows great regard for the imperial cult, often subject to the sort of dynastic limitation that was discussed earlier. And because the army was the people in military dress, it honoured certain festivals as occasions of great enjoyment. In the Dura calendar, for example, the festivals of Minerva and Neptune appear, not for any particular military reason, but simply because they were popular occasions. Also both in civilian life and in the army the new year vows of loyalty to the imperial house made January the 3rd a day of religious solemnity.[40]

The purpose of these brief sketches is to indicate how various groups – senators, provincials, freedmen, members of guilds and soldiers – contributed to religion in the form of cult acts. If we imagine for the sake of argument an unspecified time when the Empire was receiving an adequate service from these groups, we may ask what significant changes there had been since the heyday of the expanding Republic. The new gods of the autocracy attracted to themselves much of the cult but were not in principle opposed to the normal gods of the state; they were not rivals and there was nothing selfish or exclusive about the worship they claimed, which might even be called non-competitive. The Empire inherited the Republican habit of building new temples but did so more sparingly; it was, however, more officious in restoring buildings that had been ruined by time, flood or fire, but this is hardly surprising as there were now more temples anyway. These are minor changes. Perhaps a more significant change can be discerned in the financing of temples and such activities as celebratory games. In the great days of expansion these had been (very often) financed from conquest, they were manubial, derived from spoil or imported wealth. The Empire had its conquests too but these were offset by what one might call the victories of retreat. Consequently it is a reasonable surmise that the religious practices and sometimes the buildings of the Empire were paid for out of the internal economy, from the surplus that benefactors were willing to spend. In this sense the emperors, together with senators like Pliny and other religious officers, were devouring their own wealth in order to sustain the inhabitants of the Empire on its games, sacrifices, banquets and buildings. I am not suggesting that the religious energies of the Empire were inadequately financed; the imperial bounty or the high-placed individual's benefaction dipped into funds that somehow became available.[41] It is also possible that this activity was an essential stimulus to the economy. But it may be that the increased internal financing of religion under the Empire induced a certain passivity and a readiness to combine elements which were ultimately incompatible. It may be that polytheism of the Roman type is most normal when it is successfully adventurous in war, winning spoil of which part can be used to build monuments to its gods. It conquers the outside world without forgetting the deities that give success. It expects all incoming gods to be in the end compatible with its own. The tradition is that a god is certificated by a general's victory, or by the prayer that is ultimately consecrated by victory. The practice was entirely without risk for polytheism as long as wars were undertaken against powers with similar civic cults. But it was a practice that developed little in the way of self-critical reliance; it created a way of thinking that was always ready to suppose that a victory-god must be somehow compatible with the traditional interests of the polytheistic state.

The Empire, as a form of Augustanism, was an attempt to conserve what the Republic had acquired or whatever cults seemed compatible with the recognized tradition. It gave all the appearance of succeeding for many years but failed in the end. It seems impossible to point to certain clear events or processes (apart from Constantine's making Christianity official) through which we can read the various stages of the collapse of polytheism. The change was a long-term phenomenon and it is difficult, partly because of the sketchy evidence, to give convincing details of the passage from polytheism to monotheism. We may here however add some theoretical ideas about the possible weakness of civic polytheism. The following remarks are not intended to do more than canvass a few possibilities.

Conventional wisdom has offered two main reasons to account for the defeat of Roman civic polytheism. One is that it succumbed to Christianity as falsehood gives way before truth. The other is that it was an emotionally sterile religion which had little or no hold on men's minds and so it was for this reason that even upright and traditional Romans turned to the more inspiring religions of the east, including Christianity. The assumptions of the first reason will not be questioned by Christians, and the second is based (in part at least) on the idea that public ceremony means private boredom and that individual spiritual deprivation can only be satisfied outside the occasions and practices of civic arrangements. The principal defect of these explanations is that they pay no attention to the ways in which both Christianity and polytheism were expressed socially. It is at least possible that the public ceremonies of polytheism, so often decried as vices, might be shown to have something of the private benefit about them.[42]

The failure of polytheism might be attributed to a decline in the economy. The imperial system as we have described it needed men who would be willing to finance meeting-halls, dinners, gifts or games. In an economy suffering from inflation, as happened in the third century AD, the benefactor class might no longer be able to pay for the services they had traditionally supplied. After centuries of generosity they would now be inclined to be mean to their deities and more considerate of themselves. It is true that religious entertainment had always been acknowledged as 'a form of expense that should not be allowed to get out of hand'; the price of gladiators might need controlling and the emperors would try to set right the reckless extravagance of a whole area.[43] But in general the development of the economy was such that the ability of benefactors to donate was less adversely affected (by increased taxation for example) than was the ability of the poorer to pay taxes. If we look at the greatest benefactor of all, the emperor, it is noticeable that there was not much new temple-building in Rome in the third century AD before Aurelian built the temple of the Sun. But once there was a marked will to build, as happened when Constantine decided to be generous to the Christians, the money was found somehow from sources within the Empire, even though wealth from conquest had been the normal means of supplying polytheistic expansion. The lack of evidence (particularly between AD 250 and the end of the century) suggests,but does not prove, that the economy was unable to fund the activities of polytheism.

Another explanation may concern one of the end-products of the benefactor's art of giving, the desirability of the priestly offices. The benefactor, that is, might well struggle to pay if this objective were still desirable but he would surely fall away if it no longer seemed worth having. It is arguable that the honorific position of many priests (we should perhaps exempt the priestly offices in Rome, the habitual preserve of the senatorial aristocracy) had deteriorated. The reason might be that the relationship of priestly offices to other offices had now worsened since the secular bureaucracy had started to divide and multiply itself. It might have become obvious therefore that religious office had reached an even worse imbalance than before. If so it can hardly be surprising that in the fourth century there was a revival of religious institutions when the new priestly class of bishops had a coherence and effectiveness which the priests of the provincial assemblies or the freedmen Augustales never had.

A third possibility is that the Empire had exhausted the possible supply of strange or new gods even though it was confronted by new enemies, especially in the third century. The border peoples had gods who might well have been difficult to accept as recruits in an army of gods where close relationship was very much taken for granted. But the habit of assimilation would still have allowed people to see resemblances between Jupiter, let us say, and the most unpromising of the Goth or German deities. Perhaps it is more relevant to notice that the military energies of an expanded empire would only be able to express themselves by setting up a victory-god in

Rome if the army could conquer so overwhelmingly that it could afford to withdraw to the centre. For much of the third century the sustained pressure along the frontiers and their distance from Rome helped to produce different conditions for installing gods from those which had obtained when gods were won from relatively short campaigns or were not all that remote from Rome.

It may be a more fruitful approach to take a wider and more imaginative view of polytheism in its period of demise. The starting-point should be the consideration that polytheistic cult in Greco-Roman antiquity began as local cult in small populations, anxious for survival or petty territorial gains. The local gods of warring communities had many similarities among themselves, but they were not apt to be noticed internationally until conquest or destruction made their worship seem less dangerous. The tendency of the polytheistic advance was to allow for a wider distribution of identical or identical-seeming gods, with local differences of cult-name. The Roman Empire reinforced these developments. The best Jupiter was Roman but he had numerous analogies, and the Capitoline structures were emulated and repeated elsewhere.

Locality cult therefore tended at least to look like universal cult. The effect of the emperor-deities was in the same direction; the cult was gradually organized in regions, and worshippers in one area performed acts that were much the same as those elsewhere. The Roman world thus became used to a sort of hybrid, something between a local cult and a universal cult. The result was that local cults had not entirely died out but that some of the more important cults seemed to have escaped from the tyrannizing restrictions of place. Thus civic polytheism had created forms of organized cult which might seem not so very different from those of the monotheistic invader. The way was smoothed for the new god who came originally from a summit in Judaea because his worshippers had already become used to forms that were universal, first through synagogues and then through churches. The key to understanding the move from polytheism to Christianity is to remember that some of the practices and cult-acts were alike and that in other cases the changed polytheist was determined to see salutary likenesses even if they were rejected by his leaders in the new church. Some of those who became Christian did not at first realize that they were playing with an incompatible; their whole habit of mind was based on dealing in the likeness and comparability of religious things.

### *Theory in Brief*

Roman thinkers and writers of the late Republic, as we saw, found it difficult or impossible to interpret the civic gods as true representations of nature. Cicero and Varro based their defence of religion on custom or tradition, resigning themselves to ignorance of the true nature of divinity. The Latin writers of the Empire brought little that was new to the subject except for some striking rhetorical epigrams. But it is still worth considering briefly some particular views on two questions: firstly, the relationship, if any, between civic god and nature; and, secondly, the supposed lessons of divine providence to be discovered in Roman history.

The Stoic approach to the first question is most clearly exemplified in Seneca. His aim as a Roman Stoic is to find a way of understanding the Roman gods as forms of nature. He has the memorable formula 'nature does not exist apart from god any more than god exists apart from nature'. It would follow that any god with a Roman cult-epithet could be explained in a coherent way. Jupiter Stator (meaning he who stops the rout or makes things steady) is said to refer to the idea that it is through god's benefaction that all things are made stable. Thus the Roman god is deprived of his historical origin (Romulus in the tradition invoked this form of Jupiter to stop his army from fleeing) and receives the increase of a cosmological function. Again, Stoic allegory can be used with some etymological help to explain and preserve awkward traditions like the Etruscan theory of the thunderbolt. But the whole theory is exposed not only to the objections brought by Cicero but also to the argument that its wisdom is only accepted by a few.[44]

The elder Pliny's attitude (as shown in the *Natural History*) is more difficult to ascertain. His theoretical starting-point is that the universe is divine but that the human mind is too weak to grasp god in the absolute sense. Many of the particular deities invoked by states are absurd; he instances such things as Fever and animal deities, and he objects to the belief that gods have marriages or commit adultery. But although many of the civic gods are 'unnatural' – he complains too about the cults of Fortune and belief in astrology – and he does not think that absolute god concerns himself with human affairs, civic religion is still desirable. It is a good thing for men to suppose that there are providential gods, that punishment (from the gods) is sure if slow and that man is god's next of kin. Pliny's theory is summed up in the phrase: 'A mortal's (true) god is to help other mortals'. It is by this formula that he can shower praise on Vespasian and on the Roman nobles in general. The compliment to the reigning emperor is not intended to take account of his apotheosis after death but provides an elevated metaphor for esteeming his benefactions in life.[45]

Pliny is therefore a pragmatist, for whom there is an unbridgeable gap between god and nature as they really are and gods as mankind sees them.

The gods of mankind are useful but untrue. God the absolute would not work at caring for the world; and if the emperors are godlike for helping mankind they are behaving in the way that it would be unreasonable to expect of the master of the universe. The educated consensus would seem to have been that civic religion is defensible as custom, not as truth. The case is made even clearer in Caecilius' speech in the *Octavius* of Minucius Felix; for Caecilius god and nature are more unknowable than they are for Pliny, and it is for that reason that he urges a policy of non-dogmatism (directed against his Christian opponent).

Acceptance of civic religion could be simple or sophisticated. We can imagine some for whom the observances of civic Jupiter were essential, for whom it was a necessary article of faith to keep the name of Rome's guardian deity a secret. On the other hand we know of people who thought it right to keep up the civic tradition, with or without a theory that might bring the gods of the state close to nature. These different types of religious citizen would both assume that Roman history had a special place in the divine scheme of things. The Augustans had deplored the neglect of the gods during the period of civil conflicts. The heirs of Augustanism found themselves trying to explain how it can come about that Rome could suffer defeat or the reign of bad emperors. If Roman history is god-favoured (and god is in general the source of benefits to man) why have the Romans suffered? Seneca gives a feeble answer when he maintains that rulers like Caligula are allowed by the gods as a tribute to their ancestors' merits; only those bad rulers are admissible who are descended from the good and the great. This curious theory ascribes to providence an obsession with genealogy at the expense of mankind as a whole. More gloomy reasons for bad emperors are devised by Tacitus (who might have said that he had even more evidence of badness than Seneca had had). His theory is that the gods do have a concern for the welfare of mankind but that they are surely engaged in making man suffer, through war, disasters and wicked rulers. Tacitean assumptions are the complete opposite of the normal Roman view (perhaps one should simply call it the shallow human opinion); he argues for a malignant deity whereas the average patriot would have it as an axiom that the Romans should not be failed by god because they had passed so many tests in war.[46]

The practice of making some emperors into gods and damning others made little difference to speculations about god and the state. The younger Pliny, however, attempts to explain how an emperor should conduct himself in religious matters. The key to Pliny's theory is that all men, even the emperor, are under Jupiter, the god who first founded and now preserves the state. Thus he starts with a civic god whose existence he does not question. From this principle there is a simple distinction to make between bad emperors, who claim the attributes of god for themselves, and good emperors, who conduct themselves modestly and with decorum. The good order of the world is respected by rulers who are prepared to wait for post-mortem divinity. Good rulers are said to be appointed by the gods, but we are left to wonder why there can be bad rulers. Pliny's remarks show us a theorist who is concerned to stress senatorial values and to plead for the continuance of the Augustan ideal, civic moderation. But at the same time his exaggerated phrases throw the lie at all his protestations of freedom; he describes good emperors, waiting to be gods, in the pose of a courtier bent on piling up a new rhetoric of absolutism, and so his compliments to the ruler exceed what would be permitted by his sober theory.[47]

These writers of the early Empire were not political philosophers but they touched on the very question which had perplexed Cicero and Varro. What is the relationship (if any) between the civic forms of deity and deity as it really is, between the anthropomorphic cult-statue and the true nature of god? We have discovered no support among these thinkers for the theory that civic god is (even more or less) an accurate representation of ultimate reality. Also, Seneca's account of Jupiter Stator deprives this god of his historical links in order to attach him to a philosophical allegory which not everyone, not even everyone among the Stoics, would accept. Apart from this interpretation civic god survives mainly as a psychological aid, necessary only as a means of helping mankind to visualize an entity of a different order. This version of civic god and the familiar cult-statue is not intellectually admirable or even competent but it allows man some hope and admits that the feeble creature needs help to approximate to the divine.

The theorists described here were attempting to render an account of statues and gods as they should be understood in nature, by philosophers, leaving aside the gods of the poets. Poetic theology they regarded as no more than fiction in a bad sense, not even the inferior copy of a great original. As for the gods of the market-place, the versions of Varro, Cicero and Pliny were unable to discover any truth to nature in the gods actually acknowledged by a successful state such as Rome. Civic theology was left with no defence but custom, and the ordinary believer, were he to be deprived of the argument from tradition, would be left with nothing but nullified statues on his hands. If the cult-statue in its anthropomorphic guise is saved, that is not because it is necessary to explain the phenomena but because citizens are too weak to do without this psychological crutch.

But not all thinkers were so despondent about the links between human practice and the gods. The poet's god was not always left on the bottom rung, below the gods of what Varro called civic theology. Indeed the twelfth discourse of Dio Chrysostom might almost be described as an artist's charter. In this work the orator admires the great statue of Zeus at Olympia precisely because it imposes itself on the spectator as the most perfect representation of man's creative vision of god. The starting-point of his argument is the admission that all men everywhere have an innate conception of god, an idea which would certainly have been held by the thinkers discussed above. But Dio's next step takes him away from their approach. He distinguishes between different forms of social and political pressure: poetic or artistic opinion is on one side, as a persuasive influence; the political or legislative theory of god is on the other, a form of compulsion or force. Both the artistic and the political influence are said to reinforce what is present in man by nature, his tendency to pay cult to the gods as his highest relatives. But the artist's superiority, according to Dio, resides in his power of persuasion.[48] Our admiration for Pheidias' conception of Zeus (itself apparently derived from Homer as the prime source of art) persuades us to worship the gods, whereas the law-givers or politicians use 'compulsion and the threat of punishment for those who refuse obedience ...' According to this theory the anthropomorphic cult-statue (assuming it is good art) is admirable as a gentle, educative influence, appealing to the reason in man, whereas the laws lay down penalties and deterrents for those who refuse to pay cult as they should. The fact that this last is a distortion of civic practice as regards cult should not make us overlook the remarkable fact that Dio allows the artist's vision a high place.

CHAPTER FIVE

# *Religions from the East*

The religious history of the Empire, from the age of Augustus to the end of the third century, embraces three main types of cult: the traditional or inherited civic gods, to which can be added the deities specific to the imperial system, the man-gods[1] as they were called by Toynbee; the oriental cults, from Phrygia, the Middle East, Persia and Egypt; and the exclusively monotheistic religions, Judaism and its offshoot Christianity. The differences between the types will become apparent later in the discussion. At this stage it is sufficient to remember that the context of this enquiry is political. We might try to fill out this political context by keeping in the forefront of our attention the dates when new gods entered the civic system, particularly as it worked in the greatest city, Rome, and by considering the manner of their entry. A way of describing the line of enquiry is to assume that the Augustan model is a form of letting religion work in the interests of social harmony, by allowing people to cherish their past and to attach their regard for archaism to the conquering gods of the régime. Augustanism, that is, does not deny religion but gives it a safe and constructive place, subordinate to the political interest, much as the pontiff or augur is a lesser officer of state than the Republican consul. The point of simplifying Augustanism in this way is to suggest that it can be interpreted as a system of defence which from time to time admits such exotic newcomers as Cybele, Isis, Mithras and eventually Christianity. The new cults might then be seen as threats to a religious security which was determined by the first Augustus, and the entry dates of the new cults would be times of capitulation, when emperors accepted the inevitable.

These assumptions reflect the mood of some ancient critics and have helped to form the basis of several modern explanations.[2] It is indeed tempting to think of the Empire as a system that was exposed to constant religious attack much as it became vulnerable to the invasions of Goths and Germans. There is a facile comparison to be made between defending the ways of religion and protecting the frontiers of the state. The metaphor of defence and attack has (among other advantages) the merit of drawing our attention to government fears of certain religions as incitements to social disorder. But it is in the end no more than a simplification which gives to Rome and Italy an importance that belongs to the Empire as a whole; also it fails to make due allowance for a prime need of civic polytheism, the need to replenish the system by introducing new gods. Exclusion and control are not the only clues to the connectión between statecraft and religion in antiquity; the willingness to take in new cults is at least as important, and the adaptation to strange gods can be found among all orders of society. Even government was a receiver as well as a policeman.

The shortcomings of the theory that Augustanism was mainly defensive towards the eastern religions will become more apparent in the course of this chapter. In the last chapter an important theme is the way in which the Empire sought to preserve the Republican religious past, for even emperor-cult itself, though an innovation, was not an alarming or disruptive growth. The religious experience of the Empire had also a different and more adventurous tendency which in the end helped to develop a religious autonomy that would have amazed the Romans of an earlier period.

### *The Oriental Religions*

The above is the usual name, sanctified by the modern scholarly tradition, but it is not satisfactory. It puts together too many disparate phenomena and requires us to see them from the Roman point of view. Their common bond is supposed to be an origin east of Rome the city, and we are by implication expected to contrast a single metropolis with various places ranging in latitude from northern Turkey to Egypt, and in longitude from Egypt to Persia. A modern critic has suggested that we might re-name these cults the exotic religions, as a reminder that they were never really taken into the Roman pantheon in the way that the deities from Latium, south Italy and Greece had been incorporated.[3] The principal cults under review are as follows: Cybele, Dionysus, Isis and Sarapis, Mithras, Jupiter Dolichenus and Sol Invictus. This short list is far from exhaustive but it includes the more important deities, and covers a long period of time; Cybele was introduced in 204 BC and the cult of Sol did not begin to prosper until the third century AD.

Before we show how they resembled or differed from the gods who were already established at Rome, it will be useful to say more about religious Augustanism and the Roman stereotype of these cults. Augustanism was in a sense a way of adding an internal control to the Republican system of gods in which the import of new deities was determined by internal need and external supply. The imperialist advance of the later Republic brought Rome into contact with new territories, some of which could offer new gods, and for much of the time the aristocrats who led Roman armies vied with one another in their attempts to link themselves and their families with temples and gods. The system could be active or sluggish, varying with the energy of the ruling class and the expansionism of the state. The ambitions of the aristocracy had certainly made big demands on the supply of gods, but it should be remembered that through variations in titles, discovering different functions or origins in one and the same god by multiplying Jupiters almost beyond imagination, the number of gods might be greatly increased. Even so, civic polytheism of this type might conceivably run out of acceptable gods. It could therefore be counted as one of the additional triumphs of Augustanism that it reduced (in theory) the dependence on external deities, by creating gods from within, the deified emperors and the grand abstractions like Hope, Eternity and Concord. We might then be prepared to argue that the Empire had forestalled any problem of keeping itself supplied with gods, by reviving the great gods of the past and by hoping to add to them the great men of the present. Another achievement of the Empire was that it distributed throughout the provinces an organized cult of the emperor who at Rome would not be allowed to enter heaven before he had himself as a human received the last rites.

It is understandable that the deified emperors were not treated like the full gods of tradition. According to a classic formulation 'the touchstone of piety' was the votive offering to a god for supposed deliverance from danger or sickness or for benefits received.[4] The dead or living emperors were not so honoured, and for this reason they have been described as the recipients of homage, not of worship. The verdict is somewhat austere. The emperors were sometimes the target of enthusiastic veneration, and men made vows for their health or security. This was piety of a sort, even if it was piety incomplete. Tertullian criticized paganism on the grounds that the religious sentiment of populace and officials did not deter them from turning against an emperor and so destroying the god-to-be in contravention of their prayers.[5] But political desertion of an emperor should be aligned with the religious practice, not uncommon in polytheism, of threatening or forsaking a god who had not responded as was hoped. To say that this kind of religion did not prevent men from becoming political assassins is not to deny its religious quality entirely; they had made prayers on behalf of an object that was gradually found wanting; these pagans were religious and disloyal whereas the Christians so favourably praised by Tertullian practised a religion which at this stage did not incite them to political disobedience. Perhaps we should conclude that Augustanism did more than restrict the dependence of the state on external gods; it also diminished the kind of devotion shown to those who were either gods already or were about to become gods.

The standard portrait of a typical oriental religion can be found in many writers and reflects a patriotic sense of hostility towards what is felt as an alien debasement of Roman ways. Scorn of the eastern religions is marked in Juvenal. Seneca, in a remarkable flight of metaphor, draws a contrast between the calm silence that precedes Roman prayers and those noisy demonstrations with the sistrum that are said to prepare the way for the worship of Isis. The difference between the types of cult – the traditional civic and the oriental import – is emphasized by Dionysius of Halicarnassus. He says that 'even though their [the Romans'] manners are now corrupted [there are] no ecstatic transports, no Corybantic frenzies ... no bacchanals or secret mysteries ... ' Rome is said to have introduced certain rites from abroad but has toned them down in accordance with her own traditions. The rites of the Idaean goddess are a case in point:

> for the praetors perform sacrifices and celebrate games in her honour every year according to the Roman customs, but the priest and priestess of the goddess are Phrygians, and it is they who carry her image in procession through the city ... So cautious are they about admitting any foreign religious customs and so great is their aversion to all pomp and display that is wanting in decorum.

The Greek historian of early Rome is here more philo-Roman and Augustan than the Roman writers themselves.[6]

Reasons for this anti-oriental prejudice will appear later. It constitutes a literary motif of some importance but it is not of much use as a guide to the understanding of the long inter-relationship between Rome and the eastern cults. The archaeologist's exposure of the wide distribution of these cults points to a very different tale from that which seems so natural and familiar in the writers mentioned above. Like some of their modern counterparts[7] the Romans traditionally looked down upon the oriental as an outsider or an indecent invader who refused to conform to the quieter and more respectable ways of the west. The implied conception is too Italo-centric to do justice to the more complicated facts of life, at any rate in the period after Augustus. It is essential to remember that the oriental cults spread all over the Mediterranean lands; they were not simply aimed at the heart of Italy by a mysterious agent, intent on unmanning a Roman virtue which had itself undone the world.

Roman antipathy to the eastern cults is one kind of danger that may distort modern study of the subject. Another preliminary warning is perhaps necessary on the different topic of the cults as the supposed precursors of Christianity. It is tempting to over-emphasize those parts of the cults which look like anticipations of the monotheistic religion that finally overcame the rest. There was undoubtedly an increase in henotheism throughout the Empire, an agreement (especially among intellectuals) that the gods named by men are manifestations of the one god, himself unknowable. An interpretation of this kind would be too influenced by the hindsight imposed by the Christian triumph. It would be in danger of putting too much weight on, for example, the henotheistic side of Sol Invictus and so underrating its function as a form of polytheism. The temptation to look for this development within the cults is natural enough for it helps us to envisage a neat if slow transition from civic polytheism through henotheistic cults to Christianity. But the temptation should be resisted if only because the cults became historically important for reasons that have little to do with their henotheism.

An outline of the main subject, the so-called oriental invasion, can properly begin with the reasons for Augustan hostility, the sense that Roman practice is a whole heaven removed from the eastern gods. Roman attitudes were largely moulded by the Republican experience of Cybele, Dionysus and Isis. Cybele was officially summoned to Rome in 204 BC and installed through the offices of the best man in Rome, the appointed receptionist Scipio Nasica.[8] Although there are many puzzling features about the political circumstances surrounding this goddess, it seems clear that the Romans objected strongly to some of the practices as described later by Dionysius. They had no complaint that the goddess came in aniconic form, for stone-worship of this type had long been familiar in mainland Greece and in parts of Italy. We are assured that the cult of betyls was not necessarily phallic, so the authorities at Rome would not have had reason to fear a wave of sexual immorality.[9] They objected to the ecstatic nature of the cult in which there was scope for self-mutilation by males, and practice of the cult was at first restricted to the natives who had come with the 'image' from Pessinus. The Romans thereby sought to maintain a practice of a traditional kind and to domicile it without disturbing their own religious practices. Their citizens were allowed to watch the games that were held in the presence of Cybele but were not to officiate as priests. Statuettes of Cybele's consort Attis have been discovered on the Palatine though it may still be true that he was regarded for some time as an undesirable alien as he had been in parts of Greece.[10]

Rome's first public encounter with the Dionysiac religion was in 186 BC. Though the Dionysiac cult at a later period can be seen in a different light from the other oriental cults, partly because its god had an obvious Italian counterpart, Liber, it impressed the Roman authorities of the early second century BC as a cult which allowed meetings by night of both sexes, made a pretext of ecstasy and was on the side of public disorder.[11] The Romans decided once again to forbid the cult to their citizens and to license it only for those who could show it was their traditional religion. On this occasion the threatening god was discovered by accident; he did not come with an official entry-certificate, as a victory-god, like Cybele. Government preoccupation with the popular spread of cult was repeated later on, in the first century BC, when consular officials destroyed a temple of Isis and Sarapis which had been put up 'on privately owned land.' Since Augustus showed himself as the shepherd and protector of Italian gods against the threats of Egyptian Cleopatra, it is hardly surprising that his adviser, Maecenas, in a well-devised fiction, warns him against foreign religious practices which might give rise to conspiracies or political faction.[12]

These three were not the only intruders in the last years of the Republic, but they were the cults which, politically speaking, were the most noticed. They present us with different types of government action: there is first the senatorial unanimity directed against the Bacchanalia, the consular initiative against the temple of Isis, and finally the measure whereby Agrippa removed the Egyptian rites and kept them away from the *pomerium*.[13] But for all the minor differences there are some common preoccupations: fear of ecstatic and mystery religion, accompanied by a reluctance to molest and outlaw a cult that could be shown to have some traditional appeal; anxiety about the use of these religions as meeting-places for dissentients and revolutionaries; allegations of riotous sexual assembly. The senate's fear that mixed assemblies were not just for purposes of worship is echoed by the arch-Augustan Dionysius in his praise of Rome for having 'no all-night vigils of men and women in the temples', and this fear was still an important part of Licinius' anti-Christian moves three centuries later.[14]

This pattern of experience, coupled with Augustus' own religious stance in the war against Cleopatra and later, will explain why it was that the Republic and early Empire gave these foreign cults a limited reception or sought to exclude them. It is, however, unlikely that the different governments were justified in their fear of the subversive potential in these cults. Their appeal was not anti-Roman; some at least of their characteristics would surely have aroused the curiosity of people who were over-familiar with one type of religious experience (we might call it the obligatory fear of defeat followed by the victory festival) and unused to the experience embodied in the imported cults. The latter offered a form of religion with an ecstatic climax; a myth based on doctrines which were often secret, with phases of initiation; a specialized full-time clergy, with its own distinctive uniform; and (quite often) a form of daily service which was more impressive than the attentions bestowed even on Jupiter by those who had to minister to him. It is not necessary to assume that the cults appealed to people mainly or solely because they offered a form of salvation instead of a religion orientated towards success. The word mystic is often attached, rather loosely, to them, and they are sometimes alleged to have expressed a higher morality than traditional civic cult had done. It is true that the ecstatic cults provided religious experience[15] of a different type from that which had dealt mainly in civic benefits, though the latter should not be written off as merely cold and formal. But the two kinds were not exclusive of each other and we should not suppose that people took to the oriental cults because they had been spiritually starved for centuries or because they discovered in a new form of religion a means of protest against the political order. In some cases they offered reassurances that were similar to those already available; the cult of Ma, for instance, purported to give an insight into the future, and it looked after its followers through the medium of prophecies about tangible subjects. The social advantages of belonging to a club or a religious association became even more noticeable under the Empire but they had started their career in the Republic. It is therefore important to consider these cults as complementary to much of the existing religion rather than to encourage a view of them as alternatives or as forms of protest.

Government restrictive action was on the whole mostly effective in the short-term, and even when it was renewed (as with the temples and rites of Isis from 59 BC to Augustus) it had little to show for its police work. The cult of Cybele became so much an accepted part of urban religion at Rome that by the late Republic Cicero gives it an honourable mention and allows the ministers of the Idaean mother the right to make collections.[16] Time and custom worked in favour of this cult, and the process of settling to a complete social and political respectability was advanced still more by the Emperors Claudius and Antoninus Pius. The action against the Bacchanalia was at first vigorous and effective, but after the immediate onslaught (in 186 BC) the cult was left alone and it continued to spread. The Isiac cult suffered no more than minor setbacks from the consuls' hostility in 59 BC and from the exclusion imposed by Agrippa. Its entry into the inner rooms of the Roman establishment was symbolized when Caligula had an Iseum built in the Campus Martius.[17] There were in short two different ways of 'Romanizing' a cult; one might seek to let it exist only on sufferance, in a less vigorous form than it had known in its homeland, with its deity in a twilight zone, or a particular government could award the more orthodox recognition of a public temple. Initially the cult of Cybele was treated in both ways; as a victory-god she was housed in the centre of Rome but the cult was doctored, so that, though civic, its function at Rome was less central to the state than it had been at Pessinus.

The circulation of the cults was promoted by various factors. Government initiative was decisive in the case of Cybele; it sent the invitation and provided an escort, so that the newcomer would not have reached Italy at all had it not been for the senate's embassy. At a later date Claudius officially introduced other dates into the March festival. With other gods and goddesses of this oriental type government showed its approval only when the cult was fully established in Italy or near Rome. The Isiac cult, even in the first century BC, was not a newcomer in Italy, and it had spread even more widely by the time of Caligula.[18] Commodus became an initiate of Mithras and at a later date the god was honoured by Diocletian and his co-emperor as a supporter of their rule.[19] The cult of Sol Invictus, though not completely new to the west, was brought by the Emperor Elagabal, almost in the manner of Cybele, and was re-introduced more successfully by Aurelian later in the third century.[20] The emperors had more confidence than the Republican senate in accepting or authorizing cults. That is partly because most of the cults had come to seem more familiar and therefore more necessary; they had without too many setbacks become recognized as cults that could be useful to rulers.

But the role of government, whether we think of the Republican senate or the emperors, was relatively superficial. Cults were disseminated by many social groups, especially those which could be called compulsorily mobile – dispossessed natives (who might be sent west into slavery or forced by economic necessity to move) and those units of the Roman army which were transported into remote provinces. This is not necessarily a distinction between slave and free but between (in a broad sense) the defeated and the victorious. The former, who came from lands that were now Roman provinces or client-kingdoms, held on to their gods as a last shred of identity (though they were not averse to treating with new ones). Even so, their success in transplanting could only have taken place in a favourable climate, among people who were receptive to new deities. On the other hand the Roman army exhibited the opposite side of the process. Its units were composed of men who took with them a calendar of Roman type, in a form that was probably drawn up by the first Augustus, and they were also ready to acknowledge the local gods in whose area they found themselves.[21] Not all the mobility was to or through Rome, and for this reason the migration of cults should not be regarded as an eastern wave directed against Italy, but as a multifarious advance to many centres including Rome.

As a means of helping to welcome and then disseminate new cults the army was not an unwilling agent, for all its conservatism which protected the traditional gods. Thus the calendar from Dura shows that many of the cults the units would expect to celebrate were the very cults that would be prominent in the urban calendar of civil Roman life.[22] But eastern cults were, so to say, plentiful on the outskirts; the evidence from archaeology seems to confirm that oriental cults were allowed, but the dedications or offerings set up by grateful soldiers are found only outside the camp precincts. If Dura itself looks like an exception to the last point (since the camp there incorporates the cults), the appearance is deceptive; in this case the camp was using space within a city, so that the usual rules for camp measurement did not apply, and the planners had to use space that was not free but was occupied by buildings. If we assume (which is not unreasonable) that the miltary camp may be regarded as a miniature city then it may well be that the oriental gods were allowed (in the sense of not disapproved), but they were kept apart, outside the soldiers' *pomerium*, as it were. If so the army was retaining a tradition of keeping out strange gods, a tradition that in city terms had begun to look very old-fashioned indeed by the third century AD, with no more than a narrow idea of what gods might be admitted into the official pantheon.

Such a policy (if policy it may be called) would have been based on two things: on accepting as an unalterable fact of religious life the troops' appetite for the local deities where they were stationed, and on maintaining that such gods should not be admitted into the central military sanctum. We would have to assume that the authorities (commanders of legions and ultimately the emperor) might have granted full entry but that the officers and men did not press for more than an outside recognition for their cult. If so the exclusion would have been a compromise, in which the fashionable gods were not entirely denied and yet were not wholly respectable. But, on the other hand, there was almost certainly an acute shortage of space inside the camp, even if there had been official willingness to domicile all the various cults. It is possible that inside the camp there was only room for one sanctuary, to house the military standards. Thus a better model for explaining these phenomena might well be derived from the later phase of the Hellenistic city, in which the oriental cults are found towards the outskirts, as the central part has already been pre-empted by earlier shrines; if this were also true of the army it would mean that the new gods could not be brought in for reasons of overcrowding.[23] It is also possible that it would have been difficult to institutionalize some of the oriental cults inside the camp for other, practical, reasons. Ordinary traditional sacrifices required the presence and participation of the unit commander, a seer (*haruspex*) and a *victimarius*, to interpret and manage the chosen sacrifice. A difficulty in the way of introducing some oriental cults might have been their more specialized priestly organization. If none of their priests was also a serving soldier, then sacrifice would have been impossible. But it is fair to add that some of their priests may have been soldiers, to judge by evidence from the cult of Jupiter Dolichenus.[24]

Whatever the formal standing of the oriental cults in relation to the army, it is certain that soldiers were active in the process of spreading these religions and that authority did not set up insurmountable obstacles. The troops, together with the easterners so much deplored by Juvenal, were carriers of gods, they redistributed cults from their original locality and gave them a wider role in the Empire as a whole. The cults, if they were to take root as they did, had to appeal to wider sections of the more static or settled population, to be accepted by such sophisticated urban centres as those in Campania, to say nothing of less urbanized parts in the Latin west. They gave satisfactions of different kinds: they appealed to a craving for novelty, at one level of the escape from boredom; they gave the illusion of secret doctrines and the comfort of an initiation denied to or perhaps not chosen by others. The material comfort of belonging to a select club should not be overlooked. The Mithraists, for example, would often meet in relatively small groups or cells; in this case the cult satisfied a need for religious congregation, and although a particular Mithraeum might take no more than twenty it was relatively easy to set up a new meeting-place, be it a cave or a house-room, for the potential recruits. As clubs these gatherings had something in common with the guilds and funeral societies described earlier. The cults were easily included in the prayers which burdened the gods with an important charge like the emperor's personal health or welfare.[25]

I think it right to stress the opinion that the cults were complementary rather than alternatives. They spread as they did because material conditions were suitable; in the second century AD especially there was money to spend on building new temples and repairing the old. The religious monument, together with its sacrifices, was a major form of economic display and consumption. At Ostia, for example, the principal civic deity from Republican days was Vulcan, whose chief priest was appointed for life from among the leading citizens. Vulcan and other deities were not forgotten even during the heyday of the oriental cults; his temple, like those of some other traditional gods, was restored during the 'prosperity period', as the second century has been called. His survival and repair is yet another indication that the new cults came as additions rather than as substitutes. The priests of these cults at Ostia were on the whole not of the same civic rank as the leading minister of Vulcan. But they and their fellow worshippers had enough means to adorn their favourite gods and temples; one dedication to Isis consisted of 'a silver Venus, one pound in weight, with two wreaths, one of gold.' Religion therefore was a major form of spending on leisure. The oriental cults were, if not religions of the rich, at any rate prosperity religions, and they would not be likely to flourish in times of economic stress.[26] The latter part of the third century therefore offered material conditions better suited to Christianity whose public buildings did not become the recipients of lavish attention until it received state patronage.

The material conditions suitable for this oriental advance, particularly in the second century AD, were helped by the widespread habits of assimilation and cumulative syncretism. Assimilation (at one level) enables a community to accept a foreign god into its own system by apparent identification with an obvious candidate who is already present. In the terms of the traditional pantheon Hermes was identified in this way with Mercury; and among the eastern cults Bacchus was at times regarded as a form of Osiris. The god from Commagene, himself a god of summits, readily became Jupiter Dolichenus, and the Unconquered Sun (Sol Invictus) seemed less strange because there was already a cult of Sol in Italy. The psychological value of assimilation is that it eases the absorption of the unfamiliar and may well help to revive a dying analogue already within the system. Cumulative syncretism is a name for the more advanced but similar process whereby a god adds to his or her functions by taking on the powers of other gods. In North Africa at Lambaesis, for example, Mercury acquired different functions and attributes from those of the divine messenger and god of trade, and entered on an African phase as Mercury Silvanus, protector of olive-trees and oil. Neptune, who had already become the Roman Poseidon by simple assimilation, was able in North Africa to take over a Phoenician god and so to go inland, where he became not just a god of the sea but a freshwater deity.[27] Above all, the oriental gods, by a kind of religious parataxis, were accommodated as loyal additions within the existing apparatus. The dedications of the Empire look more crowded with names and more exotic than their simpler predecessors from the late Republic; it seems to be a different world when we read an inscription in which the name of Jupiter Optimus Maximus is followed by the epithets *summus* and *exsuperantissimus*, with a whole rearguard of deities, the Unconquered Sun, Apollo, Luna, Diana, Fortuna, Mars, Victoria, Peace.[28] It is however no more than a polymorphic elaboration of the original insecurity within polytheism, the anxiety to make sure that one has covered the gods or enough of those that matter.

Italy and Rome were net importers of gods under the Empire, but it would be misleading, as I indicated earlier, to see them as no more than the passive recipients of alien cults. For one thing the image of Italian passivity, which seems not inept as an account of the movement of gods produced by immigrants to Italy and soldiers sent abroad, is belied by the willingness of the home population to diversify its gods. Furthermore, it would be a distortion to overlook the fact that Rome also sent some of her own gods abroad, quite apart from the man-gods in the imperial cult. The Capitoline triad was made part of a large-scale imitation of Rome, a reproduction of something Roman that was not confined to towns with the official status of a colony. Jupiter and other gods accompanied the troops who did not always forget the gods they had brought with them even when they courted the local deities. And inhabitants of the provinces practised an assimilation of Roman gods to their own in much the same way as their victors had put a Roman interpretation on many foreign gods.

Interpretations based on such experiences as the Republican importation of Cybele are not in general a good guide to the understanding of the oriental cults as they affected the state. They err by exaggerating a western-type horror at this ecstatic religion and by dwelling too much on the factors which make it seem alien from Rome. Some of these, such as the specialized priesthood, were in the long run made to look trivial and unimportant. It was the same too with the dates or anniversaries of the goddess; she had one date which celebrated her arrival at Rome, and a whole series of days which remembered the ceremonies of Attis. The two sets of dates, the latter of which was organized by the emperor Claudius, did not coalesce into a single Roman whole. The civic inauguration of the temple was remembered annually on April 10th, whereas the long spring festival of Attis took place in March.[29] By the time of Claudius, that is, the deity's connection with Roman history was made far less apparent than it had been in the early second century, but the extended Attis festival attributed to Claudius was no longer objectionable as something alien to Rome. It is arguable that for most of these cults with buildings in Rome the great festival-days (like those for Osiris in the Isiac cult) were just as much patriotic occasions as the anniversary dates of the temples; but it would be a case of equality between covert and overt forms of patriotism.

But although Cybele would not make a good model for the interpretation of other oriental cults, this does not mean that some one other cult could be used to illuminate them all. Each of them, in its interaction with Rome, poses different problems. The extent of political manipulation by Rome was not uniform; in Asia Minor, for example, it seems that Rome advertised a connection between the deity Men, a variant of Attis, and Etruria;[30] but overt propaganda like this was perhaps unusual. For good reasons I have here tried to emphasize the conformity of most of the new cults with the existing gods of the public order. Their conformity was as variable as the fashions which ruled various gods of the staider type, such as Juno, Neptune and Venus. The new deities had each their own vogue, so that we can quite correctly speak of Mithras as the successor in the third century of the cult of Isis in the second. The eastern gods were subject to the same civic fashions that had affected the name and standing of the other gods.

The principal fact to account for is the functioning of the cults during the Empire, a period when their service in the interests of the crown was every bit as important as their (alleged) enlightenment or intoxication of the individual. The present theme, the more significant one I would suggest, is the role of religion as a public provider, as the aide of emperors and the servant of groups that were either active on state business or not wholly aloof from it. The cult of Isis, for example, was of far wider social and political importance than is suggested by the tradition of her popularity with women.[31] A brief analysis of the cult of the Unconquered Sun may help us to understand that the Roman reception of the cults was a more complex matter than might be suggested by Cybele; Sol is relevant to the political order at Rome in more instructive ways.

Cult of the Sun had been long-established at Rome; it was said to have been introduced by Titus Tatius from the Sabine people and it was the special province of the Aurelian family. This tradition seems less certain than the association of Sun with circus games (shown by coins from the time of the second Punic War), and with a consort or partner, Moon, in a special temple. But there was also a temple to Sun on the Quirinal. The indigenous Roman Sun (so-called to distinguish it from oriental Sol) emerges only dimly from the traditions; by the Augustan age it was in civic terms an enfeebled cult, shining a little more brightly perhaps, with some light borrowed from the Apollo of Augustus, but dim nevertheless compared with other gods, whether or not they had been imported.

The more important was the invader, Sol Invictus, whose effective floruit spanned the third century and lasted well into the fourth.[32] In his first period of political importance the god was introduced to Rome by the young emperor Elagabal (AD 218–22), who succeeded Caracalla and Macrinus and was himself priest of the aniconic god from Syrian Emesa. The emperor sent ahead to Rome a portrait of himself sacrificing to the god so that senators and other functionaries would become accustomed to seeing him thus associated with the statue of Victory in the senate house. The emperor is said to have angered public opinion at Rome by giving precedence to his priesthood of Elagabal over his position as pontifex maximus; by having the symbols of other cults brought to the new temple constructed for his god on the Palatine; and by arranging one marriage between himself and a Vestal Virgin, and another, celestial, partnership between his god and the patroness-deity of Carthage. If the tradition is to be believed (it is extremely hostile), the ruler was an enterprising mixture of personal depravity and religious zeal, taking every step to entertain himself and to hoist the alien dominance of a Syrian god.[33]

The god was deported or restored to Emesa after the emperor's assassination.[34] But the cult was safely installed in several other shrines as well as in the home temple of Emesa, and did not become completely unpopular. Sol also appears on coins of Gallienus and Claudius Gothicus. It enjoyed a further period of reviving political fortune later in the century when Aurelian celebrated his victory in Syria by proclaiming his allegiance to Sol Invictus. The god received a new temple in the seventh district of Rome, and a special board of priests, pontiffs of the Sun, was created, separate from the existing pontiffs. It is claimed that there must be a direct link between Aurelian's apparent enthusiasm for the solar cult and his claim to be god (*deus*) in his lifetime.[35]

Some of the traditions about the two emperors tend to suggest that both had strong and clear religious policies; that both, though in different ways, were so ambitious for their gods that they might be called religious imperialists, who were determined to set up their versions of Sol over all other gods.

The ancient critics of the Emperor Elagabal assume in their readers a shared aversion for the affronts to Vesta, Jupiter and other gods. They assume that eastern religion was all of a piece and that hostility to it had the potency of the senate's horror of the ecstatic Cybele. But it is far from clear that Elagabal's ambitions for his god had the political importance that has been ascribed to them. He was killed because some of his appointments had angered the army whose creature he was, and it is possible that only the senatorial-minded among the civilians were deeply offended by the eastern deity and the introduction at Rome of this part of Syria. If the ancient historians of Elagabal are under the spell of Roman prejudice against the Orient, the modern admirers of Aurelian are eager to discover in him a passion for henotheism; they suppose that paganism (both Roman and eastern) was everywhere tending to the same end, 'solar monotheism'. Yet it is hard to find compelling evidence for this view; whereas it is possible to see Aurelian as a conqueror who set out to honour the god whom he, for good local reasons among others, connected with his victory.[36] It was entirely traditional that he should take back to Rome such a god and honour him with quadrennial games. His precursors are therefore the Republican generals and emperors concerned to honour their victory-gods.

The significance of the cult of Sol during the reigns of Elagabal and Aurelian does not stand or fall with the view that these rulers sought supremacy for their god. There is more to be gained from considering the other temples to Sol built by Elagabal and the priesthood invented by Aurelian. The spread of the other cults before Sol and the advance of the newest religion, Christianity, alike showed that in the Roman Empire a single locality-cult was not enough to guarantee success for a religion. Even two important centres, such as Emesa and Rome, would not suffice to ensure a favourable reception for the cult elsewhere. Elagabal (or his advisers) seems to have decided to make plans for setting up other temples, though this is not to say that his god was therefore to be none but an ousting god. Secondly, the fact that Aurelian set up a special priesthood may suggest that he saw it was no longer good enough to hand over a new cult to priests of the old order; pontiffs of the traditional kind did not give and take lustre as they had in the days when religious posts were held by men with a great political past or future. If a religion were to succeed it needed many centres of worship and a more vigorous priesthood.

Interpreting civic polytheism, both in its local and imperial phases, is extremely difficult for those who have known nothing but monotheism or a culture secularized from monotheism. We cannot easily adapt to the habit of finding no gods superfluous or unnecessary. Some such incapacity, a lack of sympathy in effect, may lie at the heart of modern views which emphasize Roman prejudice against eastern cults or which claim that solar cult, for example, was an oriental preparation for Christianity. Most civic polytheists (with few exceptions even among the philosophers) found it almost impossible to reject gods, either by excluding them or by reducing them to subordinates of a One. They found no problem in employing additional gods, without worrying too much about their order of appearance. It is in short all too easy to patronize the Greek and Roman ways with their gods, to excuse the ancients as seeking for an intermediate stage between polytheism and Christianity. Henotheism, the idea that there is a single deity to which the existing deities are subordinate, can be represented as an obvious or natural stepping-stone for those who were on the way from the many to the One.

Some moderns have tended to exaggerate the importance of classical henotheism as a form of intellectual tidiness, a way of bringing order into the apparent irrationality and chaos of polytheism; and others, as the assured followers of Christian monotheism, have found it natural to assume that henotheism of this type was the necessary spiritual preliminary to belief in a personal deity. But the ancients were not disturbed by the numbers of gods within a polytheistic system, and not all of those who became Christian needed to pass through the gate called henotheism.

### *Imperial Persecutions*

To judge by Roman attitudes towards the oriental cults religious persecution was not a mainstay of Republican and imperial policy taken as a whole. In the Republic measures were taken to circumscribe the cult of the invited god Cybele, and in two other cases, Dionysus and Isis, the Romans attempted to limit the spread of deities who were already advancing without warrant. Most such prohibitions were in the nature of police measures, they called for active supervision for a relatively brief period only, after which vigilance lapsed. It seems right to say that in general the oriental cults were not seen as threats but as adventitious supports; whatever else they did for the devotions of their adherents they performed the essential public service of adding themselves to the Jupiter tradition. It is perhaps hardly surprising that cults of this kind, which were originally civic, could make an accommodation with Rome.

It was in the nature of the polytheistic state to accept new gods, not to decline them. Persecution of other religions, except for relatively short-term political reasons, was therefore an alien way of behaviour. Yet it is perfectly clear that for three centuries the emperors either persecuted Christians or connived at their maltreatment; and it is clear too that for much of this period Jews felt and were oppressed to such an extent that it is reasonable to speak of persecution. We have therefore to explain what was entailed by persecution and in what sense Jews and Christians were made to suffer.

The term persecution itself implies a degree of assent to the viewpoint of those who felt wronged by extreme authority. There is bound to be sympathy if only of the humanitarian kind for the loss of life sustained in the two great Jewish wars and for the destruction of the Temple at Jerusalem; for the ruin of Christian churches, and for the lists of martyrs, though they may have been lengthened by hagiographers. There are three (at least) ways of considering persecution and its effects; the Jewish, with its emphasis on territory and the Judaean homeland; the Christian sense of an unsettling adversity within the provinces of the Empire; thirdly, the imperial attitude assumes that what will be noticed as persecution by the subjects or outsiders is no more than an administrative necessity when examined from within. It is far more difficult to make an accurate assessment of rulers' theory than of the realities as they were perceived by subject minorities. Roman theory (could we consult it) would try to allow the conduct of affairs within some such framework as this; its statement of policy would find it reasonable to allow practices that could be shown to be traditional, but it would be remarkably vague about the length of time needed to constitute a tradition. Christianity was suspect as a deviation from Judaism, suspect not only to Jews but also to the rulers of the Empire; it was an offence against the parent cult and against an approved tradition. Reliance on custom was carried to the length of assuming that the many varieties of religion could be disciplined within a Roman context. It was supposed that the gods of defeated peoples would accept the verdict of history on their worshippers and would be able to join the Roman pantheon. Roman confidence in Rome's generosity to other cults was accompanied by a trust (in two cases misplaced) in the willingness of others to settle down with the gods of the conqueror.

The Jewish and the Christian points of view were entirely different and could dwell on facts that for them were full of the sense of grievance. The Jewish experience of imperial Rome had, however, made an auspicious start; Jews were granted privileges by Julius Caesar and Augustus, a special status which was confirmed by many subsequent rulers. But before long, by the time of the war against Titus (AD 66–74), the revolt of 115–17 and the revolt against Hadrian (AD 132–5), the Jews felt harassed instead of protected.[37] They felt their religion had been oppressed not only in Judaea but also in Alexandria and in the Diaspora generally, in spite of the fact that they were controlled by a power which countenanced separate cult provided it was long-standing. How then did it happen that Roman tolerance as we have described it was no longer upheld, with the result that Jews, both in the homeland and the Diaspora, felt wronged and persecuted?

Within the Judaean homeland Jews were conscious that their religion was allowed and that Rome was often prepared to comply with the important, though difficult, rules governing access to the Temple. These indications of tolerance on the part of Rome were offset by other conditions which exacerbated Jewish bitterness and sense of inferiority. The whole of the Judaean area was still, in the age of Augustus, subject to an invasion by different forms of Hellenism. The imposition of these alien ways had provoked a nationalist resistance under the Maccabees in the second century BC; but this had merely postponed the advance of Hellenism which continued under Rome's protégé Herod the Great. It was now presented in a more palatable form, as the following will show. Augustus himself observed the courtesy of making gifts to the Temple, rather as other kings had made presents to the temple of Jupiter in Rome. Herod the Great, though never completely accepted by the Jews, was careful in observing important taboos and employed none but priestly labour on the reconstruction of the Temple. A school of Jewish thought was prepared to accept the rule of a Herod, as an authority of which it disapproved, on the grounds that such injustices were a sign of divine punishment and should be endured willingly.[38] And Jewish common sense, which might not be prepared to agree with this Pharisaic view, took comfort from the fact of Roman protection and from some at least of Herod's offerings to the national religion.

But the system was essentially unstable. The permanent factor in the middle East was Hellenism, with its games, gymnasia and forms of deity that could easily give offence to Jews; the Hellenized were often all too ready to deride the Jewish dietary taboos and to make fun of those who were intolerant of the pig. The threat to Jewishness was a deep-seated ailment, and Augustus' courtesy and the diplomacies of Herod were no more than palliatives. Changes of personnel could prove fatal; in Caligula the Jews encountered an emperor who was ready to violate their religious self-respect by having a statue of himself prepared for the Temple; in the Governor Florus, sent to Judaea in AD 66, they had to deal with a Roman who was probably anti-Semitic through clumsiness rather than policy, though he ended by acting in the full consciousness that he was offending Jewish opinion to the point of causing rebellion.[39]

The Temple was destroyed in Vespasian's war; there was a widespread revolt in the middle east in AD 116; and from AD 132–5 the Romans again quelled a revolt in Judaea and Hadrian was then able to build his projected Roman town on the site of Jerusalem, Aelia Capitolina. The Jews felt they had been persecuted even though their privileges as a tolerated religion were confirmed by later emperors. They were able to accept many forms of Hellenism, but one particular version, man-worship in its contemporary Roman form, proved intolerable. Persecution of this type can be analysed into several components: government will or reluctance to take steps which it knows will be offensive to a significant group; the degree of willingness on the part of soldiers and administrators to act for the government; the presence of another, significant group, which enjoys the humiliation of the victim; the inability of the victim to accept what is proposed. It seems that over the period from Augustus to Hadrian there was not often a positive determination on the part of government to impose an offensive policy; there were, it is true, clumsy governors, but there were also sensible administrators like Petronius, who delayed carrying out Caligula's order because he could foresee the consequences.[40] In this kind of persecution the role of government is mostly passive rather than active. Caligula's statue and Hadrian's town are exceptions to the general rule of letting the Jews practise what is seen as their peculiar religion. The provocative factors are found among the Greeks and Jews; the former provided the element that government could, if necessary, look to for popular support, with an endemic and at times sly aggressiveness; and the Jews themselves developed an even greater sensitiveness to the various kinds of insult offered by the rulers and the alien immigrants.

It is not surprising that the conflict became extreme. Roman government, even when it was not in the hands of autocrats, was faced with a dilemma over the Jews. It allowed them their religion and various privileges many of which were resented by Greeks; but it was in general committed to extending its version of the imperial cult in ways that sometimes seemed not to be contentious to the Romans and yet were sacrilegious to the Jews. It is reasonable to distinguish between various forms of persecution, such as the tribal, the political and the theological.[41] In the relations between Jews and the Roman Empire, for instance, the tribal clash between Greeks and Jews is particularly strong (I mean the irritation of one group over the different ways and conduct of another); the theological animus is powerful on the Jewish side, with its convictions about Jehovah; and the political will to persecute, or to impose solutions that awaken and maintain a sense of injustice, emerges only gradually among the Romans.

An admired historian[42] of the Jews has remarked that in Roman terms Vespasian could have made one of two choices after his defeat of the Jews in AD 70. He could either have introduced the Jewish deity into the Roman pantheon or he could have annihilated it; instead of this he set up the Jewish treasury (*fiscus Judaicus*) into which Jews were required to pay a poll-tax, for the benefit of Jupiter. Adoption or destruction by other powers were fates that often beset the destinies of polytheistic gods. But in this case the choice was unreasonable or impossible. Unreasonable, as an emperor could not have introduced to Rome a god whose claims on a part of Roman territory were still cherished by his worshippers; and impossible, in another sense, as the large numbers of Jews in the Dispersion had created an institution which enabled them to dispense with the Judaean Temple. The synagogues of the Diaspora were able to do without the Temple; they had originated as substitutes for the Temple in the God's homeland, and though they soon flourished on their own account, they kept alive the territorial ambitions of the God. The Romans therefore had a far more complex problem than they had faced in earlier days when they had taken gods from defeated towns in Latium. They were now dealing with a God whose territory, so to speak, was both local and international; it would not have been enough to destroy the Temples at Jerusalem or at Leontopolis in Egypt; the organization that had been developed through the synagogues could only have been overthrown by a government with far more men and arms at its disposal, to say nothing of the commitment necessary for such a project.

In its dealing with Jews the Roman government showed only faint-hearted support for toleration. In Alexandria, for example, it protected Jews as against the Greeks, but because of the peculiar tax introduced by Augustus, the *laographia*, it made them feel inferior to the Greeks who formed the dominant élite in the city.[43] The Alexandrian Jews, whose social standing made them equal to Greeks, were made to look and feel like the Egyptians who were despised by both. The taxation policy therefore created (no doubt this was not the government's intention) a sense of resentment which undid the safeguards provided for the Jews by other means. This is not to say that blunders of this kind were avoidable, but to suggest that they were not recognized as blunders until much later. Gradually the Jewish sense was that Rome passed from deeds that might not have been intended as deliberate acts of persecution to aggressive proposals such as those of a Caligula intent on installing his own image in the synagogues. There were various motives that might have been ascribed to Caligula or his unfortunate representative in Alexandria, Flaccus; but Jews could only be indifferent to establishing the exact Roman motives when the consequences for them seemed so grievous. The feeling of resentment against Rome as a representative of Hellenism grew; the talent for a compromise with Hellenism, in the way that Philo, for example, expounded Jewish values in the medium of Greek ideas, gave place to an increasing sympathy with zealot extremism.

In trying to explain the nature of Roman dealings with the Jews the historian is bound to have at the centre of his attention the loss of the Temple, the risings under Trajan and the revolt of Bar-Kochba. One is justified in using the term persecution because of the *effects* of Roman policies, even though, as was suggested earlier, it took a long time for Romans to become quite as self-conscious in their anti-Jewishness as were the immediate Greek neighbours and rivals of the Jews. But Jewishness itself was in theory protected by Rome, unlike the name of Christianity, and for that reason a study of imperial persecution in the fullest sense must give pride of place to Roman dealings with Christians. It is still unclear whether Roman proceedings against Christianity were deemed to come under a general law, or whether on various occasions the questioning of Christian suspects was justified by the powers of arrest and enquiry that belonged to a Roman magistrate, though most opinion inclines to the latter theory. The shelter of tradition could not be made available to a cult so new, once it was seen as a thing distinct from its parent Judaism. The legal grounds of the persecution may be left aside, while we try instead to outline a sociology of the persecutions.[44]

The persecutions lasted from the time of Nero to the great persecutions under Diocletian and Galerius. They varied widely both in their incidence and duration, though it seems difficult to argue with the view that they became worse and more ferocious. A likely course of events might be as follows. An officer or magistrate would put to a suspect the explicit question, 'Are you a Christian?' On receiving the answer yes he would often allow time for reconsideration or would offer the chance of taking an oath by the emperor's Genius or of sacrificing to the gods and the emperor. If the suspect was still obstinate he was either beheaded (if a Roman citizen) or obliged to fight with animals in the arena. Roman officials and many who were not officials considered that they were disposing of criminals, but in the eyes of the church these criminals were martyrs, the children of whom she was most proud. To come to an understanding of these phenomena, however inadequate, we need to consider them under at least three heads: popular antipathy to Christians; the kind of zeal shown by subordinates and soldiers in carrying out arrests or conducting enquiries; and the reasons why governments initiated persecutions when they did so.

It is difficult for a government and its officials to conduct a persecution without some form of popular support. In Alexandria, as we saw, there were always Greeks to support or even incite a governor against the Jews they hated. Similarly, the accounts of martyrs and of persecutions often refer to the crowd or mob as a presence hostile to Christians. Anti-Christian feeling seems to have been caused by many factors. Petty economic jealousy made the statue-makers at Ephesus express their fears of missionaries who would, if they had their way, deprive them of a living; there would soon be no market in images if the realities were supposed not to exist. Some of the crowd (perhaps not many) were genuinely incensed that Christians had attacked their gods and were keen to see them punished; 'everybody acted as though it were a serious fault and impiety to fall short in their viciousness towards him [one of the martyrs of Lyons], for they thought that in this way they could avenge their gods.' The non-conformity of Christians was sometimes an offence; and some believed that Christians met as they did in order to perform acts of sexual licence.[45] Hostility founded on these rumours probably became less as Christians became better known and did not seem to be so threatening. Christians were not usually as separate in their way of life as Jews were.

Whatever the reason for the hostility, crowd anger was often both spontaneous and genuine. Christians were an obvious target of resentment for people who had been frightened by earthquakes, plagues or famines. There were also times when resentment was instigated from above, by rulers or officials with a will to persecute. But in these cases too crowd sentiment might be nonetheless alarming even if it had not started of its own accord but had been pushed. Factionalism at Alexandria, for example, was always terrifying and had an energy all its own, even when, as in the Decian persecution, someone had deliberately worked the people up to the point where they 'convinced themselves that the only true religion was this demon-worship.'[46]

It is doubtful whether, with our sources for the persecutions, sources which are both partial and biassed, we can do more than register the fact that the crowd reactions were extremely variable and differently motivated. Crowd anger quickly becomes autonomous, so that we hardly need a Eusebius to warn us that in some cases (perhaps in many) the feelings of the crowd were worked upon. In some of the persecutions, however, from the second and early third centuries, it seems that officials were either reluctant to act as persecutors or were determined to proceed with prudence and caution. The model interpretation here is suggested by the younger Pliny, faced with the task of investigating those who were alleged to be Christians in Bithynia.[47] Trajan explains that Christianity is an offence but that proper legal forms should be observed; Pliny ought not to listen to anonymous accusations, he ought not to initiate persecution by seeking Christians out, and he should allow those who confess a chance to repent and to re-join the community of pagan gods. Similarly, we hear of other governors who acted with caution; in the case of the Scillitan martyrs the proconsul allowed a reprieve of thirty days, and the proconsul Perennis allowed the martyr Apollonius a stay of execution. At one extreme, we might suggest (it is an extreme composed of Trajanic patience and Plinian moderation), there is an admission by the emperor that Christianity is wrong, but it is coupled with a reluctance to persecute, and impresses on the ministers of state a need of decorum. The result would be a slow or quiescent persecution, in which the state and its principal officers do not do more than react to complaints against Christians (*they* cannot be said to be going out and making the heretics come in) and offer them a period of grace for recantation.

In calling the Plinian or Trajanic model an extreme I am referring only to a typology of persecutions as it might be designed in theory. It is a way of drawing a distinction between persecutions in which government initiative is more or less pronounced, whether or not there is popular support. The distinction can also be set into a chronological frame as the persecutions of the mid-third and early fourth century came to be more severe and more general than earlier ones. There is a case for maintaining that from the time of Decius onwards (AD 250) imperial policy became a more important and a more energetic constituent of persecution.[48] The emperors came to perceive the Christian menace as more significant and were anxious to counter-attack it over a wide area. The difference would be that the emperors Decius, Valerian and Diocletian were no longer content to wait for popular pressure or even for the persuasive influence of a governor, but that they themselves set out to impose on their subjects the duty of hunting out the Christians. The suggested pattern (to put the matter in crude or simple terms) is that the emperors became increasingly concerned about the presence of Christianity and that the degree of imperial initiative for persecution is far more marked towards the time of Diocletian than it was before. Even so it is still unclear why the later emperors came to express their anxieties about the Empire's religion so much more positively. The argument that they did so is made to rest on somewhat facile assumptions, that Decius or Diocletian were in the nature of things bound to condemn the new cult, as they wished to restore the old Augustan Reich. But the particular evidence that they hungered and thirsted after the archaic in this exclusive style is unconvincing. It is possible too (a possibility that should not be discounted) that the very idea of initiating persecutions became more attractive as the government added to its bureaucracy and as it also looked for more areas in which to exhibit its diligence. In general oppressiveness or in mere industry government action or assertiveness became more pronounced in the later Empire, and it would be entirely in accordance with events elsewhere for the rulers to try to demonstrate their apparent control in religion as well as in the fields of taxation and employment.

But it is far from clear why the persecutions continued for as long as they did or why they were intensified under Decius, Valerian and Diocletian. We have seen that it is difficult to detect a common theme that makes the persecutions under Decius and Diocletian comprehensible. Decius started his attempted purge early in his reign whereas Diocletian did not begin his persecution until he had held power for about twenty years; and one would have thought that Diocletian's persecution, if it were intended to put back the religious clock, would have been more opportune at an earlier stage, as propaganda to help his well-advertised allegiance to Hercules and Jupiter. On the other hand one of the earliest interpretations of the persecutions is based on the idea that rulers persecuted in order to mark a difference between themselves and their more tolerant predecessors; in this way Eusebius tries to account for the vindictiveness of the Emperor Maximin the Thracian and of Decius.[49] But if the regnal difference suggested by Eusebius seems too naive, the assumptions behind modern accounts of Decius and Diocletian are also unsatisfactory.

The political motive of persecution is, or may be, to statesmen what the tribal one is to the superstitious multitude.[50] At its lowest level this principle would only mean that statesmen (though they perhaps have more thought for the means at their disposal) will object as strongly as the mob to a parade of non-conformity. The Church as a whole (before the intervention of Constantine) was treated as a dissident sect,[51] as reprehensible as the heretics of the fourth century who were to be condemned by the holy alliance between Catholic Church and Empire. The reasons why rulers and ruled passed a judgment of dissidence are reflected in some of the propaganda and polemic from the age of the beleaguered Church. Critics maintained that Christians did not pull their weight in the ordinary affairs of life, that they refused magistracies and the official posts that were a necessary burden. Soldiering became a key-issue in these attempts to say what was wrong and what was right with Christianity. For Tertullian it is axiomatic that military service is not allowed for those who called themselves Christians. And Origen, replying to Celsus, is content to plead that the emperor's armies will benefit from the prayers offered by Christians, indeed he thinks they are indispensable, but the Church's position is essentially that of an outsider; serving Christians are not themselves to be soldiers though the emperor's troops will benefit from Christian overtures to God.[52]

But the reality was probably quite different from the extremist position taken by Christians who proscribed war as a tainted form of sharing in the life of the world. Christians in fact became more common in the army. In the Alexandrian persecutions under Decius we hear of a soldier who protested at the insults that were rained on the persecuted, as well as of a whole squad of men who protested audibly when 'a man accused of being a Christian was on the point of denying Christ.' Several of the saints' tales from the martyrdoms at the end of the third century concern the particular problems of army men, their reluctance, for instance, to return and serve as veterans.[53] And it is clear from the events in the final persecutions that Diocletian's aim was (at first, at any rate) to purge the army and the imperial entourage of Christians. His purpose would only make sense if there were a significant number of Christians in the imperial civil service and in the army.

It is not easy (the difficulty arises mostly from gaps in the sources) to present the main phases of government initiative in persecution as reasonable or intelligible. The effectiveness of the persecutions is also highly debatable. The Empire did not have the bureaucratic or scientific technology to make the investigations really thorough. It had to rely on the sometimes reluctant service of minor functionaries, men who were loyal enough but frequently slow; one of the accused Christians stayed at home for several days while a government agent looked for him everywhere else. In particular the Decian system of requiring certificates from people to show that they had sacrificed would have been an imposition on a far more literate society.[54] The persecutions were really too ambitious to be sustained for very long, and it follows that the enquiries often petered out before the government itself announced the official all-clear.

To some extent government aims were helped by the ideology of those whom it set out to molest, the bravado of people who courted martyrdom. There were a number of people who refused to hide from authority, men and women whose resistance has been enhanced in the stories of the saints. The willingness to confront (together with some understandable backsliding) is well attested. Christian experience of this sort can be paralleled from outside the Empire. In Gothic territory, for example, we hear of an instruction sent by the central authority (the tribal council) to the local authority, ordering the village council to see that all villagers should consume sacrificial meat.[55] The villagers themselves are prepared to use unconsecrated meat, as a concession to their resident Christian Sabas, but he refuses the favour. He forces the tribal representative to be made aware of his 'guilt', his Christianity, and his execution therefore comes about only because he has sought to make the consequences of his beliefs fully public. There is a picture of harmonious relationships at the local level disturbed by a clumsy or aggressive intrusion from on high. Incidents like this were repeated inside the Empire. As far as Christians in the army were concerned some ceremonies were fraught with danger or opportunity for those who sought to combine Christianity and war: the commander's sacrifice; the offer of a donative; carrying the standards; even the question of which god to thank after victory. Some Christian soldiers learned to live with most or all of these. Even the chance of promotion could be made into a means of exposing a Christian. When Marinus at Caesarea was about to receive the office of centurion, to which he was entitled by seniority, another man who wanted the job denounced him on the grounds that 'he did not sacrifice to the emperors.'

Presumably the persecutions were intended to deter people from becoming Christians, by killing some and forcing others to lapse. But the intended consequence did not come about. The numbers of Christians grew, though slowly. There is no doubt that the persecutions were serious and alarming, even in a group which valued martyrdom. They gave rise to major questions of community discipline within the Church, the problem when to receive back into membership one who had survived by denying his faith. All the time the Church itself was learning the reasons why it too might have to persecute the disobedient and heretic, developing a far more confident ideology than any that had been known to the pre-Constantinian state, in spite of all its numerous gods. It would be uncomprehending, a form of modern rationalism, to say that more people came to think that the religious hypothesis they were defending was unverifiable while the human cost of rooting out the non-conformists was all too visible. Reasoning of this sort did not apply at the time when the persecutions ended. Once the Christian God had been given full civic stature, He had on His side not only the confidence of theologians but also the voice of law and order.

The persecutions failed partly because they were incompetently managed, partly because there were long periods of respite. In Gaul, for instance, the Christians were unmolested between AD 258 and 303; and in fact the period of grace in this part was longer still as the ruler in 303 was Constantius Chlorus who was only half-hearted in carrying out the edicts of Diocletian. Christianity in Gaul, as in other near-frontier areas, was helped by the inactivity of government and by the invasions of the barbarians. The former left Christians alone and the latter's fury fell more on the visible amenities of the towns, the temples of the old gods, so that the new religion could never have been faced with the heavy expense of restoration and repairs.[56]

But even so the periods of respite, like the government's inability to make a persecution last a long time, do not explain why men and women took to Christianity and why they persisted in it.[57] It is probably misleading to think of the religious motive as separable from the social and economic. The dichotomy, in my view, belittles a considerable part of pagan or polytheistic civic cult and makes it difficult to approach the task of describing how the Church formed a social compromise with the world. It is tempting, for instance, to attach a lot of importance to the claim, which is a long-established tradition with the apologists, that the saviour in Christian faith was a recent historical figure invested with deity. The implied contrast here is with the pagan gods, and the assumption is that Jupiter and Christ would have been quickly recognized by Romans of the Empire as non-comparable. We may readily accept that it would have been easy to pierce the flimsy constructions of euhemerism, and so be able to expose Jupiter as a bare figment, with no history of his own except the history of his statues on earth. But it is not so easy to accept that men and women then cared about the historical reality of their gods at a time when the sense of historical truth was poorly developed even among the educated.

One of the greatest strengths of Christianity was its social organization. It was, from near its beginning, when it broke the early synagogue-link with the Temple, a universal religion whose missionaries developed their own local centres and persuaded their followers to maintain relations with one another. Here was a remarkable 'advance' on the isolated scattering that had seemed to be the characteristic of many pagan cults. The new religion was freed from ties with homeland and had a greater mobility. The local centres of Christianity were made to observe what might be called the secular pattern; the Christian provinces, the bishops' districts, were in a sense as the emperor's provinces. Within this organization the bishops played an important part, in distributing some of the economic benefits in peace and in providing leadership in such crises as persecutions. Part of the reason for the lasting success of Christianity was its particular form of congregational appeal. It provided far more than had been available through the most traditional civic cults, in which many of those present had been little more than transient spectators. It created more opportunities for active participant good. The congregations therefore stood in a different relationship to their priests and bishops. The latter were masters of the arcane, it is true, but their knowledge was not the tricky restrictive set of rules devised by pontiffs and augurs, nor was it the amazing charade performed in some of the eastern cults. The priestly officers of the Christian congregations were expected to be men of influence in the world (they were sometimes appointed as well as respected for it), and the social return to a congregation esteeming its leaders was more tangible than in the days when religious office was far more closely tied to the political ambition of the politicians.

CHAPTER SIX

# *The Fourth Century*

This account of the basic structure and the historical practice of civic polytheism will indicate that in late antiquity the pagan deities were not just ghostly survivors from an age of faith. The loose expansionism of the system was still dynamic under the Empire even if the tempo of acquisition was slower than in the Republic; and the imperial proliferation of gods should not be written off as no more than a collection of trophies, with the deified emperors and their deified ladies all arranged in families. The religious experience of polytheists disposed them to welcome novelty; both as public figures holding high office and as private citizens men started from the premiss that new gods were necessary. The outsider gods invited by Rome, especially those which were allowed *inside* the sacred precinct (the *pomerium*), may be divided into two broad groups: those which were ceremoniously installed and authorized without much delay and those which sometimes spent many years in a pagan limbo before the senate or the emperors ordered their release. In much the same way human outsiders had either received full citizenship at once or had had to advance more slowly, from slave to freedman, and so on.

The Christian God acknowledged by Constantine in AD 312 was thus, judged by the traditional practice of Rome, a second-class god, a deity whose full political advent was delayed. The cult that became official so late co-existed with a civic polytheism that was far from exhausted.[1] The vitality of polytheistic habit showed in its appetite, not to say its greed, for fresh cults. In the fourth century, as we shall see, the government looked to the new religion to function in part as earlier cults had done. Neither the emperors nor the church could be blamed for having failed to anticipate that the relationship would make different demands on them; Constantine, for example, could hardly have foreseen how bishops would learn and perfect the arts of political intervention. The continued survival of polytheism is shown by the fact that a long time was needed to convince men why exactly the new cult was incompatible with the old. Christian intellectuals and theologians had confidence in the exclusive superiority of their God, but they lived and worked among men who were used to taking in new idols without discarding the old. The fourth century showed up the unforeseen problems in the novel partnership of church and state, and revealed various ways of testing the polytheistic assumption of compatibility.

Slower Christians were not at one with their sharper brethren whose powers were used to refine theology and to give reasons for rejecting pagan practices. Similarly, polytheists of the traditional kind included both those who disallowed the Christian cult and those who wished to live in the usual compromise with the new. Christians with the habit of compromise might be called the church of the multitude,[2] to distinguish them from the purists, the church of the martyrs, and to designate them as people whose conformity to Christianity reproduced with advantage a good deal of their conformity to paganism. There is therefore no simple contrast to be made between extreme Christian and extreme pagan at this stage. The complexity of paganism is shown by the different forms of revival, in which anti-Christian sentiment was socially derivative from the new practices and was informed by Christian institutions. These themes are discussed in the second part of this chapter.

In much of the writing about Constantine it is assumed that Christians were still in a minority when the emperor made their cult official, though little or nothing is usually said about Eusebius' account of Maximin's persecution in which this Augustus admits that he has finally had to leave ill alone because of the large numbers of Christians.[3] The effect of this assumption is to draw attention to what can look like a paradoxical gamble on the part of Constantine. But in the absence of reliable figures there is no warrant for making an uninformed guess about the relative numbers of Christians and pagans. Even if the size of the Christian minority were certain, we would then wish to know how in the case of the army it was divided among officers and men. To suppose that numbers were important is in effect a modernism, the fallacy of supposing that weight of numbers moulded the taking of decisions then as it sometimes does now. It is more in tune with the facts of fourth-century life as they are known to us to refer the power of decision to élite factors such as the individual ruler, or to an episcopal will imposing its fiat or arguing a case from enthusiasm or conviction. Generals and emperors tended to choose their own deities and tried to make sure that their choice would be ratified by victory. Curiosity about the proportions of pagans to Christians is understandable but is impossible to satisfy; the emphasis should be on the social comparability between fourth-century innovations and earlier phases of religious cult.

### *Christians' Progress*

Major historians of Constantine have tended to speculate on the nature of his conversion before his defeat of Maxentius, and on the subsequent course of his relationship with the new cult and beliefs between AD 312 and 337. For accounts of the former we are obliged to make what sense we can of Lactantius, writing a few years after 312, and of Eusebius, whose version appeared after Constantine's death. Lactantius alleges that Constantine was instructed in a dream to re-equip his troops with a new military standard, the *labarum*; and Eusebius describes how Constantine saw with his own eyes a vision of the cross, inscribed with the words, 'in this conquer'. Neither authority is entirely easy to accept. We may not put much value on dreams as evidence, and even if we do we might well suppose that most men of this period (including Constantine) would be, if anything, predisposed to see not Christian but pagan statues in their sleep, in the manner described in the dream-book of Artemidorus. The credibility of Eusebius is not improved by his clerical self-assurance, his trust that the report of conversations with the late emperor will seem quite as reliable to his readers as to himself. Doubt on this score may well have more weight than confidence that Constantine had a genuine religious experience based on a happening which can be given a modern scientific explanation, that what he saw was a form of the 'halo phenomenon' in which a cross of light with the sun in its centre may be observed. It is more reasonable to distrust a historian, who has obvious reasons for brandishing his credentials as the friend of kings, than it is to accept a story in which the miraculous element is sweetened by science; whatever the merit of the modern scientific account, it does nothing to explain what was for Eusebius (and for Constantine presumably) the vital experience.[4]

The later history of Constantine's religion is also beset with difficulties. It is clear that in his campaign against Licinius (in 324) he came forward as the defender of the faith against an opponent who had re-opened, somewhat half-heartedly, the files of persecution. After this victory the first Christian emperor convened and encouraged the first oecumenical council. But it is less obvious how we should relate the religious attitude of the emperor in and after 325 to his attitudes in the period immediately after 312. Then he certainly favoured the church even though his religious position was equivocal. The Edict of Milan, put forward by Constantine and Licinius in 313, urged a tolerance for religious practice which seems at variance with the aggressive spirit of Christianity in the fourth century. It may be that here the emperor was different from or better than his supporters, that he had not yet discovered the increasing extent of their demands. It seems too that for some years after 312 the emperor was portrayed in a way that would (to say the least) lead to an understandable confusion between Sun and Christ, as the symbols of solar cult were still displayed. Also the panegyrist who spoke of the 'divinity' in reference to Constantine's deeds chose an enigmatic form of words; he might have been using an ambiguous phrase into which the adept of any cult could read his own deity, or (as one view suggests) he might have been using a term that would satisfy Christians without doing too much violence to his own (pagan) views.[5]

I mention these problems mainly to suggest that it is lost labour to puzzle over the conversion psychology of Constantine, or to present an interpretation of his religious biography in which all the pieces are persuaded to fit together. These are fascinating subjects but they are more suited to speculation than to historical argument. It is less important to determine the kind of faith which moved the emperor personally than to estimate where he stands in relation to the social and political advance of Christianity, as it was to be shown in the number of its churches and the power of its bishops. The new cult (new to official life, that is) had already made an impact on society by its organization which provided some practical daily welfare and which had on the whole stayed intact through the persecutions. Constantine took the decision, as other generals had done before him with lesser or at least more tractable gods, to attach it more closely to the emperor himself. This is not to say that had Constantine been defeated by Maxentius the Empire would never have become Christian; the likelihood is that Christian organization would have outlived that setback and would still have found, sooner or later, an imperial general in search of a cult to patronize. It was a habit of the polytheistic Republicans and emperors too acclaim a deity as helper before a decisive battle and to award the prizes after victory.

The immediate context of Christianity's political advent was therefore military; the Christian God began his official existence within the Roman system as a victory-god. Constantine did not go up to the Capitol to pay his respects to Jupiter after the defeat of Maxentius, and this fact may suggest that he realized some of the new demands and exclusions that the religious ally might make on the government.[6] But, however his absence from the Capitol is interpreted, it is of course highly unlikely that he foresaw to their full extent the new relationships which were to develop between state and Church. For the government, especially for the emperors, Christianity could be described as a target religion. A new cult would attract to itself those hopes of deity which had been satisfied by the pagan gods of the past; and would expect to receive some of the usual prizes in the form of religious buildings and favours for the priesthood. The cults of polytheism can therefore be described as the source religion for the new adventure, but not in the narrow sense in which origins are often discussed. The terms target and source are an attempt to indicate the formal quality of the relationship between old and new. In this system people (not only emperors, it should be said) transfer to the new god expectations which are moulded by the national experience of earlier gods. The new god cannot be at all lively within the system unless there is some transfer of expectation. This is one of the reasons why many of the gods in polytheistic Rome were relatively short-lived or were forced into the background; they handed on their credit to newcomers. Constantine, on the eve of the battle, was looking to his target religion for a traditional good, victory in war. The ruler's choice of course influenced more lives than the choices made by humbler people who had become Christian; but they too had come with expectations of comfort or material assistance that had first been developed in a pagan cult. To say this is not to exclude the factor of novelty; ordinary people had become used to things that were not expected, such as the surprises of martyrdom and persecution, and emperors were now to experience the remarkable force of ecclesiastical politics.

Apart from victory in war the emperor's other main hope was for the support of the new priesthood, a hope which in Constantine's reign and later was often frustrated. Constantine on his side showed that he knew how to give as well as to expect; the arrangement between man and God was reciprocal, it postulated an exchange of gifts in which the worshipper should not be too mean or parsimonious. An emperor measured or rather poured out his bounty by favouring a new cult; in this case imperial munificence was expressed in building churches for God and in granting privilges to the clergy. These might be called the costs of the new deity, though to speak of costs is perhaps to introduce a form of calculation which was foreign to the Greek and Roman way of bargaining with god. Religion was in a sense like success in war and it counted as an imperial exploit; an emperor therefore would demonstrate his own worth and grandeur by erecting magnificent shrines and by granting special favours to the clergy. The true witness to the full social and political incorporation of Christianity is apparent in the Constantinian benefactions to Church and clergy. We need to see how churches and the bishops contributed to the life of the community much as we saw how in an earlier period the temples and pontiffs of other religions had adorned the cities of the Empire.

I do not mean that the evaluation of Constantinian religion should confine itself to thinking about its function against the background of target cult and source cult; the novel factors peculiar to Christianity must also be understood, but it may still be important to interpret the acquisition of a new cult in terms of a long tradition. Some habits of polytheism had persisted even though the religious topography of many cities had been reshaped after centuries of introducing new gods. In discussing the architectural advent of Christianity we should remember that Rome itself, more than other cities, had been considerably changed through civic growth. The Aventine district, for example, had once been a plebeian stronghold and housed the temples of gods who were either the favourites of plebeians or were not prestigious enough to find a home within the *pomerium.* But long before the fourth century the extension of the civic boundary and the growing acceptability of its cults had transformed the Aventine hill. Indeed, after Constantine, this district contained the residences of fashionable pagan aristocrats. Thus the Christian invasion of Rome the city, as authorized by Constantine the benefactor, meant that the builder had to modify a larger city, a city which was now encumbered with temples as once, in the first century AD, the calendar had become congested with festivals and official sacrifices. The development of Rome into an ecclesiastical metropolis was bound to be a long-term project; there were consequences to honouring the new God with buildings, consequences which had to be measured in fallen temples, and the loss only became apparent as the Christian refusal to juxtapose churches and temples gradually took its toll of the latter. At the beginning, however, the emperor found it both acceptable and traditional to set up where he could buildings in honour of his deity.[7]

The tradition here mentioned was that of pagan munificence to a god. Other emperors before Constantine, as a mark of relinquishing a persecution, had restored its property to the Church, but Constantine was the first to lavish new buildings on the persecuted and to improve the clerical lot with tax-exemptions and special grants. The emperor's generosity could not be satisfied by humble house-churches of the type which had been used for many years. Christian cult had held its first meetings in the rooms of private houses. A later stage was marked by the house-church, sometimes purpose-built or at least acquired for the special function of Christian worship. House-worship of this type was not a novelty in the late Hellenistic world, since other cults too had at first held meetings in a room in a sympathizer's house and had only entered the public domain when their adherents felt more secure and perhaps more wealthy. The purpose-acquired house marks an intermediate stage – it indicates an advance on the time when the congregation was too small and too poor to have its own special place for worship – before the imperial intervention, which allocated land for the building of magnificent churches. St John Lateran and St Peter were among the most striking monuments of Constantine's Rome, and the religious generosity of the ruling family constructed like memorials to piety in the Judaean homeland.[8]

The Christian basilicas were grand enough to please the emperor's sense of architectural splendour. They showed too that the new cult had different congregational needs from the temples of the past; the home of a pagan god was suitable for a committee or a dinner-party, it could admit a fugitive population which came to thank or beseech, but as a form of building it was inadequate to house the worshippers of the new cult. The new religious functions – prayer, reading a text, singing, hearing a sermon and observing the administration of practical charity – meant that the congregation (it probably grew in size as the religion enjoyed more of the imperial esteem) needed a more spacious edifice. Thus the imperial tradition of munificence to a deity on the grand scale was matched by the needs of the enlarging church. Even so the house-church did not become extinct overnight, and in come communities it remained as the small-town equivalent of the basilica.[9]

As mere space-units, since their capacity was for different religious quanta, the temples might have endured for centuries without disturbing the churches. Their overthrow was in fact only gradual and the Christian onslaught was in practice less devastating than theory prescribed. Constantine is alleged to have ransacked the pagan temples, for emperors when they chose could overstep the property-rules which kept out lesser men; the presumption is that they were more important to him as a financial source (for Constantinople, for example) than as a means of venting ideological hatred. Being responsible for running things eventually shortened the Christian temper and led to the destruction of pagan monuments. But even Eusebius reports that at this earlier stage only three temples were destroyed by Constantine, and at least one of these may be dated to a later period.[10] The temples were plundered (as they often had been before) but the emperors were on the whole more conservative than the religious mobs which destroyed some of the greater shrines. Attacks on pagan temples were, it seems, often inspired by irrational outbursts directed against the obvious symbols of the old cult; the temples were not required for Christian congregational purposes, and so there was no question of commandeering older buildings for a more vigorous religion.

The Christian basilicas were built on a larger scale than the temples, but like the latter they were a form of exploit and display. There were other features in common, whatever the difference between the deities themselves and their various followers. Locality cult was still important even though some of the pagan cults had achieved a kind of *de facto* universality, with some degree of freedom from the constraints of a particular place; Jupiter cult, for example, and even more the imperial cult, had become detached from too close a dependence on a single locality, the city of Rome. In theory, at any rate, Christianity was nothing but universal and was not restricted by those habits of locality which had determined the embryonic or youthful stage of many pagan cults. But in practice the architectural shaping of the new religion gained from exploiting the more obvious associations with locality. The Holy Land was especially favoured as the seat of churches that were inseparable from the life of the founding deity. And in other places too locality contributed to make one church more important than another; many of the new buildings were monuments to martyrs and were venerated as memorials that had been raised on holy foundations. Locality in this sense was not a disadvantage to the cult as a whole; instead it endowed with the humanity of a particular presence what would otherwise have been too remote from local experience.

As a religion Christianity had more in common with Judaism, which saw its Temple as a replica of the heavens, than with Roman civic polytheism. Even a Roman temple could only be prepared by one who had an official position and consequently the ability to map out the sky. It provided for man as well as for god; a late effect of its functional diversity is shown by the fact that former polytheists, as they came to frequent the churches, brought with them some of the practices which had been common in polytheistic temples. There were banquets which continued to be held in spite of the fact that they were forbidden by the decrees of church councils. Pammachius' wake as a homage to his departed wife provided food and drink for the poor and was compared with Christ's feeding the people on the loaves and fishes. Dancing in church was sometimes allowed in connection with the festivals of martyrs. The church as a building was not only a house of worship, it also allowed incubation (for which there were plenty of pagan precedents), sanctuary (for which there were some), and it provided living and sleeping quarters, most often in emergencies.[11] Thus some of the purposes to which church buildings lent themselves resemble the more secular functions of pagan temples. But the likeness can only be taken so far. In the churches many of these activities were in conformity with the new religion and only betrayed it (if at all) through a sense of exuberance. Thus, although the church building was indeed multi-functional, the function of worship was more important than the other uses which make it appropriate to invoke the polytheistic tradition with its wide range. Churches, it should be remembered, were not prescribed as the meeting-place of Christian administrators, in the way that a temple was the *sine qua non* for a meeting of the senate.

Both the emperors and the leaders of the Church had an interest in building grand basilicas to house the new faithful. And yet church buildings were not strictly necessary; some of Christ's words suggested that God could be worshipped anywhere and there was a traditional Christian saying that 'walls do not make Christians'. In the fourth century the former pagan

Victorinus used to protest jokingly that he did not need to go to church to prove his Christianity, though in the end he too accepted the need to go. But it will be clear from this account that there was much sociological ground in common between the temple and the church. It is true that the different needs of the Christian congregation led to the creation of a different type of building, but mobility of faith was encouraged by the fact that some familiar practices were admitted within the holy walls. At a later date it was recognized by Pope Gregory that the British might be more easily converted 'if the people sees that its sanctuaries are left standing ... They will more easily come to those temples which they used to frequent.'[12] The fourth century was in general less tolerant; it was determined to have distinctive buildings of its own; and perhaps even Gregory's tolerance was intended as no more than a temporary measure. In the fourth century the first requirement was to make a clean break with the gods that had recently been identified with the persecution of the faith.

It was easier to dispose of a statue than to knock down a temple; and in the fourth century statues were moved about by the depredations of building emperors or were destroyed by enthusiastic crowds. Aesthetic conservationists were few; most people were motivated by hostility towards the images of gods which (in the view of some) had magical powers. Christian attitudes in the fourth century were in part the product of a long tradition of Christian theorists committed to presenting a powerful case against the hated cult-objects. Clement of Alexandria wrote that it was ridiculous for mortal man, as the plaything of the deity, to manufacture gods and thus turn god into the plaything of human art or technique. Tertullian's scorn for statues was followed by the argumentative indignation of Arnobius. The latter is aware of a pagan apologia for statues of gods, based on the idea not that the materials are gods but that the gods are thought to be in the materials; he replies with the question, why should the supposed gods leave the heavens in order to limit themselves in the strait-jacket of man-wrought matter? He also shows that he knows the political argument for statues of gods and for temples, and answers it by saying that man has not behaved any better because of an increase in the number of gods and temples. Both pagan and Christian theorists agreed that the anthropomorphic image of god is untrue to nature; the Christian went further and denied its relevance to the moral and political life.[13]

It is unlikely, however, that theory of this sort made men destroy the statues. Fear of the magic power, turning later into contempt, was perhaps more effective. Eusebius tells us that Constantine sent out troops to show that the feared instruments of theurgic worship were full of tricks. They held up to public scorn the bones, skulls, clothes and straw that had been concealed in the images as part of the miracle-worker's stock-in-trade. The casuistry of destruction was clearly expressed by Augustine:

When temples, idols and groves are destroyed, once we are given the power, even though it is plain that by so doing we are not honouring those things but showing our hatred, we ought not to take anything for our own private use, to make it clear that we are destroying from piety not for greed. But when they are put to public use or changed to do honour to the true God, they are treated in the same way as living persons when they are converted to true religion from sacrilege and impiety.

The biblical warrant for the Christian re-use of traditional pagan culture comes from Deuteronomy and is here extended to allow for the Christian re-cycling of building material. But iconoclasm was not given a charter; a canon of the Elvira council shows that statue-smashing might cause difficulties as between owners and their slaves, and another disallows it as an entitlement to martyrdom.[14]

Eusebius' story portrays an active emperor confronting a passive but educable throng with the sordid evidence of the stage-properties from inside the statues. The alleged passivity is probably not typical of popular attitudes to idols in the fourth century. The people at times started the destruction, and it seems likely too that in this period there began the popular transfer of certain practices from pagan statues to images of saints. Polytheistic man had shown his reverence for some gods by immersing their statues as a form of renewal or purification; in much the same way the statues of saints were dipped into purifying water, and the chief honour on these occasions could be given to the symbolically pure, a young female virgin. These immersions were performed in a spirit of reverence as an attitude common to both pagan and Christian was fearfulness and awe before the deity. But it was also possible to punish or threaten a statue with the legitimate excuse that the god had failed to perform his part of the bargain. Augustus, for example, withdrew a statue of Neptune from a procession of the gods because of his misfortunes in naval battles. This form of threatening a statue recurs in the Christian tradition in which it might be quite proper to immerse a saint's portable image if prayer had failed to stop a storm at sea. Even when idols were destroyed, a process which took place unsystematically throughout the fourth century, sometimes to the discomfort of rulers, pagan practice was at least in part transferred to new and purer objects. It is well known that hymns and the use of incense were a common feature in both pagan and Christian divine service.[15]

The transference of imperial bounty and popular attendance from temple to church was one of the successes of the Constantinian age; the like transference from god's statue to holy image took longer and was more uneven. But Constantine's hopes of the Church as an institution were less readily met. It seems from his address to the bishops at Nicaea that he had envisaged a clear role for the episcopacy; it was to be parallel to his own function, described by himself in terms which have been much debated, as 'bishop of those outside'. Even before the Council of Nicaea the state had been disappointed in the co-operative activity of the Church. The end of the persecution and the beginning of imperial favour were not able to produce a unified organization that would give the emperor the support for which he looked. At this early stage the Church was already divided on the question whether to accept the emperor's advances; in North Africa for example the Donatist schism developed into a struggle between Catholics, who looked forward to a future of co-operation, and their Donatist opponents, for whom an alliance between the state and the Church of the pure was a form of the most abject collaboration.

There have been various interpretations of Constantine's claim that he was 'bishop of those outside'. He may have meant that he was to look after pagans and heretics; or that he was himself a bishop, even though he had not been consecrated; or that he held a commission from God for the temporal government. It is fairly certain that he did not expect to have on his hands an insubordinate institution; no one who thought of pontiffs and augurs and Arval brethren, men in religious posts that had become more and more ceremonial over the centuries, would have imagined that the chief priests of the new cult would prove so difficult. Undoubtedly Constantine expected the bishops to resolve their theological disputes and present the emperor with their unified support. But in place of an obedient Church he brought about an independent priesthood that looked to him to back the right theological party but did not allow him the right to decide without episcopal guidance. His successor Constantius was no more successful; he was blamed for obscuring the 'plain and simple religion of the Christians' with controversies and arguments.[16] But the Christian elaboration of the truth was the responsible party; all that Constantius can be blamed for is that he 'sought to make the whole ritual conform to his own will.' The bishops, that is, expected the government to be on the right side – an unfair hope when so many of them were often in the wrong – and they resented active intervention that made hostilities within the Church even worse. Competition for a bishopric was sometimes as fierce as the Republican elections for the pontificate, and some bishops wielded great political influence.

The favours and the genuine donations of Constantine helped to make a priestly class with a sense of its own independence. He can hardly have wanted the sort of episcopal activity that is so noticeable at the clerical extreme, in the careers of Athanasius and Ambrose, who became considerable politicians as well as bishops. In the Hellenistic world the royal and Republican experience of priests would not have disposed a ruler to expect this change; that it happened may be ascribed to complex social factors as well as to the Christian obsession with its own theory.

The strength of the episcopacy was in part derived from the conviction of an unbroken dynasty. The bishops went back to the apostles and St Peter whereas the imperial dynasties were no more than disjointed sequels to the first Augustus. Secondly, the pagan priesthoods had fallen even further behind in political value to their holders as they had been greatly outnumbered by the increased posts in the military and the civil bureaucracy; their political role had declined from the not very high level of the late Republic; there was room for an institution such as the episcopacy to show that its members could be politically effective. The bishops, therefore, were able to minister to spiritual needs and to demonstrate their ability to influence rulers. The quasi-political priesthood of the polytheistic state was to be replaced by an autonomous caste which became politically important even though it began life as a body outside politics. And the economic favours granted the clergy gave them a sense of being a class apart, but essential to the welfare of the Empire. The moral and spiritual authority of the bishops won them an influence over imperial policy, and was at times more of an effective constraint on policy than the procedures and rituals once imposed by the authorities in charge of the Sibylline books.[17]

If it is likely that Constantine had hoped for an obedient clergy, he and still more his successors were surprised by the unforeseen power of the bishops.

A profit-and-loss account of Constantine's endorsement of Christianity would be a complicated matter. Undoubtedly the Empire lost some talented men, at all levels of administration; there were minor officials, such as those who were won over to the monastic life by hearing about St Antony, and, higher up, career administrators like St Ambrose, who was the social equal of Roman aristocrats. Society as a whole was anxious about ensuring a supply of manpower for the cities and the army, yet it lost some men it could ill spare to the desert life. A society that was faced with invasion along miles of frontier was probably not helped by some of the theological arguments within; but the debates about God varied in their social consequences: the wider Arian heresy, which translated bishops somewhat roughly but hardly touched their congregations except spiritually, was less destructive of property than the localized Donatist dispute in Africa. Endowing the churches with land and making exemptions for the clergy had something of an adverse effect on the returns from taxation, and at times the government attempted to block this form of outlet and so to keep land or money at the disposal of the treasuries. There was also morale to consider as well as money; the emperors, except for Julian and one or two others, believed they had their God's support, but they were fighting against barbarians many of whom were also Christian; and Jerome's declaration that Gothic valour, known to be formidable, was a function of Gothic faith, can hardly have pleased a government that was trying to keep out this Christian enemy. Pure Catholic priorities were in theory different from those of government; the Goth therefore, though an enemy, was valued as a fellow-Christian, and preachers esteemed 'soldiers of Christ' before those who were soldiers of the 'saeculum'.[18]

But it is all too easy to represent the Church both in its architecture and its institutions as nothing but a drain on the inadequate resources of the Empire. It is true that Constantine's own city foundation was expensive, but this was not specifically because of expenditure on and for Christianity; Constantinople would have cost a lot anyway.[19] Loss of manpower, for instance, was not as simple as it looks. In high politics Ambrose the bishop was not completely lost to the world but served as an ambassador for the court; when the Emperor Valentinian heard that one of his appointed judges had been made a bishop, he showed his pleasure, even though he was losing an Ambrose. At a more local level Synesius as bishop in Libya helped to maintain law and order against invading tribesmen. Churchmen therefore were still engaged in the support of the realm,[20] and there were many degrees of adherence to the more solemn dicta of theologians. As a local institution the Church undertook and fulfilled many of the responsibilities which in the past had been carried out by private enterprise. It looks plausible to suggest that the cost of church building might have become a burden on an economy that could only manage holding victories and so was deprived of manubial resources. But the suggestion would only have had weight if the Empire had continued to accumulate pagan temples at the same time. The rich, such as Melania and Pinianus, gave endowments to the churches rather as their wealthy predecessors, the Plinies, had followed the example of temple-building set by the emperor.[21] There is in fact much to be said for the view that both intellectually and socially Christianity was of great use to the Empire. With all the theological hatred and envy, its ideas and institutions helped to sustain people in their congregations, and it improved on some of the services that had once been offered by the pagan temple; and in some places, because there was a delay in executing theological writs, one of the more popular pagan amenities, the games, survived and flourished, to the indignation of Church leaders. In these parts pagan entertainment was still for many an acceptable complement to Christian service.

A principal theme of this chapter is that imperial benefactions were readily transferred from temples and priesthoods to churches and bishops. If we may assume that they were expected to produce similar satisfactions – I mean here the buoyant sense of a supporting or present victory-god and the political delight in a special relationship with a priestly class – Constantine and other rulers were not wholly satisfied. As an organization the Church was both too strong and too weak to suit the emperor's requirements. Its strength resided in certain qualities which made it like a military state within the state; it already had a sense of discipline, *esprit de corps* and loyalty, and the gradual defining of the hierarchical relationship of provinces to Rome and Constantinople reinforced this autonomy. But it was also divided as an institution and could not heal its divisions just to make a concordat with the emperor; and though it was grateful for the benefits it received it did not take imperial dictation when required. The episcopacy was the main instrument of an ecclesiastical submission to the will of God which did not shirk the consequence of arguing against the state. It acquired political influence not because it was from the beginning a quasi-political office like the pontificate, but, surprisingly, because it was sure of its independence and was confident enough to set a limit to the emperors' demands.

The bishops therefore were a major political novelty of the fourth century. They were on occasion able to make a ruler bow to religion, as Ambrose exercised authority over Theodosius in a way that seems entirely foreign to the former polytheistic collusion between office-holder and advisory priest.[22] It is however a mistake to think of government and Church as set on a collision course. There were subjects on which they found no difficulty in reaching agreement, though the initial approach was slightly different; magical practice, for example, was feared by the emperors as a token of conspiracy, and it was hated by the clergy as an extreme instance of the paganism which ought to be eradicated. Political and theological anxiety in this case shared a common ground. The world of the fourth century was extremely complicated. On their side the leaders of the Church were often separated from those whom they sought to instruct and guide, with the result that the Christian front was not unified. Christians were divided into those with unimpeachable doctrine and those who were hazy about what polytheistic practices were compatible with the new orthodoxy. It was possible at one stage for a Christian to belong to a pagan funeral club or to hold pagan priesthoods. These combinations did not last very long but they may help to show that for some, the palaeo-Christians as they have been called, the experiment with Christianity started as a test of compatibilities.[23] Some practices were quickly discarded in the light of episcopal criticism. Others enjoyed a longer life in spite of objections from the pulpit. Thus the exchange of presents on New Year's day was a long-standing polytheistic custom, popular and exciting as a special form of the gift relationship. It was criticized on the grounds that it encouraged self-seeking, that it would lead men to hope for a more valuable 'strena' (gift) than the one they had donated. The contrast with Christian charity, with its emphasis on giving, not on receiving (whether or not in exchange), was clear-cut. This particular festival was also thought to be objectionable because it caused indiscipline in the army, created tension between urban sophisticates and simpler country-folk, and imposed a vain expense on the consuls.[24] But many of these polytheistic activities survived the transference to a Christian milieu and became accepted, so that the dates of some pagan festivals were honoured with Christian processions; perhaps a better way of putting it is to say that without these transferences, even if they did not survive for long, the social form of the move from polytheism to Christianity would have been too rich in novel content.

*Pagan Revivals*

The argument so far has concentrated on those demands and expectations of polytheism which were either satisfied through their new Christian milieu or which were not at once denied. To many people, that is, the new cult did not make itself manifest by an overwhelming difference from the old or traditional cults. They became Christian not from a sense that paganism was wholly wrong and that Christianity was exclusively right, but in the hope that the rightness of their tradition might be fortified by an additional increment. They would not have sympathized with the judgment of a great modern who was himself deeply religious:

> The heathens were easily converted, because they had nothing to give up; but we ought not, without very strong conviction indeed, to desert the religion in which we have been educated. That is the religion given you, the religion in which it may be said Providence has placed you. If you live conscientiously in that religion, you may be safe.[25]

It does not take much of an acquaintance with the fourth century to see that pagans and their like had something considerable to surrender and that some of its famous conversions, though in a sense sudden, were not easily made; Victorinus and Augustine, for example, were converts who needed a preparation lasting years.[26] Likewise men on a humbler level of intellect were often conscious not that 'they had nothing to give up' but that the new might give them even stronger hopes of enjoying what older cults had promised and had sometimes even performed. A striking way of expressing this is to remember that only a minority of converts fled to a desert refuge and that for many conformity to a new cult did not compel them to forsake the army or the bureaucracy. It is better to think of fourth-century men as people who did not at first see themselves as betraying or deserting their past; they had been brought up to suppose that new gods could and should be invited as official consorts. They were not yet as certain of the falsehood of their tradition as leading Christian intellectuals both then and later required them to be.

Paganism in this sense was defined only gradually through the adversity of persecutions that were sometimes conducted by the state in response to the ideological demands of the Church. Among those who could be called pagan there were considerable varieties of practice and of belief. Thus it is misleading to speak of 'pagan revivals' if the expression is taken to mean the attempts to restore practices that were *uniformly* non-Christian, as if there were an agreed body of doctrine which could somehow be reinstated or fashioned into a new institution. The phrase may still be useful as long as we remember that a greater concern of the fourth century was with the degree of compatibilities between pagan and Christian practice; it can serve to designate those periods of disturbance in which the reassertion of pagan practice was usually accompanied by a persecution of the Church or by a reduction of its privileges. These upsets may not be of major historical importance, but it is still desirable to exhibit their character in order to assess more accurately the polytheist's sense of loss within a Christian Empire. Since the divisions between pagan and Christian were frequently blurred, an account of the resurgence of polytheism should be preceded by a version of the strange relationships between the old and the new.

It is right to speak of a choice between polytheism and Christianity provided that we bear in mind some of the peculiar features that affected the circumstances of decision. Choice of this kind was not exercised between equal things and was in that sense, if in no other, not free. Both socially and politically the bias was towards Christianity and away from polytheism of a type that either excluded the new cult or had not yet sought to accommodate it. The general drift was from polytheism towards a form of Christianity in which varying amounts of polytheism could be retained. The opposite formulation seems almost inconceivable, for it would hardly have been possible to return (or go on) to a polytheism in which the exclusiveness of the Christian God would be as prominent as the polytheistic traits retained in Christianity. Change or conversion from polytheism to Christianity had no counterpart in a corresponding movement from Christianity to polytheism; in the second case, when people lapsed, they went into heresy, becoming Arians or Manichees, or into schismatic movements like Donatism in north-west Africa.

The new cult provided most of the public religious goods that had been sought by polytheistic cult; also it enhanced some goods and added new ones. Among the improvements we might cite the more elaborate forms of the congregational act. Religion was granted its independence and (without disloyalty to the best interests of the state as the clergy envisaged them) it helped develop a more complex sense of group identity within a local membership. Its prayers, supplications and sermons were regular rather than occasional; they became para-civic instead of being wholly begotten by the state. Religious goods should not be understood in the material sense alone, even though the tangible evidence of God's support was not forgotten; men still expected that God would send the emperors victory in war and that the church commissioners would receive enough from the emperors and others to assist the poor.

It might be thought that Constantine's support for the Church, such as his gifts to Anullinus for the African churches, could be regarded as the first of many similar inducements.[27] The assumption would probably be too coarse to do justice to the temper of an age which increased its hold on an other-worldly religion when it was itself hard pressed for its existence as well as for victory. It would also exaggerate the importance of a man's religion to his political and military career in a misleading way, though the interconnection grew. The phenomena to be explained may be supposed to lie between the so-called Edict of Milan (AD 313) and a law of AD 415, which explicitly puts a bar on the non-Christians, the 'gentiles'; they, as the followers of rites profane, are excluded from military service with the emperor, from civil governorships and from the position of judge.[28] To put it bluntly, by this date, even if we make allowances for the undoubted fact that in practice the measures in the Theodosian code were only partially effective, there were more and more political and social disadvantages to being a Jew or a pagan, quite apart from the difficulty of finding temples. One of the ways in which the legislation advanced towards its Catholic perfection was by becoming more anti-Semitic and more anti-pagan.

But although the Empire became more restrictive by then we should not infer that for most of the fourth century advancement of a career was closely linked with a man's religion. Christian emperors were practical politicians who employed the able when and where they found them; the career of Tatianus under Constantine, for example, describes a man who became eminent as a governor and was commemorated for his religion, a religion defined by his offices as 'pontiff of Vesta, member of the pontifical college, priest of Hercules'. He does not seem to have had in his make-up even the merest trace of Constantinian Christianity. Other men, even more eminent, seem to have had no religious posts at all. It was not necessary to become Christian in order to get on; pagans were not as such the prime enemies of officials who were Christian; indeed one might say that from the point of view of an Athanasius an indolent pagan was greatly preferable to an over-active Arian.[29]

On their side too most pagans in public life, even though they were enthusiasts for their own cause, did not make polytheism and Christianity their sole or even their principal tests of what was acceptable in public life. Libanius was on good terms with several Christians and had a strong dislike for at least some of his fellow-pagans. An analysis of his correspondents suggests that at Antioch there were numerous Christians as well as pagans in high and low places. When Ambrose as bishop of Milan decided to oppose the Roman senate's request to have the altar of Victory restored to the senate house, he put his case before an imperial council which included Bauto and Rumoridus; these were both pagans, friends of Ambrose, but they do not seem to have made the senate's request their own cause.[30] The great pagan exception to this lack of intolerance is undoubtedly Julian, since it was clearly his aim to reward pagans with political appointments. It seems likely that Julian gave considerable offence to all, not by taking religion seriously, since other emperors did this, but by making it an obtrusive issue yet again in the manner of those who had persecuted the Christians. The social upheaval caused by his policies was too uncomfortable for either side.[31]

The spokesmen on the pagan side in the fourth century give an impression of timidity and caution. The judgment is perhaps somewhat unfair to them as they were men of custom and tradition, with whom enthusiasm appears in the polished tones of formal rhetoric. Libanius speaks with respect of the civic gods of his own Antioch, and his religion has been described as mainly Hellenic and cultural;[32] if these terms are imprecise, the scope of his attitude is better defined by his hostility to the monks, not so much as Christians, but because they are the supreme enemies of the highest good, life in the city-state. Libanian religion therefore envisages man only as a political creature. Symmachus, for all his different culture as a Latin-speaking aristocrat close to the centre of things, has a similar regard for custom and pleads for his cult without wishing to exclude Christianity. It is an argument for the past that presupposes the rightness of a multifarious approach to the deity. These men put their main intellectual point – the variety shown by mortals in their submission to the one mysterious god – in a rhetorical form that had been wrought by years of practice. The defence of paganism was therefore both theoretical and aesthetic. The two features reappear in the case of Maximus, a grammarian who pleaded with Augustine that there must be more than one avenue to god and who made fun of the names of Punic martyrs; understandably enough, since the familiar sonority of the names Hercules and Juno could not be expected to give place to such Punic oddities as Namphamo and Miggo.[33] The new religion came with weird rhythms and outlandish sounds, with the result that it baffled men like the young Augustine, with their highly developed sense of classical decorum in language. But the artistic consciences of Libanius, Symmachus and Maximus were ineffectual and did not assist their convictions to any practical extent. They wrote well but they were on the defensive; they do not strike us as men who were as passionate for their customs and ideas as the martyrs, for all their ludicrous names. Perhaps only Julian and Virius Nicomachus Flavianus ('in life and death ... the last Roman') were committed men, in the style of Ambrose, Augustine and Basil. Even Julian was prudent about the timing of his pagan confession and he could not persuade all the intellectuals he wanted to join him.[34]

On their side the bishops were far more assured of their dealings with the emperors even if they failed at times to get their own way. Their confidence owed something to the elaborate network of dioceses which made religious organization another community within the state. They were often conscious of extensive popular support. It has been suggested that one of the ways in which Christianity bridged the gap between the learned and the vulgar was through miracle; the former, that is, were serious students of the miraculous deeds of saints and martyrs, to which the man in the street was also attached, though more uncritically. On this theory the allegories used by the Christian were intended to bring together both the preacher and the taught, whereas pagan allegory was a mode of refinement for the initiated, a kind of pedagogy in aloofness. But there could well have been other reasons for the popular support enjoyed by some of the bishops. Roman society as a whole had for long been deprived of the opportunities for factionalism that had once been so vigorous in the primary assemblies, as in the Republic. The fourth century gave scope (to all, including those who were only nominally Christian) for processions and demonstrations; the slogans chanted by crowds were sometimes obscure claims concerning the relative status of the Father and the Son, but there was the chance to show great enthusiasm and energy, to be a visible religious crowd with a sense of participation.[35]

Bishops also enjoyed economic power. The Church's right of inheritance and the imperial bequests both helped to swell the properties which came under episcopal jurisdiction. Bishops were in control of considerable funds, and sometimes a knowledgeable congregation attempted to detain a wealthy visitor in the hope that he could be cajoled or even forced into becoming the local bishop, when his own wealth might be conscripted into the service of the church.[36] The imperial generosity created – without perhaps intending to – a subsidized priestly class, with its own resources used, quite properly, for the local good. It is difficult to say whether this was weakness or generosity on the part of the government; the result, in part at any rate, makes the late Empire bear some resemblance to those Hellenistic kingdoms in which the ruler restored or donated lands to the temple states. Yet the Roman Empire was unlike the Seleucid kingdom in that it had itself encouraged the priestly class and had created those ecclesiastical domains which are apparently like the enlarged temple-lands of the dying Hellenistic states.[37]

The institutional success of Christianity in the fourth century enshrines the masculine invasion of an area which had been traditionally female. I mean that men now began increasingly to make religion a way of life in which the offices were ends in themselves, not a quasi-political means to a wholly political objective. It is of course true that some of the new developments allowed women a greater variety of religious expression. They increased their modes of patronage and cultural association; widows and virgins were attracted to the company of clerics who were in turn drawn by the prospect of wealthy female converts. They shared in religious experience and accompanied men in the devout life. They were equal in the eyes of God but their equality was determined by ecclesiastical males; and they were praised for having masculine virtues, although they were women. The new priesthood, both in theory and practice, was controlled by men, and the canons of the Church councils, with treatises on widowhood and virginity, restricted the conduct of women more than that of men. The increase in women's freedom was therefore more apparent than real. The female martyrs and saints, from this point of view, are insignificant compared with the great numbers of male priests and bishops and monks who held power locally and sometimes over wider areas.[38]

For much of this period the government and the Church had a similar interest in checking or discouraging paganism, but the tempo of the Christian crusade only became more pronounced at the end of the fourth and in the early fifth century. It took time for the government to offer the whole-hearted support expected by its protégé; the state for instance was hostile to magic because it feared conspiracy, whereas the Church's condemnation of magic was more widely based and included the white, non-political practices described by Eunapius; the state sought for a time to preserve temples as long as they were empty of illicit objects (idols) and could be put to a public use;

temples were acceptable to government as the source and occasion of public entertainments that were still popular, and the state could not easily dismiss a traditional form of amusement even though churchmen thundered against games and theatres.[39] The state therefore approved of the motives which inspired church feeling against such pagan practices, but it weighed the implementation of them against a political background which mattered far less to the Church.

It is roughly true to express the difference between the age of Constantine and the reign of Honorius as follows: to think of the former as a time when the state encouraged the activities of the Church, and of the latter as a time of encouragement accompanied by increased legislation against pagans; a change from benefactions that sought to remedy the ills of persecuted Christians, to benefactions abetted by active interference with paganism. There is no doubt about the differences, the question is how to explain the transition. One way is to express the facts in simple regnal terms, by arguing that the subordination of Church to state, which was the aim and achievement of Constantine and Constantius, was disrupted by Julian's paganism; that in the reaction to this an enraged Church put more and more pressure on a compliant or obsequious court. The theory may however be criticized for making too much of Julian and for creating a false antithesis between directing emperors and those who were directed.[40] Episcopal power was nourished as well as checked by the first Christian emperors, and both factors, state support for the Church and differences of opinion with the state, helped the bishops to grow in confidence. Secondly, in the period from 377 onwards there are several events which suggest (but perhaps no more) that the Church's demand for state intervention became more effective. The city prefects of Rome in 377 and 378 destroyed or moved pagan statues, the Emperor Gratian stopped wearing the toga of the chief pontiff and soon after the altar of Victory was removed from the senate house.[41] Changes that were at first confined to Rome became later more general in scope. Some, perhaps all, of these events were demanded by the Church, as through the personal influence of Ambrose. On this view of things the church became more demanding not because of Julian and his doings but because a strong bishop overrode weaker emperors. Perhaps both types of explanation put too negative a value on the government's co-operation with Church authority. It was not all reluctant consent on the emperors' part to the compulsion exercised by the Church. We should therefore allow the possibility that the government's role (in sending troops and passing laws requested by the Church) was a successful piece of internal policy. A way of interpreting the late Empire is to begin with admiration for its administrative energy which strengthened these internal institutions that were capable of growth;

not to condemn it for wasting on the Church what might have been spent on repelling the barbarian invaders, who were likely to succeed whatever was done against them.

This preamble may seem long but it is necessary to set out at length the general nature of fourth-century changes in religion; to point out that abandoning Christianity to the extent of becoming a persecutor was likely to be less common than extending a welcome to the new God, however slow or quick the converts might be at realizing the demands made on them. One must start from the idea that Christianity was now establishing itself as the civic norm and that pagan revivals were disturbances of the new relationship between Church and state. The revivals may be considered in three broad categories, imperial, aristocratic and popular.

The major episodes are linked with individual emperors, with Maximin Daia (309–13), Licinius (in 324), Julian (in 361–3) and Eugenius, pretender or usurper between 392 and 394. In three cases, the first two and the last, civil war is the apparent motive for returning to paganism; pagan Maximin was engaged in a struggle with Christian Licinius; Licinius went pagan in his war with the Christian Constantine; and lastly Eugenius supported pagan measures against Theodosius the Great, the most docile of the Christian emperors. It seems natural, as the age was so preoccupied by theology and Church issues, to suppose that paganism here was revived as a means of defining a counter-policy to Christianity. Yet there is not much evidence to indicate that declarations of paganism won much support among the population, and the degree of the emperors' pagan conviction must often be in doubt. The Licinius episode is in a way the least interesting and the most obscure. It is not clear whether his anti-Christian moves began the conflict with Constantine or were no more than a further expression of the disagreement once the break had become unbridgeable. His measures were all anti-Christian with no encouragement of paganism in a positive sense. He stopped the bishops from meeting in synods, interfered with congregations in which the sexes were mixed, excluded Christians from his personal service, and was prepared to allow Christian meetings only outside the walls of a city; in city-state society to expel a god in this way or to keep him in extramural banishment was a way of demoting a cult. But there is hardly enough to suggest that the war between Licinius and Constantine was a 'war of religion' and that paganism was defeated when Licinius lost at the battle of Adrianople. Perhaps Licinius' measures were directed against what he considered to be the over-intimate relationship between Church and state that had developed since the Edict of Milan.[42]

On the other hand, if we look at the last of these occasions, the war which ended with the victory of Theodosius in 394, there seems to be a clear case of pagan against Christian. Eugenius' army was protected by a great statue of Jupiter, and he had threatened, if successful, to enrol the clergy in the army and to use the churches as stables. But once again, even if we allow for the fact that Eugenius had supporters among the pagan aristocracy, it does not seem as though the declaration for paganism helped to make his cause popular. What is common to Maximin, Licinius and Eugenius is that they were either emperors who felt on the defensive or a usurper (Eugenius) in a weak position. They all made the mistake of trying to make a name for themselves as being utterly opposed to the Christianity of the other camp, and it was a mistake in part because their deities were short of victories whereas the Christian God was not. The emperor who was most committed to paganism was Julian; and he did not proclaim his faith, even though he was leading an army that had recently defeated Germans, until *after* the death of the emperor Constantius. The conclusion should be that measures against Christianity and for positive paganism were, understandably, invoked by the weaker side. They were propaganda measures of a somewhat desperate kind and should be contrasted with the patience of Julian; an emperor who had won wars and was also (after Constantius' death) unchallenged, would naturally be able to commend his favourite deities to his army; it is not surprising that Julian's army, as he tells us, was content with the return to the old gods.[43]

Licinius' attack on Christianity and Eugenius' threats were inadequate as the foundation of a possible pagan revival. Persecution of the new God would only destroy the social and political institutions developed by the church; it was necessary to foster paganism if there were to be any hope at all of its rising again to confront the established forms of Christianity. Two of the emperors, Maximin Daia and Julian, showed how the religious counter-revolution might have been handled if either or both of them had had more time. (Maximin, Augustus from 309 to 313, had barely two years in which to promote an overt paganism, rather like Julian between 361 and 363.) A comparison of the two shows that they both objected to martyr-cult as a focus of the new religion. In order to turn their peoples towards the old, they adopted similar procedures, including restoration of temples and encouragement of sacrifice. Both were aware that pagan institutions had to be improved. Maximin appointed as high priests in the provinces under his command men who were 'chosen from the public servants of the first rank'. Julian's objectives were comparable. His priests were to be the religious counterparts of the provincial governors, they would be expected to lead pure and holy lives and would deserve to be treated with as much respect as the other civic officials. They should be removed from office if they were convicted of misconduct. Men of substance had been the obvious choices for preferment in, for example, the imperial cult; now they were to need piety as well as substance before they could be assured of their political reward, advancement in their careers on returning to ordinary life.[44]

It is in a way not inappropriate to describe these ideas as attempts to develop a pagan church. The model for these elevated and purified priesthoods appears to be the Christian clergy which had won a following and had earned respect. But the indications are that the conditions put forward by Maximin and Julian would mainly have catered for the well-to-do. The new priesthoods would still have looked too political, a stepping-stone to the life of the world, even though they were not formally co-ordinated with the secular offices of the bureaucracy; it is far from clear whether these Julianic priesthoods were meant to be (to glance back at the Republic) precursors or rewards of high office. They must be regarded as no more than a feeble imitation of part of the Christian institutional framework, and it was a mistake to leave their political quality more or less intact without revising the relationship to other offices. It was not understood (by these emperors) that the Christian priesthood was strong not merely through purity but also by virtue of life-tenure; but their pagan priesthoods were designed in terms of a civic political model, as awards that were too brief to be illustrious.

Popular support for these projects is hard to estimate. Maximin asserted that his persecution of Christians was an imperial response to complaints at city level, but Eusebius, admittedly a hostile witness, says that the cities' protestations were engineered either by deception from above or as judicious flattery from below.[45] By Julian's time it was certainly harder to get this sort of support. Army approval was perhaps easier to obtain than that of the cities, for the troops followed the deities of a successful general and readily consumed the sacrifices for which the provinces paid. The difficulties that faced a would-be pagan are shown by Julian's unpopularity at Antioch. The emperor's version of paganism required priests, in the interests of the higher purity, to keep away from the shows and the theatre. But Antioch at this time seems to have been a happy mixture. Its churches were flourishing, and though its temples were neglected the games were popular. It therefore seemed odd both to Christians and pagans that a pagan emperor should encourage a return to civic ceremony and civic religion and yet show his disapproval of the traditional amusements. Even Christian institutions had not yet everywhere attained the salutary objective of setting up their God without games.[46]

Towards the end of the century the senate in Rome was deprived of the altar of Victory, and certain funds, originally legacies, were confiscated from the Vestal Virgins. Both these losses were matters of symbol rather than substance (for even Symmachus, who pleaded with the court for restitution, admits that the sums were not considerable) but even so they angered pagan senators, and made it natural for them to support the usurper Eugenius in 392 and after against the orthodox and pious Theodosius. Eugenius was backed by the eminent pagan Virius Nicomachus Flavianus (who committed suicide after the defeat) and openly proclaimed his hatred for the Catholic clergy. These facts make it plausible to suppose that a conflict of religion was an important factor in this civil war, and this view of events is (not unnaturally) confirmed by the Christian version of Theodosius' triumph.[47]

It is, however, difficult to see exactly what the senatorial pagans contributed to the resistance against Theodosius. The senators had no divisions of their own to persuade. The usurper Eugenius and some senators were satisfied that they could announce a state of harmony between government and chief city; Eugenius returned some religious funds to individuals, and Flavianus invoked Bellona and employed Etruscan ritual in order to cajole the gods. But the dispute between the two emperors was not primarily religious; Theodosius, naturally enough, was concerned about the prospects for his dynasty, whereas Eugenius and Arbogastes, the power behind the throne, wanted recognition as rulers. Flavianus too had grounds for political resentment: Theodosius had replaced him as praetorian prefect, and one of the fruits of his support for Eugenius was reinstatement in this important position. Flavianus was accused of making converts to the cause of paganism but it is unlikely that the movement to the old gods assumed significant proportions.

We might well make the bold conclusion that the usurper was pushed further into paganism by the circumstance of opposition to Theodosius, and that the 'pagan reaction' among senators, though real enough, did little to effect events. The pagan senators of whom we hear most were religious hybrids; they combined the traditional posts of religion with a variety of the new cults. Ceionius Julianus Kamenius, for instance, was an epulo, a quindecemvir and a pontifex; he was also an initiate of Mithras, Liber and the Mother of the gods.[48] Men like him prided themselves on the religious titles they had accumulated; their religion was expensive, a way of proclaiming their continued participation in the well-to-do club of the aristocracy. Whereas Christians read pagan authors in order to document their polemics, there seems little evidence that pagans were opening Christian books to provide themselves with counter-material.[49]

The analysis suggests that a pagan counter-revolution could only have had a chance of succeeding if several factors had been present: a determined ruler or victorious usurper; army support; a programme for changing religious institutions; propaganda; and popular dislike of Christianity on a scale large enough to be effective.[50] In the episodes we have discussed these elements occurred only partially, if at all. Even so their value was known, as we can judge from the importance of propaganda and the nature of popular protest against Christianity. The pagans used both forged and accredited documents. In the first of these so-called revivals Maximin displayed in public what purported to be the memoranda of Pilate and also had rescripts posted up which explained the grounds of persecution. The vehicle of his propaganda was therefore the official document or a document with an official sanction. Julian used the same methods and augmented them with letters and pamphlets. Julian realized that it was necessary not only to sustain the pagans but also to penalize Christian literacy; his famous edict, which aimed at disbarring Christians from teaching pagan literature, irritated Christians and pagans alike.[51] It presupposed a union between pagan literature and cult which was far from apparent even when it was not denied. Later pagans extended this conservatism in literature as well as in cult, and tried to exploit the *Life of Apollonius of Tyana* as a pagan counterpart to that of Christ. The pagan prescribed texts have an unrespectable look about them, and it is difficult to think of them as much more than *ad hoc* offerings, not really able to support the superstructure of commentary and exegesis that was being heaped on the Testaments. Fake prophecies about the duration of Christianity were shown up for what they were at least by the year 399, if not before. The older pagan books were no better than the new; one could not have much confidence in the lore of the pontifical books when they declined to say anything specific about earthquakes for fear of naming the wrong god. Julian's attempt to deny Christians free access to the pagan literary heritage might have been effective in the long run, but it would also have needed a concerted exposition by all the pagan priests he could appoint. Pagans imitated Christian literary activity by reading out allegories of gods in the temples, but as Augustine pointed out they must have had problems with Jupiter Adulter.[52]

Spontaneous popular outbursts against Christianity and in favour of pagan cult occurred here and there, but in general their range was local and limited. According to Ammianus the mob at Alexandria took their revenge on Bishop George when his protector had died. George was hated as a destroyer of monuments and is said to have incited his followers to knock down what he dubbed a 'tomb', the temple to the city's Genius. Shortly after, two more Christian iconoclasts were despatched, and their ashes were thrown into the sea to prevent their admirers from building a church in their place of martyrdom. Pagan violence brought more serious loss of life farther west, at Colonia Suffectana, where in AD 399 pagan reprisals for the loss of a Hercules statue caused the deaths of sixty Christians. At Calama, in 408, anti-Christian riots took place in front of the local church which was stoned on several occasions, and some Christian defenders were killed. These protests were undoubtedly genuine but, politically speaking, they led nowhere; their main effect was to involve the offenders in appeals to the great Augustine to show mercy. There was at times, as might be expected, a gap of misunderstanding between the government law forbidding a particular pagan rite and the popular reception of the official edict. One's impression (it can hardly be more) is that active pagan resentment of this kind is insignificant compared with the enthusiasm shown to martyrs' relics and churches. A pagan protest of more than local import was raised after the sack of Rome in 410, when some people complained that the troubles of the age were caused by desertion of the old gods; but it made less impact than it might as it was accompanied by a strong Christian grievance, directed against the justice of a God who could let his faithful people suffer.[53]

For understandable reasons the pagan revivals have proved an attractive subject. They made dramatic episodes, and some are well provided with contemporary sources: Julian's own works, and the letters of Ambrose and Symmachus are all valuable aids. But their prospects of a meaningful success were probably slender. The spectacular but brief acts of aggression by pagans are less important than the 'blurring of the sharp distinction between the pagan past and the Christian present'.[54] Even though some pagan senators were extreme and there was one notable suicide, the gradual process of 'accommodation' to the new ways went on not only in the aristocracy but also among the people.

### *Christian Interpretations*

The fourth century has usually been studied by political theorists as the starting-point of new developments in the relationship between Church and state. Some events can be read as prefiguring a characteristic of the Byzantine theocracy, in which the emperor appears as the director and arbiter of the Church; the emperor, as the royal and priestly counterpart on earth of God in the universe, must be supreme like a fully-fledged Constantine, and is both the secular and the spiritual controller of the state. Some such theory as this may be held to be implicit in Eusebius' version of Constantine's role, which the bishop may have conceived as a way of persuading the emperor to intervene against the unacceptable parts of the Nicene Council – unacceptable, that is, to Eusebius. On the other hand a different type of relationship can be detected in the western part of the

Empire; the stand of Ambrose against the Arianism of the young Valentinian and against the sinful orthodoxy of Theodosius points to the claim made by the Church to be the sole interpreter of God's will and to convey it to the emperor. This second model is derived in part from the increasing ambition of the bishop of Rome to be the independent voice of Christianity, to assert that there is a domain of the *ecclesia* which is distinct from that of the emperor, and inviolable.[55]

It is entirely legitimate to turn back to the fourth century as the source period of these major changes in the relationship between Church and state. But it is also proper to consider the first age of official Christianity as the climax of a long history, at the end of an evolution through different forms of polytheism. The Christian thinkers of the period were concerned with some of the arguments and anxieties about the function of religion which had been formulated first by Greeks and then by Romans. Christians such as Lactantius, Eusebius, Ambrose and Augustine knew that they had to contend with the heirs of an inadequate but long tradition, and they tried to show that their cult was both true and politically superior to the polytheism it was displacing. In this part I shall sketch the Christian approach to some of the polytheistic preoccupations discussed in chapter two: such questions as whether religion is true and necessary, whether it can be explained and defended philosophically, whether there is a difference between 'religion' and 'superstition'.

The contrast between polytheism and Christianity is the sum of the particular contrasts at various levels of intensity: contrasts between church and temple, between pagan priests and Christian clergy, between Catholic theology and the various apologias for the civic gods. It is clear from the earlier studies in this chapter that even within one and the same contrast there can be a lack of homogeneity; that the pace of separation is uneven, with the result that there is no uniform measure of the differences between monotheistic Christianity and pagan polytheism. If we take buildings as an example and consider the architecture of temples and churches, the conclusion will be that the separation of the new is complete, and the result may seem to be confirmed by functional consequences (such as the removal of cult-statues) within the new churches. But it is also true that the members of church congregations went on expecting the performance of activities which had been common in pagan temples. For this reason the contrasts exhibit a great deal of internal variability; similarly, the religious offices or posts of the Christians are in theory worlds apart from the civic priesthoods of the pagan state, but in practice the political power of certain bishops is much closer to the influence exercised by some of the augurs and pontiffs.

Polytheistic worship, centred on the temple with its cult-statue, might be described as roughly midway between the earlier stage of numinous cult and the later stage of Christian monotheism (to speak chronologically, without reference to religious value). Primitive man is lost in his ignorance, in a twilight without images; his successor, polytheistic man, strives for the civic perfection of, in the literal sense, *homo idololatres*[56] (man the idolater); and then he enters the Christian state with the decision to dispense knowingly with statues of the deity. This is not just a picturesque summary of a development from life without statues (because they have not been invented), through life with statues (because man knows no better), to life without because the theory of God not only does not require but also no longer allows the anthropomorphic cult-object. It shows us an extreme case of the contrast between Christian theory and pagan theory. The former forbids a practice, asserting that it cannot be justified in reality, whereas the latter, knowing, but for different reasons, that it was untrue, countenanced it on psychological grounds: man needs to imagine gods in the human form once he supposes that he himself is the aesthetic perfection of what body and mind there is. The above outline is admittedly crude, and, as was indicated in chapter one, perhaps not wholly historical, with its simple and clear-cut version of a move from the numinous to the anthropomorphic phase. It may remind us, however, that here too polytheism and Christianity are not just in opposite corners; the enthusiasm for disposing of the hated cult-statues was accompanied by a readiness to look up to and learn from the images of saints. One of the strengths in polytheism was that it had domesticated god and had localized the human sense of awe in understandable ways; the weakness of its *practice* was that it reduced and diminished the gods, making them accessible to sometimes trivial aspirations. Christianity (at least in theory) put back the terror into God; but the theory was not able to withstand the long-established civic habit of making religion look more solid through pictures.

Christian theory was expected to account for its religion as true and also as necessary to the good life of the state. A common pagan view, it should be remembered, held that religion, though untrue, was necessary as a discipline to keep the turbulent masses in order; an extreme version in effect denied that religion had any value on its own account, and would therefore not be required in a mature society. Christian theologians had no doubts about the exclusive reality of God; they put their trust in revelation, in argument of a philosophical kind, and in historical witness derived from the prophets and the life of Christ. It is not meant as a disparagement to say that their persuasive energies were often more successful in annihilating some of the pagan arguments and practices than in expounding the merits of their own monotheism. Lactantius, for example, poured scorn on the sophisticated case for representing god anthropomorphically, especially that form of it which takes for granted that a representation of this kind is an impossible reflection of ultimate reality; better, he thinks, to believe in your portrayal than to practise a double standard, deceiving others by what you know to be false but require them to believe.[57] This particular instance of theoretical statue-smashing is offered for the purpose of showing that in practice (in the fourth century) the pure and holy concern with truth expended at least some of its vigour in destroying the pagan case. The gods of paganism were denied but they were still allotted a role as malevolent tempters. Christian theory took with alacrity the pagan idea of euhemerism; but as it was convinced that the gulf between man and God is unbridgeable, it forced euhemerism to become an argument in its own cause. Euhemerism is no longer a means of pleading for deity to be conferred on deserving cases, but a proof that all pagan gods were once human; the doctrine is used to sweep away all the pagan gods as man-made.

In much the same way Christian philosophical assurance about the reality of God is only one side of the coin; the other is the Christian conviction that pagan multiplicity of cult and proof is erroneous. A typical argument is as follows: since we assume (rightly) that the deity is perfect, there cannot be many gods, each with different functions, as that would imply an unthinkable imperfection in the godhead. And the variety of pagan philosophies (the theoretical maximum is given by Augustine as 288) is contrasted with the one true Catholic faith (though this is to overlook the multiplicity introduced by the heresies).

'Religion' therefore, or 'true religion', was the label to be applied to Christianity, and 'superstition' became the name for polytheistic cults whatever their ancestry or origin. The Christian objective was to eliminate 'superstitions', that is wrong ideas about the nature of death and salvation. Cicero's use of the distinction between 'religion' and 'superstition' is turned against him. If 'superstition' means a practice or belief that is unwarranted by the *nature* of things, then Cicero should not have applauded Roman custom (*mos*), for that very custom was responsible for the anthropomorphic cult-object which is a lie in the face of nature. The hostility to polytheistic 'superstition' is enacted in some of the imperial laws.[58]

The value of the true religion is not that it is the only way to prevent anarchy from breaking out again, but that it bestows on the state which adopts it the order of a just society. The Christian worship is both true and necessary; it differentiates the intentions of this new society from the 'lust for conquest' which characterized polytheistic Rome. The doctrine is said to be necessary not merely for the sake of temporal satisfaction; since beings have a life to come, the quality of their lot in eternity will also be affected.

The theory of the political value of religion must here be confined to a discussion of what Augustine called the 'earthly city', temporal society with its present mixture of good and bad Christians and good and bad pagans. Augustine argues that Christian society is bound to be more pious and harmonious than a polytheistic state; the latter portrays a Jupiter taken in adultery and allows citizens to worship this god, whereas the Christian state's vision of piety will not, in a literal imitation, disrupt family life. Secondly, the Christian state will by definition be able to make juster and more pious treaties with its enemies. It will be obvious from this that a Christian theory of the state does not put the highest value on victory in war, even though the fourth century has its fair quota of tales about emperors praying to God before battle. The Christian state could well be made to look too pacific and uncompetitive for everyday reality. The long-term necessity for this kind of state may be one thing, the question whether Christianity is in fact useful for competitive survival may be quite another. Augustine answers the objection in at least two ways. He argues from early Roman standards to remind his opponents that poverty is not as such a curse, and thus agrees with their sentimental premiss (admiration for the virtues of a hard primitivism) to show that they have no reason to fear the practical effect of Christianity. Secondly (more seriously, perhaps), he reassures critics that Christianity is not incompatible with the military life. The object here is to show that certain Biblical texts do not forbid the armed defence of the state, that 'returning good for evil' does not mean that Christians should throw down their arms.[59]

Christian theoretical dicta in the sense discussed here are a mixture of pure doctrine and the practical need to set the newly created Christian state in a different historical context. By doctrine is meant the expounding of Christianity as true religion, the arguments against idolatry, the reasons why the new cult is necessary and not harmful to the state. A new historical perspective was needed to replace the traditional picture of the Roman Empire as the favourite of the gods, to show that Rome itself was not the centre of history and that success (in the obvious sense of winning wars or becoming wealthy) is not the measure of value. Christian theorists were obliged to produce versions of history that would account for a surprising phenomenon, their consciousness that man's religious history was progressive. They believed, as we have seen, that the contemporary world was better than the past, since the moral economy had improved and the revelation of God had become more widely known. On this view of history man's increasing knowledge of nature (it is assumed that nature here must include God) is accompanied by an increasing awareness of true religion.[60] Society knows more than the remote past had known, and is also more pious, for Christianity, though in different ways in each case, makes the modern age the superior of the early Roman kings and the early Jewish prophets. I call this a new phenomenon since a characteristic theory of paganism, as discussed in the first century BC, had been conscious of a different development. It had discovered a conflict between the increased understanding of nature and the first religious practices of the kind introduced by Romulus and Numa. Paganism was not progressive[61] as Christianity was, it was illuminated only by custom, not by any light of reason within custom; it might be said that pagan theory (by the first century BC) had found no good reasons for certain traditional practices even though more gods had been imported. Improvements in man's knowledge of nature had *not* been accompanied by a sense that religion was thereby made more credible or more reasonable. Religion was left as a 'political invention of statecraft' defended only by the argument from custom, and theorists had lacked the Christian confidence that knowledge of religion and nature were at one. The new cult, as the friend and no longer the adversary of reason, called for a different version of Roman history in which Rome and the great Roman past were no longer at the centre of things.

In the new schemes Rome and the Empire were set in a different time-scale, as the last, up to that time, of the great empires. Rome was still favoured in a way because of the great Augustan coincidence which Christian apologetic liked to play with, the imperial peace and the birth of Christ; but pre-Roman time, so to speak, now assumed far more importance. The antiquity of Rome had been the coping-stone of the appeal to custom and tradition. The course of Rome was now no longer regarded as the whole of antiquity but was treated as a mere part of a receding chronology, and an even smaller part of the time ahead. Rome therefore was deprived of her sense of international priority and of her perfection as the empiric centre of the gods' attentions. Christians asserted that they were entitled to the claim of priority, since their prophetic ancestors, with their prescience of Christ, were known to antedate the foundation of Rome the city.[62]

Roman archaism had often been applauded as the bulwark of religious tradition and commendable moral virtues. The customs and the heroes in the Roman traditions were judged, sometimes harshly, in the light of a Christian valuation. Some of the great Roman exemplars, Lucretia and Cato, for instance, were now found wanting; these political suicides could be interpreted as case-histories of self-love, not the heroic and unselfish love of liberty for which they were praised in Roman literature. More than any other thinker Augustine, with his satirical talent, sought to diminish the past of Rome, so that its human and religious grandeur was made to decline in intensity. But it is fair to add that he did not make Roman history entirely destitute; it was left with serious imitation-virtues, virtues from which the validating love of God was absent but nonetheless they were virtues of a positive kind; Rome was commended for having the constructive ambition that built the Empire. Her heroes, like Cato and Regulus, were better than her gods who were exposed to damaging ridicule.

It was not easy to offer a consistent explanation of the conduct of the state in relation to the Church. Within the lifetime of the fourth century many had experienced the state first as persecutor and later as benefactor, and different theories were evolved to explain these contrasting functions. Understandably the contemporary theorists who had experienced state hostility delighted in maintaining that the persecutors had been punished for their misdeeds by horrible deaths; they dwelt with satisfaction on the sufferings of Galerius and others. But if such persecution of the Church by the state were to stop entirely, it would deprive the Church of its greatest glory, the martyrs. Thus persecution by the state could be said to have produced more admirable works than did 'the peace of the Church'.

The danger (it is a danger to orthodox Christian thinking) was that rulers might be tempted to become Christian for the sake of temporal reward, in order to avoid the sufferings of the wicked (like Galerius) and to earn the same prosperity as good Christian emperors such as Constantine and Theodosius. Augustinian theory requires men to become Christian for the sake of eternal felicity. Augustine points out that not all Catholic emperors have prospered; Jovian's reign was short and Gratian, though a good Christian, was killed by a usurper. His point is that the justice of God does not make a clear-cut division between rewards for the good and punishment for the bad. History is full of instances in which the apparently good are not rewarded as they deserve to be. Events of this type are, for Augustine, an indication that the good are not as virtuous as they should be or that their virtue is being tested.[63]

Thus some Christian theory presented a view of history which was quite different from the kind of pagan approach which saw Rome's victories as rewards from heaven and her defeats as punishments for neglect of the gods. In the Augustinian view temporal success and failure are no longer matters of the first importance to society. The theory requires of its believers that they should see disasters such as Alaric's sack of Rome in the perspective of divine justice; it is no longer the case that religious optimism and confidence can be restored by repeating a few ceremonies with the right ritual. The emphasis is on the ultimate goal of the citizens in a state. But, as in other matters, Christian theory, while laying down pure doctrine, also had its anti-pagan side; it set about a revision of Roman history in order to show that disasters and hardships were not an intrusive novelty, the depressing consequence of a Christianized Empire. Thus it sought to demonstrate that defeats in war did not have the importance they had been given by polytheists, and that they were far more common even in pagan Roman history than had been believed.[64]

# *Conclusion*

It may be of some help if I attempt to discuss how the approach in this book departs from received ideas and unquestioned assumptions that are often found in other works on religion in this period. This is not to admit to heretical views that fly in the face of an orthodoxy but to question whether the orthodox interpretations are worth considering any longer.

There is not much point in interpreting ancient religious behaviour on the simple assumption that belief in a god (or set of gods) comes into being, grows to an acme and declines. Those who make this assumption will readily entertain the further idea that new belief is mainly accepted when an old belief has withered away. In the subject covered by this book examples of these assumptions would be: that Rome in the middle and late Republic imported gods from Italy and overseas because citizens had lost faith in the country cults with which Rome began; that Rome acquiesced in the cult of imperial man-gods when the Olympians or their civic namesakes were discredited; and that the advance towards Christianity was equal and opposite to the withdrawal from belief in the *divi*. On this theory new beliefs come as substitutes for the old and in an extreme form of the doctrine *only* as such substitutes.

The theory, though attractively simple, should be doubted on grounds of history and commonsense. People can well accept new beliefs and practices without having lost touch with established or traditional ideas and without realizing at first that a complete readjustment is necessary. Civic polytheism in all its baffling complexity was founded on the hope that the new gods would at least be compatible with the old. This supposition should be applied not merely to the normal case when a polytheistic state invites or accepts a deity who has been worshipped by other polytheists but also to the more adventurous affair of trust and convenience between Rome and the exclusive God of Christianity. Here too the habits, both social and private, produced by centuries of civic polytheism made it natural for many to take to Christianity as another form of religion, capable of much the same juxtaposition that had been tolerable in the case of other cults. The polytheist, that is, even in the periods of persecution before Constantine, is unpractised in the habits of consistent exclusiveness and is unlikely to exhibit the fierce rigour that is common among competing sects of the same monotheism. The latter have one thing in common with one another, the understanding that their claims are mutually exclusive. The convert from polytheism would not at once have assumed that he must leave behind all his pagan ways, and it might take some time for him to learn the intransigence of monotheism. To put the matter in general terms, the polytheist of this type assumes, or is prepared for, a compatibility of cults and religious practices; his course of adaptation is different from that of the rebellious polytheist whose starting-point is the certainty that other cults are all wrong.

Interpretation of the phenomena should therefore be based on the idea of gradual and imperfect transference, not on the principle of a substitution that carries all before it by overwhelming compulsion.

In the second place, to make a simple assumption about changes in belief is to be in danger of conceiving the history of religions as a sort of barter or trade in experiences that are somehow thought to be equal. An important point about the introduction of Christianity is that it stood for a quantitative increase in the social impact of religion. An altar erected to Jupiter could well be the expression of great fervour, but the worshipper's substance and sacrifices need not be called for more than once a year. In this system a cult-activity, such as a sacrifice or banquet, is marginal to other social activities in the community. This is not to deny polytheism its likely share in enthusiasm or devotion (there is for instance no need to disparage the imperial cult as a political religion) but to concentrate on its social expression. There may be a great many cults, that is, but they tend either to require a few participants or not to be celebrated all that often. The common meal brought by Christianity was of course meant to be different in kind from the banquets in guilds and colleges; but the difference was social as well as symbolic for it was held more often and among more people.

We should therefore think of religious changes not as simple replacements but as a set of coexisting innovations. The new god acquired by a polytheistic state was expected to be compatible with the gods already present. There were many accidents and surprises as a result of this expectation, not least when the Christian God was made official. For most of the period discussed (from about 200 BC to AD 400) religion was deficient in autonomy. Compared with politics it lacked independence. It was usually expected that religion was a means which would help men to live the good life within the state, but religion was not something to be pursued apart from the values and objectives of the state. But it is unlikely that anyone foresaw that the Christian form of development would take the precise direction in which it came to affect public life; it is doubtful whether Constantine, however committed he was to the new God, could have supposed he was authorizing a religion in which the political effectiveness of the new priests, the bishops, would be independent of their achievements as politicians, and *more* effective than that of the pontiffs.

The history of polytheistic cult in the Roman world has been exposed to other misleading ideas. One is the prejudice against cult as an activity concerned with the welfare of the whole community, the prejudice that cult by officials for the sake of the people collectively is bound to exclude any religious satisfaction of an individual kind. From the same cluster comes the idea that the eastern religions offered something which was not obtainable in civic cults of the home-grown variety. These are misleading conceptions which have on them the stamp of a religious individualism that is alien to the Greco-Roman world. The starting-point of classical antiquity is the conviction that individuals do not have religions that are independent of the community, that they only practise cult which has some collective authorization. A common modern assumption, that the individual's religion shows its superiority by its difference from and indifference to that of the state, is no use as a guide to the general interpretation of classical antiquity. The distinction between public and private was present, but not in a way that is familiar to us. It distinguished the celebrant as office-holder from the citizen observer, it separated land consecrated by the state for the state from land reserved (often by pious hopes) for an individual family. It is only prejudice against the polytheistic collective when critics assume, as they do, that civic cults are nothing but state occasions of public frigidity whereas eastern religions alone have the means of satisfying emotional needs. Some of the civic occasions quite obviously gave emotional satisfaction of a kind related, not all that distantly, to the more exciting initiations offered by the oriental religions. It would be a vulgar modern error to identify the secret with the ecstatic and to suppose that the great religious occasions of state were always unemotional.

These ideas about the way belief declines and about the emotional failures of civic polytheism, are congenial to moderns with a particular kind of religious upbringing. A third kind of distortion is present in the idea that in antiquity simple belief was corroded by the complex scepticism of philosophy. It is often supposed that in the late Roman Republic religion declined because it was manipulated, and that it could only have been so mishandled because men had learned to doubt. But most philosophy, including doubt, was in Roman antiquity on the side of the gods. Ciceronian doubt was directed against philosophy that claimed too much or too little for the gods, and it was prepared in the end to admire custom and tradition. Philosophy as a means of secularization is familiar to us from the modern world but should not be exported without modifications to the Roman experience.

I have argued against the interpretative use of certain fixed ideas: the idea of a uniform decline in belief; the prejudice that state cult was quite unable to yield emotional satisfaction so that individuals in search of religion were compelled to seek eastern gods; the supposition that Greek philosophy in some way secularized Roman beliefs.

We should instead attempt to understand the political involvement of religion in the light of certain characteristics of civic polytheism. Firstly, it functions as a centre of instability which attracts new gods, often because of anxiety before battle or because of relief in the hour of victory. The instability is shown by the fact that there are fashions in gods; a new god is not imported in order to expel an old but he may make other gods seem less vital just as surely as he will in time come to lose vitality himself. It is perhaps right to think of the system as insatiable, since it is rooted in the conviction that deity is an uncertain matter of which man or the state can never really have enough; the state therefore should have an appetite for gods and expect to make an ally of the unseen by domesticating more of its manifestations.

In the second place civic polytheism began its career as the religion of a confined locality cult. The gods surveyed the city and the terrain from which their worshippers were drawn, and a god could only be properly authorized when he had been installed in an overlooking temple. The practical requirements of a large empire did something to attenuate the close relationship between locality and the act of cult. Thus Jupiter received altars, in remote lands, away from the Capitol, and the emperors received cult in many different regional centres. Locality cult was still flourishing in the later Empire but it no longer monopolized the terrain of the city-state as it had done before one of them, Rome, had expanded by conquest. To recognize this is to reflect that the usual question about why or how a monotheism came to replace polytheism can be replaced by the study of locality cult, to exhibit the social consequences of offering cult to a god in various places, some of them remote from the original centre. Offering cult to the same god in many centres is at least something of a preparation for accepting that a homeless god with no statue (a pagan way of describing the Christian and Jewish bar on graven images) can be diffused and worshipped as a simultaneous presence.

A summary of the last change within the Empire, the change to an exclusive monotheism, might well start by considering the strangest fact in the history of Roman civic polytheism: that a Roman emperor acknowledged a new deity with a different cult, a deity whose followers were unable to comply with the normal rules of entry into the system. A system that was heavily dependent on new gods ought to have been manageable in such a way that rulers would find and welcome none but acceptable guests. Even if we omit the deities produced from within, Rome was still encountering other peoples with their own gods who might have been assimilated to something Roman and might then have been granted an establishment within the walls, within the boundaries of other cities as well as of Rome. Even in the difficult period of the third-century disasters Rome was still winning victories which could all have been commemorated in the traditional manner, with prayers and supplications before battle followed by different supplications, together with temples, on the outcome. When this was the usual pattern, it is hard to suppose that Constantine made Christianity official in the full foreknowledge (or even a mere foreboding) of the attendant difficulties. It seems likely that he at first turned to the Christian God as a deity who could be reliable in war.

In some ways the polytheistic system was weaker by the early fourth century. In some areas the temples, for example, had been damaged in the course of the barbarian invasions. Secondly, there had been changes in the priestly offices. They had functioned best during the later Republic, when they satisfied the aristocracy's need for religious ceremony and its appetite for imitation political offices. The Empire continued these practices, as a way of offering honours in advance to close relatives of the emperor and as awards for distinguished service to those who were lesser by birth but greater in merit. In this different political system the priesthoods, though still recognizable as ornaments, were hardly the same objects that had been so useful to the ambitious politicians of the Republic. The inventiveness of the Empire multiplied posts within the bureaucracy but it had done hardly anything to alter the religious honours. The new religion, which surprised people by its intolerance of other cults, also surprised them by the organization of its clergy. The priesthoods developed by Christianity created new career outlets, especially for those who were reasonably well off and were in demand as bishops. The religious institutions received money and endowments from the government but soon showed they could function as an independent counterweight to imperial aims. The episcopacy may have been intended by Constantine to unite the Empire behind a dynastic emperor, but its prime allegiance was to another power.

The result was an unpredictable change, an institution which would attract men with a capacity for the religious life and some talent for politics. Innovation in this part was balanced by conservation; in some ways the new cult took over and enhanced the social vitality of pagan forms, it increased the services that many expected from civic polytheism. Thus the churches came in a new style of religious building but they provided at least some of the customary religious blessings that had once been dispensed through temples.

Although most of this book is concerned with the public aspect of religion, it is worth remembering that pagan attempts at theory make it clear why polytheism became a failure. Varro, for instance, put forward three different theories of the gods: poetic theology was unsatisfactory as it allowed the gods moral relationships that were condemned by ordinary civic morality; and philosophical theology left too wide a gap between god as he was supposed to be in reality and the anthropomorphic gods of the state. The residuum was civic polytheism, a collection of forgettable practices and rites, with little by way of rational explanation to guide the visitor or even the citizen through the maze. Its capacity for absorbing new gods and its increased diversity of cult provided for the faithful a range of emotional certainties, but accounts of its practice were theoretically feeble. Some versions concentrated on the place of Rome in patriotic history; others, more esoterically, considered man's spiritual place in the universe; but the two sorts of accounts were not united into a greater whole.

# *Notes*

See Bibliography for more details on publications

ABBREVIATIONS

| | |
|---|---|
| *AB* | *Analecta Bollandiana* |
| *AJA* | *American Journal of Archaeology* |
| *AJP* | *American Journal of Philology* |
| *ANRW* | *Aufstieg und Niedergang der römischen Welt* |
| *BCH* | *Bulletin de Correspondance Hellénique* |
| *BICS* | *Bulletin of the Institute of Classical Studies* |
| *CIL* | *Corpus Inscriptionum Latinarum* |
| *CP* | *Classical Philology* |
| *CTh* | *Codex Theodosianus* |
| *DAC* | *Dictionnaire d'archéologie et de liturgie chrétienne* |
| *EPRO* | *Etudes Préliminaires aux Religions Orientales* |
| *ESAR* | *Economic Survey of Ancient Rome* |
| *HA* | *Historia Augusta* |
| *HTR* | *Harvard Theological Review* |
| *ILLRP* | *Inscriptiones Latinae Liberae Reipublicae* |
| *ILS* | *Inscriptiones Latinae Selectae* |
| *JHS* | *Journal of Hellenic Studies* |
| *JRS* | *Journal of Roman Studies* |
| *MAAR* | *Memoirs of the American Academy in Rome* |
| *MDAIR* | *Mittheilungen des deutschen archäologischen Instituts (römische Abteilung)* |
| *PBSR* | *Papers of the British School at Rome* |
| *PG/PL* | *Patrologia Graeca/Latina* |
| *PLRE* | *Prosopography of the Later Roman Empire, 1* |
| *REA* | *Revue des Etudes Anciennes* |

| | |
|---|---|
| *REL* | *Revue des Etudes Latines* |
| *RHR* | *Revue de l'Histoire des Religions* |
| *SIG*[3] | *Sylloge Inscriptionum Graecarum* |
| *TAPA* | *Transactions of the American Philological Association* |
| *YCS* | *Yale Classical Studies* |

CHAPTER ONE

1. The most familiar exemplar of the approach is H. J. Rose, *Ancient Roman Religion* (1948) esp. ch. 1. His enthusiasm for the numinous and for 'polydaemonism' is criticized by G. Dumézil, *Archaic Roman religion* (1970) 1. ch. 3, 'The Most Ancient Roman Religion: *Numen* or *Deus*?' Cf. n. 3 below.
2. Ovid (*Fasti*, 4. 901f.) describes 'the procession, which was apparently quite new to him' (see W. W. Fowler, *The Roman Festivals*, 88–91).
3. For Varro's opinion see Augustine, *City of God*, 4.31. G. Dumézil has insisted (against those whom he calls the primitivists, such as Rose) that the early Romans knew gods even though they did not show them as images; his approach compares the fact that Latin has a word *deus* with the fact that 'the word is found in the majority of Indo-European languages, whereas the primitivists concentrate on comparing *numen* with Melanesian *mana*'. See G. Dumézil (1970) esp. 27–31, on Varro's view and on *deus*.
4. Succinctly put by the *Encyclopaedia Britannica* 15th ed.s.v. Nippur: 'Although never a political capital, Nippur played a dominant part in the religious life of Mesopotamia.' On civic or poliad deities see U. Brackertz, *Zum Problem der Schutzgottheiten griechischer Städte* (1976) 11f. A. J. Toynbee, *A Study of History, Somervell Abridgement of Vols 1–6*, gives more illustrations of the change whereby 'the once local divinity ... takes on characteristics borrowed from the rulers of the universal state in which the local community has been engulfed.'
5. On the evocation of Juno see Livy, 5.21 and V. Basanoff, *Evocatio* (1947) esp. 42f; on Vortumnus (Vertumnus) see Basanoff, 56f and 67–8; and L. R. Taylor, *Local Cults in Etruria* (1923).
6. Arnobius, *Against the Pagans*, 3.38. See M. van Doren, 'Peregrina Sacra', *Historia* 3 (1954) 490 nn.6 and 7.
7. This neat arrangement is outlined by C. Koch in 'Gottheit und Mensch im Wandel der römischen Staatsform' (1942), republished in *Religio* ed. O. Seel (1960) esp. 100–1. One might more profitably compare the success of the numerous immigrant gods with the social advance of non-Italian slaves and freedmen.
8. This view of 'Olympian' is akin to the sociological definition advanced by R. Robertson, *The Sociological Interpretation of Religion* (1970) 82; '*Olympian religious culture* is distinguished by the centrality of orientation to a pantheon of several high gods.'

9. Cf. the development of the Janus festival into the elaborate ritual on the 1st of January in the later Empire; M. Meslin, *La fête des Kalendes de janvier* (1970).
10. For Neptune, Dio Cassius, 53.27. For Venus in the late Republic see R. Schilling, *La religion romaine de Vénus* (1954), esp. 272f., 'Vénus et les grands conquérants'; the statesmen of the late Republic pursued a political Venus and were indifferent to the modern philologist's indecision whether it was an Italian or a Hellenizing Venus. On the connection between public monuments and personal fame see W. V. Harris, *War and Imperialism in Republican Rome* (1979) 20, and his additional n. 6.
11. For Cicero on Ceres see *in Verrem*, 2.4.103 and 108. The Athenian relationship between city and country is described by H. W. Parke, *Festivals of the Athenians*, 100: 'The (country Dionysia) ... was in many parts influenced by the development of the city festivals ...'
12. A. J. Toynbee, *An Historian's Approach to Religion*, 27f. esp. 33. The statement sounds persuasive but is perhaps too theoretical. Hellenistic cities in the Roman Empire for example were not burdened by a sense that their civic gods were inferior to those of Rome. What mattered was pride in the civic god, who made a link with the past, and readiness to accept the emperors as new man-gods, the international gods of the present. See A. D. Nock, 'Early Gentile Christianity etc.', in Nock (1972) 1. 49f esp. 52.
13. But Rome's political hegemony in Latium is not directly connected with control of this festival; see E. Gjerstad, *Early Rome*, 5.42.
14. The quotation is from Hobbes, *Leviathan*, ch. 12. Even if Jupiter's claims to be an agrarian and a warrior god are disallowed (G. Dumézil (1970) 1.181f), his remaining functions as a sovereign god (*optimus maximus*) still count for much in the civic scale.
15. The political implications of myth are well brought out by H. Tudor, *Political Myth* (1972). See also M. Grant, *Roman Myths* (1971).
16. R. Meiggs, *Roman Ostia*, 384, rightly draws attention to the part played by the cheerful crowd in Roman religious practices.
17. In spring the Salians' dance invokes Mars, before the campaigning season starts, and in autumn the rite of the October horse is a device for magically preserving the forces of victory for next year's campaign. See H. le Bonniec in *Problèmes de la guerre à Rome*, ed. J. P. Brisson, 101f; and Y. Garlan, *La guerre dans l'antiquité* (1972) 25f. The phrase 'sacral rhythm' is from J. Bayet.
18. Livy, 10.23.
19. On fetials, Livy, 1.24; see W.V. Harris, *War and Imperialism in Republican Rome* (1979) 166f. On oaths C. E. Brand, *Roman Military Law* (1968) 91f.
20. Aulus Gellius, *Attic Nights*, 14.7. See the account and discussion in J. E. Stambaugh, 'The Functions of Roman Temples', *ANRW*, 16.1 (1978) 554f.
21. Virgil, *Aeneid*, 1.505f. and 7.170f, tr. Jackson Knight, Penguin edition.
22. The rules for the siting of public buildings, especially temples, are set forth in Vitruvius, *On Architecture*, 1.7. On the *pomerium* see esp. the accounts in Livy, 1.44 and in Aulus Gellius, *Attic Nights*, 13.14; it seems that Augustus may have been more strict than Republican practice warranted in excluding foreign rites;

see A. D. Nock, 'The Roman Army and the Religious Year', *HTR* 45, in Nock (1972) 2.758 n.99. On Venus Erucina there is a convenient account in Platner-Ashby, *A Topographical Dictionary of Ancient Rome* (1929) 551.

23. See H. Bardon, 'La naissance d'un temple', *REL* 33 (1955) 166f; and, more fully, Stambaugh, in n.20 above.
24. Tacitus, *Histories*, 4.53, tr. Michael Grant.
25. On Aventine Diana as a model for temple charters see *ILS*, 112, 4907 and 4908.
26. The principle is boldly stated by Trajan in Pliny, *Letters*, 10.501: 'the territory of a foreign community (*civitas*) is not able to admit of a dedication made in accordance with Roman law.' On control of sacred places see *Digest*, 43.6.1–2.
27. Macrobius, *Saturnalia*, 1.12.25; Seneca, *Letters to Lucilius*, 97; Juvenal, *Satires*, 6.339f.
28. See E.G. Hardy, *Roman Laws and Charters* (1912), 'Three Spanish Charters', esp. 64–5 (sacrifices), 66–8 (pontiffs and augurs), 70 (games), 72 (use of money – surplus left over from sacrifices).
29. On the gods' property see Mommsen, *Römisches Staatsrecht* (1887) 2.1.59f, 'Das Göttergut'. The quotation is from the *Rules of Ulpian*. On Vestals see Labeo in Aulus Gellius, *Attic Nights*, 1.12.
30. Valerius Maximus, 7.6.4; Suetonius, *Julius*, 54; Dio Cassius, 41.17 and 39; Tacitus, *Annals* 15.45. On the figures see T. Frank, 'The Sacred Treasure and the Rate of Manumission', *AJP* 53 (1932) 360–3. See also Pliny, *Natural History*, 33.14.
31. Herodian, 7.2.5 ('M. melted down everything ... offerings in temples, statues of gods and objects in honour of heroes').
32. On Hellenistic banking see *ESAR*, 4.888f. On the temple as a place for 'deposit of treasure' see Strabo, 640f. and esp. Dio Chrysostom, 31.54f. On temples as landowners see M. I. Finley, *The Ancient Economy* (1973) 70 n. 17 and 102 n.22.
33. For a brief survey of *asylia* see Rostovtzeff, *The Social and Economic History of the Hellenistic World*, (1941) 901–3; on the arguments about *asylum* in early Rome see F. Altheim, *A History of Roman Religion* (1938) 255f. See below ch. 4 n. 27.
34. Livy, 4.54.
35. Livy, 27.8 and 31.50; Valerius Maximus, 1.1.2.
36. Tacitus, *Annals*, 3.58 and 71.
37. Livy, 27.25; H. Bardon (n.23 above) argues that the pontiffs were urged on by the senate, to which body he attributes a policy of seeking to stop the generals from becoming too dominant in civic religious life. There probably was *political* opposition but we do not have to assume that it was group policy rather than local sniping by individuals.
38. Cicero, *Laws*, 2.31–33. Cicero's qualified defence of divination here should be compared with the views expressed in his *Divination*, 2.73f. See R. J. Goar, *Cicero and the State Religion* (1972) esp. 108f. See below ch. 2 n.81.
39. See L. R. Taylor, *Party Politics in the Age of Caesar* (1949) 82f.

40. See E. Rawson, 'Scipio, Laelius, Furius and the Ancestral Religion, *JRS* 63 (1973) 161f., esp. 166, with her reference to R.M. Ogilvie, *A Commentary on Livy 1–5* (1965) 128.

CHAPTER TWO

1. On the 'critical' period of the second Punic War see below 33f; and see e.g. J. Bayet, *Histoire politique et psychologique de la religion romaine*, 149f. J. Carcopino (*Histoire romaine*, 3.2, p. 52f.) takes a stern view of second-century Pythagoreanism, calling it 'le mysticisme contre l'État'. It is, I suggest, a mistake to think of Greek cults, Greek rituals and Greek rationalism as alien intrusions, tossing simple Romans between excessive religiosity and disbelief; the point to be stressed is that the Roman polytheistic system was essentially receptive. I doubt whether M. Weber, *Sociology of Religion* (1971), 11 is right when he says that Hellenic conceptions at Rome attained little more than an aesthetic existence.
2. For references see G. Wissowa, *Religion und Kultus der Römer* (1912) 202.
3. Livy, 31.9; J. Briscoe, *A Commentary on Livy 31–33* (1973) 80. J. Heurgon (cf. n. 31 below) considers that the pontiff Licinius Crassus was opposed to 'le scepticisme naissant.' The problem however was not just a losing battle between a few religious conservatives and a group of reckless innovators. The demand for changes of this type came about for political reasons which do not necessarily impugn the religious *bona fides* of those who sought to benefit.
4. L. R. Taylor, 'The "Sellisternium" and the Theatrical "Pompa"', *CP*, 30 (1935) 122f., esp. 127 '... a Roman custom to carry chairs of the gods into the theater at *ludi scaenici* ... '
5. On resistance to a stone theatre in Rome see F. Altheim, *A History of Roman Religion*, 290. The claim that 'the connection of theatrical performances with religion is not only basic, but also lasting and specific' is examined by J. A. Hanson, *Roman Theater–Temples*, 43f. esp. 47 and 55. In his discussion of Pompey's theatre he criticizes the views of Marchetti-Longi for over-emphasizing the factor of religion and concludes that 'despite Pompey's assertion that he was dedicating principally a temple, the theater was now the dominant element ...'. See also Tertullian, *de spectaculis*, 10.5.
6. Cicero, *prov. cons.*, 26–7. For Pompey see S. Weinstock, *Divus Julius* (1971) 63; for a list of supplications in Republic and Empire see L. Halkin, *La supplication d'action de grâces chez les Romains* (1953).
7. For expenditure on temples see *ESAR* 1, 183, 286 and 370f (this last on the period between 80 and 50 BC), and I. Shatzmann, *Senatorial Wealth and Roman Politics*, esp. 90–1: 'it can be asserted that proceeds of booty covered the expenses of these works' (mostly temples, he means).
8. Valerius Maximus, 9.3.8; Pliny, *Natural History*, 7.138 emphasizes the allegation that Sulla was eager to have the credit of the dedication for himself.
9. Livy 24.16.19; possibly a temple of Jupiter Libertas; see Platner-Ashby (1929) s.v.

10. For Caesar's remark see Suetonius, *Julius*, 77. D. E. Strong, 'The Administration of Public Building in Rome', *BICS* 15 (1968) 97f. (nn. 39–41) points out that in some cases the temple advertised the family, not just the individual – the Claudii, for example, maintained the temple of Bellona.
11. These examples are taken from M. Crawford, *Roman Republican Coinage*, 727 and 733.
12. Livy, 26.18. R. Seguin (*Latomus* 33 (1974) 3f.) thinks that Scipio combined respect for tradition and a sense of his personal religious mission; R. Combès, *Imperator*, 66f considers that the title of *imperator* created the special link between Scipio and the god.
13. Plutarch, *Gracchi*, 39. For Caesar see e.g. Appian, *Civil Wars*, 2.616 and S. Weinstock, *Divus Julius* (1971) esp. 364f.
14. Caesar, *Civil War*, 3.83.
15. For the Jupiter-banquet see Aulus Gellius, *Attic Nights*, 12.8. L. Robert (*BCH*, 59 (1935) 442) uses the expression of occasions which concern the whole community; it is also appropriate for the aristocratic order on its own.
16. Macrobius, *Saturnalia*, 3.13.11; Cicero, *haruspicum resp.*, 12. See L. R. Taylor, 'Caesar's Colleagues in the Pontifical College', *AJP*, 63 (1942) 385–412, who discusses the order of names in Cicero's list from 57 BC.
17. The comment is from E. Badian, 'Sulla's Augurate', *Arethusa*, 1.29, in a discussion of Dio Cassius, 39.17.2; the '*gens*-law' did not apply to the pontificate.
18. Cicero, *ad familiares*, 3.10.9.
19. E. Badian (n. 17 above) supports the explanation of the symbols put forward by L. R. Taylor, 'Symbols of the Augurate on coins of the Caecilii Metelli', *AJA*, 48 (1944), 352f; for the opposite view, that the symbols of the augurate mean that the office was actually held, see T. J. Luce, 'Political Propaganda on Roman Republican Coins: 92–88 BC', *AJA*, 72 (1968) 25f.
20. For changes in election procedures see (on 103) Cicero, *de lege agraria*, 2.7.18; Velleius Paterculus 2.12; and cf. Cicero, *de amicitia*, 96, on 145 BC; (on 81 and 63) Dio Cassius, 37.37. For a brief account of these changes see G. J. Szemler, *The Priests of the Roman Republic* (1972) 30; for an account of whether priests had a privileged seat on the senate, see G. J. Szemler, 'Sacerdotes Publici and the Ius Sententiam Dicendi', *Hermes*, 104 (1976) 53f.
21. D. E. Hahm, 'Roman Nobility and the Three Major Priesthoods 218–167 BC', *TAPA*, 94 (1963) 73f. ends his study with the remark that in this period the priesthood was bestowed early as 'a form of patronage' on aspirants to political office.
22. On the incident in 131 BC see Cicero, *Philippics*, 11.18; and on the resolution of conflicts see J. Bleicken, 'Oberpontifex und Pontifikalkollegium', *Hermes*, 85 (1957) 345f. esp. 356.
23. Livy, 22. 9–10 and 33; for Fabius' remark on 'neglect of ceremonies and auspices', Livy, 22.9.7.
24. Livy, 27.25 (Virtus); 36.36 (Iuventas); 29.10 (Cybele).
25. According to R. Schilling (*Kokalos*, 10. (1964–5) 259) the Venus of Eryx was

'romanized' in the shrine on the Capitol whereas in the later temple (ded. 181 BC) outside the Colline Gate Rome recognized the *Sicilian* character of the goddess; see also Diodorus Siculus, 4.83 and Strabo, 272.

26. The significance of the new deity in internal politics is emphasized by Th. Köves, 'Zum Empfang der Magna Mater in Rom', *Historia* 12 (1963) 321–47.
27. According to E. Montanari, 'Mens', *Religioni e Civiltà* 2 (1976) 173f. Mens was a senatorial choice and was intended as a divine counterweight to Hannibal's fortune.
28. The idea is borrowed from S. E. Finer, *The Man on Horseback* (1976) 40. Later Romans who went overseas for longer periods may have said an emotional farewell to their temples in Rome, but they took naturally to the local gods; see A. J. N. Wilson, *Emigration from Italy in the Republican Age of Rome* (1966), 116.
29. The morality is from Seneca, *Letters to Lucilius*, 18.1; for a discussion see M. le Glay, *Saturne Africain: Histoire* (1966) esp. 468–70: 'D'une fête "paysanne" en déclin, la réforme de 217 vise à faire la grande fête "populaire" ... ' On carnival in general see P. Burke, *Popular Culture in Early Modern Europe* (1978) 178f.
30. On *lectisternia* Livy, 22.10; 25.12; 29.10; notice especially the games for Apollo (212 and 208) and for Cybele (204). On *stips* for Cybele, Cicero, *Laws* 2.40.
31. Livy, 22.9 and 34.44; see the study by J. Heurgon in *Trois études sur le 'ver sacrum'* (1957) 36f. The chief pontiff, P. Licinius Crassus, who argued for a renewal (*instauratio*) of the ritual in 194, had also been on the side of rigour in 200 BC – cf. above n. 23.
32. P. Fabre in 'Minime romano sacro', *REA*, 42 (1940) 419–24, argues that Livy's objection is not to human sacrifice in general but to human sacrifice in which blood is shed.
33. Valerius Maximus, 1.1.1; Festus, *de significatu verborum* s.vv. *Graeca sacra* and *minuitur populo luctus*; Livy, 22. 56. For discussion see A. Merlin, *L'Aventin dans l'antiquité* (1906) 140f. and H. le Bonniec, *Le Culte de Cérès à Rome* (1958) esp. 386f; the cult was exclusively for women whereas the earlier rites for Ceres were celebrated by both sexes.
34. Livy, 25.1.7.
35. Livy, 21.62; 22.1.18; 26.9; 27.37. The use of cypress wood was not just an economy; it was meant to evoke the style of antiquity; see J. Cousin, 'La crise religieuse de 207 avant J-C', *RHR*, 126 (1943) 15f. esp. 25–8.
36. Virgil, *Aeneid* 2.501 and 515; 11.477.
37. Livy, 27. 50–1.
38. Tacitus, *Germania* 8. R. Pichon, 'Le rôle religieux des femmes dans l'ancienne Rome', *Conférences au Musée Guimet* (1912) 77–135 perhaps overestimates the value of priesthoods as a means of expressing social ambition for women; wealth and family (cf. Seneca, *Helv.* 14.2) were always important, both in pagan Rome and in the Christian circle of Jerome.
39. See the *laudatio Turiae*, 1.30; *ILLRP*, 311 and 316; Pliny, *Natural History*, 7.142f. on masculine aristocratic values. G. J. Szemler, 'Religio, Priesthoods

and Magistracies in the Roman Republic', *Numen* 18 (1971) 103f. esp. 105 explains why membership of the colleges was valued; see also Harris, *War and Imperialism in Republican Rome* (1979) 261.

40. For Cicero see *ad familiares*, 14.4 and 7, and Dio Cassius, 38.17 for the statuette of Minerva. For Cato, Sallust, *Catiline*, 51.29; Allecto, Virgil, *Aeneid*, 7.440f.
41. See A. J. Toynbee, *Hannibal's Legacy*, 2.378, for a hostile assessment of senatorial control. His views and assumptions are challenged by J. A. North, 'Conservatism and Change in Roman Religion', *PBSR*, 44 (1976) esp. 9–10.
42. Livy, 25.1 and 12.
43. Livy, 39.8f. *ILS*, 18 gives the *senatusconsultum de Bacchanalibus*. A. Bruhl, *Liber Pater*, esp. 115–16, stresses government fear of a plot against the state.
44. L. R. Farnell, *Cults of the Greek States*, 5.135f. gives instances where Dionysus became the 'paramount divinity' of the state. But see I. M. Lewis, *Ecstatic Religion* (1971) esp. 101, who follows E. R. Dodds in contrasting Dionysus as 'a god of the people' with Apollo who 'moved only in the best society.' On the whole (at this stage) Dionysus would have appealed to such groups as poorer women and men of low social status. Cf. E. R. Dodds, *The Greeks and the Irrational* (1951), 76.
45. NB. the invitations to freedwomen to make their contribution; Livy, 22.1.18. and Macrobius, *Saturnalia*, 1.6.13.
46. For a sympathetic version of the earlier Roman religion see e.g. W. W. Fowler, *The Religious Experience of the Roman People* (1922); his sense of a decline is well illustrated by the heading to his lecture 12, 'The pontifices and the secularization of religion'. But we should remember that the eastern cults were civic as well as exciting, and that the urban rituals at Rome were not all solemnity.
47. On the Gracchan troubles, Appian, *Civil Wars*, 1.25. 113–14; on the times of Apuleius, *ibid.*, 1.32. 143f; on the Sullan proscriptions, *ibid.*, 1.95. 443; and on Marius, *ibid.*, 1.73. 337.
48. On the attempt to find refuge with Vesta, Appian, *Civil Wars*, 1.54. 236f. On Julius Caesar, Ovid, *Metamorphoses*, 15.763 and 801–2; Augustine, *City of God*, 1.2.
49. The temple had been vowed and built by Camillus (Plutarch, *Camillus*, 42); on the restoration by Opimius, see Plutarch, *C. Gracchus*, 17; Appian, *Civil Wars*, 1.26. 120. On the subject of concord see M. Amit, 'Concordia', *Iura*, 13 (1962) 133–69.
50. Cicero, *de domo*, 116; Plutarch, *Cicero*, 33; Dio Cassius, 38.17.
51. S. Weinstock, *Divus Julius* (1971) 287f. documents the case that Caesar was not a 'passive recipient' either in the east or the west; see esp. 297 and 303f. For a criticism of his arguments see the review by J. A. North, *JRS*, 65 (1975) 171f.
52. For Ateius, see e.g. Cicero, *Divination*, 1.29; Plutarch, *Crassus*, 16; for Bibulus, Dio Cassius, 38.6, Suetonius, *Julius*, 20. J. Bayet, 'Les Malédictions du Tribun C. Ateius Capito', *Latomus* 19 (1960), reprinted in *Croyances et rites dans la*

*Rome antique* (1971) 353f., thinks that Plutarch's version helps us to understand popular religious emotion of the time.

53. See the study by A. E. Astin, '*Leges Aelia et Fufia*', *Latomus*, 23 (1964) 421f.
54. The basic evidence on intercalation is conveniently presented by A. K. Michels, *The Calendar of the Roman Republic* (1967) 145f. Appendix 1.
55. Cicero, *ad familiares*, 3.4 and 9; *Divination*, 1.105 and 132; 2.75.
56. For Nigidius Figulus see the study by A. della Casa, *Nigidio Figulo* (1962), esp. 101f. For Caecina's views on lightning see Seneca, *Natural Questions*, 2.39.
57. Cicero, *ad familiares*, 6.6.
58. On this subject see E. Courtney, 'Notes on Cicero', *Classical Review*, NS, 10 (1960) 98; J. O. Lenaghan, *A Commentary on Cicero's Oration de haruspicum responso* (1969) 142–3 agrees with Courtney against the usual explanation that the house was that of Q. Cicero.
59. For the towns in Latium (Gabii, Bovillae, Labici) see Cicero, *Planc.*, 23; on Delphi, Plutarch, *Moralia*, 394D; on Sicily, Diodorus Siculus, 4.7 and Strabo, 272.
60. See the account in Harris, *War and Imperialism in Republican Rome* (1979) 67.
61. On Cornelius Merula's death see Velleius Paterculus, 2.20; Appian, *Civil Wars*, 1.65.296. On the vacancy Dio Cassius, 54.36; Tacitus, *Annals* 3.58.
62. Cicero, *Divination* 1.28. On the general's auspices R. Combès, *Imperator* (1966) 388f. has useful remarks on Cicero's laments and inconsistency, esp. 393 with n.
63. Caius, *Institutes* 2.4 and 6.
64. For Lutatius Catulus and Fortuna see Plutarch, *Marius*, 26; Cicero, *Laws*, 2.28. For Pompey see Pliny, *Natural History*, 8.20; Tertullian, *de spectaculis*, 10.
65. For the Faesulae inscription see *ILS*, 3084; for Etruscan theory see Servius on *Aeneid*, 1.422. On the distribution of Capitolia the older work by Kuhfeldt (*De Capitolis Imperii Romani*) (1883) is useful; but see esp. M. C. de Azevedo in *Atti della Pontificia Accademia Romana di Archeologia, Memorie* 5 (1941) esp. 64–7 where the development and the spread of Capitolia are succinctly discussed.
66. For Ephesus see R. Mellor, *Thea Rōmē: the worship of the goddess Roma in the Greek World* (1975) 15, 56f. and 199f. P. Servilius Isauricus was proconsul 46–44; the cult of Roma at Ephesus is 'first attested at the beginning of the first century BC' (Mellor 57).
67. Plutarch, *C. Gracchus*, 17. The later date, connected with Saturninus, has been suggested by E. Rawson, 'Religion and Politics in the Late Second Century BC at Rome', *Phoenix*, 28 (1974) 193f. esp. 207.
68. For the altar see Appian, *Civil Wars*, 1.4; 2.148; 3.2. For the temple of Divus Julius, Dio Cassius, 47.18 and Augustus, *Res Gestae*, 4.2.
69. Plutarch, *Marius*, 27.8; Pliny, *Natural History*, 34.27.
70. Plato, *Laws*, 10.885b; Polybius, 6.56.6f and cf. 16.12. 9–11; Strabo, 1.19–20 stresses the need for 'myth and marvels' to reinforce the effects of religion.
71. For Varro's theologies see e.g. Augustine, *City of God*, 6.4; Cicero, *Laws*, 2.23. P. Boyancé, 'Sur la théologie de Varron', *REA*, 57 (1955) 57f. esp. 62 argues that

Varro made a different use of the tripartite theology from that made by Scaevola ('he wanted civic theology to be regarded as a mixture of the other two rather than as something distinct and separate' – Augustine, *City of God*, 6.6).

72. Augustine, *City of God*, 4.31, refers to Varro's theory about early Rome. See Cicero, *Laws*, 2.26 on the theme 'species deorum in oculis, non solum in mentibus'.
73. See Augustine, *City of God*, 4.27.
74. On Amphiaraus see *SIG*[3], 747; F. F. Abbott and A. C. Johnson, *Municipal Administration in the Roman Empire* (1926) no. 18; Cicero, *Nature of the Gods*, 3.49.
75. Cicero, *Philippics*, 1.13 and 2.110.
76. The theory that Roman religion is exempted by Lucretius is put forward by S. Weinstock, *Divus Julius* (1971) 2.
77. E. Benveniste, *Le vocabulaire des institutions indo-européennes* (1969), 2.265f. thinks that the pejorative meaning of *superstitio* developed at Rome because of the discredit attaching to seers and the like; see also D. Grodzynski, 'Superstitio', *REA*, 76 (1974) 36f., who distinguishes between the use of the word superstition in the 1st century BC to mean deviation from the 'national religion' and a later usage, 'la mauvaise religion des autres' – but this is too restrictive on 1st century usage. See Varro in Augustine, *City of God*, 6.9; Seneca, *Letters to Lucilius*, 123.16 ('superstitio error insanus est'). For Ulpian (*Digest*, 28.7.8) the dangers are (a) contempt of *religio*, and (b) fear of the gods 'usque ad superstitionem'.
78. For Cicero's distinctions between religion and superstition see esp. *Nature of the Gods*, 2.71 and *Divination*, 2.148. For a Christian view see e.g. Lactantius, *Divine Institutes*, 4.28; for Caesar on Gallic religiosity *Gallic War*, 6.16; for Cicero on Sicilian fears *Verrines*, 2.4.105.
79. Cicero, *Flaccus*, 67 and 69.
80. The passage on the Druids is from Pliny, *Natural History*, 30.12f; *Digest*, 48.12.30 gives the lawyer's view; on Marcus Aurelius see M. Beaujeu, *La religion romaine à l'apogée de l'empire* (1955) 349.
81. For Cicero's views see *Laws*, 2.19: 'let no one have gods on his own, or new or foreign gods unless they have been sanctioned by the whole community (*publice*)'. See Festus, *de significatu verborum* s.v. *religiosus*.
82. See esp. Cicero, *ad Atticum*, 12.36; Cicero wants to 'achieve apotheosis as far as may be. That I could do if I built within the actual precincts of the house, but ... I am afraid of changes of ownership'. On the legal aspects of *res sacrae* see W. W. Buckland, *A Text-Book of Roman Law* (revised 1966) 183f.
83. Suetonius, *Nero*, 56 and *Domitian*, 13.
84. See Cicero, *On Divination*, 1.105 for a defence of divination, and *ibid.*, 2.70 for Cicero's counter-attack. At *Laws*, 2.27 Cicero defends divination in reply to Atticus' question.
85. See Minucius Felix, *Octavius*, 6; and Maximus (Augustine, *Letters*, 16 and 17) defends the images of the gods in the market-places.
86. Seneca, *Natural Questions*, 2.30f.

CHAPTER THREE

1. G. Boissier, for example, *La religion romaine d'Auguste aux Antonins*, 1.59, makes a great deal of the Epicurean Cassius' remark (Plutarch, *Brutus*, 37) that he would like to believe that the gods support the juster cause: 'les sceptiques eux-mêmes se sentaient ébranlés dans leur incrédulité'. It is doubtful whether he had enough evidence to entitle him to write: '... beaucoup devaient éprouver comme Cassius le besoin de croyances solides ... ' The case of Cassius hardly justifies the 'beaucoup' of Boissier. The key distinction in any attempt to explain the religious attitudes of Romans is not that between doubt and belief but that between observing traditional religious practices and accepting new (or as yet unauthorized) cults. Pagan doubt was often moderate; it objected most to those who claimed certain knowledge. Cf. the pagan Caecilius in Minucius Felix, *Octavius*, 5–6 and the Christian characterization of him at 16.2: 'he wavered from belief in the gods, at one moment, to keeping the question open at another ... ' and see J. Beaujeu, 'Les constantes religieuses du scepticisme', *Hommages Renard* (1969) 2.61f.
2. W. M. Watt, 'The Place of Religion in the Islamic and Roman Empire', *Numen*, 9 (1962) 110f.
3. A. N. Whitehead, *Religion in the Making* (1926) 42–3. Whitehead was drawing a distinction between two types of 'modified communal religion', the Roman and the Jewish. His view of 'the cult of the Empire' (I take him to have in mind mainly emperor-worship) as a lawyers' construct may seem dismissive; it should be remembered that he also criticizes the Jewish version (of communal religion) as one which embodied general ideas 'entirely expressed in terms of their relevance to the Jewish race.' Whitehead's axiom ('religion is solitariness', *ibid.* 17) is not the best starting-point for a consideration of religion in antiquity.
4. For the 'older view' see A. Bouché-Leclerq, *Les pontifes de l'ancienne Rome* (1871) 347; for Augustus' behaviour 'circa religiones' see Dio Cassius, 52.35 and Suetonius, *Augustus*, 90–94, esp. on Aug.'s fear of lightning, his interest in dreams and omens and his scorn for foreign rites except for those that were long-standing. On the stories of religious prowess attached to Aug. see W. Deonna, 'La légende d'Octave-Auguste', *RHR* 83 and 84 (1921) esp. his no. 50 on the superstitions of Augustus and his belief in omens.
5. See K. Scott, 'Emperor-Worship in Ovid', *TAPA* 61 (1930) 43f. esp. 48. To doubt whether Romans saw divine sonship as a form of legitimization does not mean that one rejects the Roman sense that the world mission of their Empire had a religious character; on which see A. Zwaenepol, 'L'inspiration religieuse de l'impérialisme romain', *Antiquité Classique* 18 (1949) 5f. Cf. Watt (n.2) 123.
6. See L. R. Taylor, *The Divinity of the Roman Emperor* (1931) 74, who makes a comparison between Caesar and Alexander, named as the son of Zeus by the oracle at Ammon.
7. H. Weinbrot, *Augustus Caesar in 'Augustan' England* (1978) 5f. asserts that in the eighteenth century 'Augustan' implied a variety of excellences, but may be

reduced to the omnibus belief that during the reign of Augustus Caesar the throne was a center of value'. He argues that the idealizing picture of Augustus as a benefactor needs to be modified; that conventional panegyric of the golden age of Augustus should be set against the considerable evidence of those classical historians who were critical of Augustus and against the need of Whigs and Tories to see Augustus as a 'usurping tyrant'.

8. P. Lambrechts, 'Auguste et la religion romaine', *Latomus* 6 (1947) 177f. argues that Augustus' Apollo was an Italic form of Vediovis and was regarded as the deity of the Julian gens (*ibid.*, 185 n.2), with the result that he took Jupiter's place. This last seems doubtful. On the temples as buildings see *Res Gestae* 19 and F. W. Shipley, *Chronology of the Building Operations in Rome etc.* (1931) esp. 49f.
9. On Jupiter Tonans see Suetonius, *Augustus*, 29 and Dio Cassius, 54.4. Suetonius records Aug.'s alleged escape from lightning; for the dream see *Augustus*, 91.
10. On the temple of Divus Julius, Dio Cassius, 51.22 and *Res Gestae*, 19. According to Dio Cassius, 54.8 Augustus ordered a temple to Mars Ultor to be decreed on the Capitol; until recently modern scholars have assumed that it was actually built and was used to house the standards until 2 BC when the 'second' temple of Mars was built in the Forum of Augustus. The corroborating evidence for the supposed *aedicula* of 20 is only the legend MAR ULT on coins of 19–18 BC; and it might well be that the standards were first kept in a temple of Jupiter. See F. E. Romer, 'A Numismatic Date for the Departure of C. Caesar', *TAPA* 108 (1978) 192–6 esp. nn. 13 and 14, and C. J. Simpson, 'The Date of Dedication of the Temple of Mars Ultor', *JRS* 67 (1977) 91–5.

    S. Weinstock, *Divus Julius* (1971) esp. 131 rejects the tradition that Augustus vowed the temple in 42 BC and treats the vow as a joint undertaking on the part of all the triumvirs.
11. Suetonius, *Julius*, 6 shows that Caesar made the claim in a funeral oration. For Greek tributes see *SIG*[3] 760 (Ephesus).
12. Ovid, *Fasti*, 4.959; *Metamorphoses*, 15.864; Dio Cassius, 54.27; *CIL* i[2] 213, 236.
13. P. Gros, *Aurea Templa* (1976) 79f. remarks that Greek and Hellenistic cities had not as a general rule given a distinctive place to urban sanctuaries. Augustan Rome sees the start of an urban, imperial development which uses temples not only as ornaments but also as constructive features along the important roads and lines of communication.
14. *Res Gestae*, 24; Dio Cassius, 52.35, 54.35, 56.46. See K. Scott, 'The Significance of Statues in Precious Metals in Emperor-Worship,' *TAPA* 62 (1931) 101–23.
15. On Concord see Dio Cassius, 55.8 (on 7 BC); and on the dedication see Ovid, *Fasti*, 1.640f; Dio Cassius, 56.25; Suetonius, *Tiberus*, 20.
16. *Res Gestae*, 19; cf. Ovid, *Fasti*, 2.63 on Aug. as 'templorum positor, templorum sancte repostor.'
17. For fires see Dio Cassius, 5.10 (31 BC); 54.19 (16 BC); 54.24 (14 BC); 54.29

(12 BC); 55.1 (9 BC); 55.6 and 8 (7 BC); Ovid, *Fasti*, 4.347 (AD 3); Dio Cassius, 55.26 (AD 6).

18. For 'magnificence' as a complimentary term, Tacitus, *Annals*, 1.9.7 and Vitruvius, *On Architecture*, 7. *pref.* 17. On 'golden' temples, Propertius, 4.1.5 and Ovid, *Fasti*, 1.223–4. There was, however, marble in Rome before Augustus; see M. G. Morgan, 'The Portico of Metellus', *Hermes* 99 (1971) 480–505.
19. On Salus, Dio Cassius, 37.24. On the fetial procedure for declaring war, abandoned after 171 BC until Aug. revived it, see Harris, *War and Imperialism in Republican Rome* (1979) 166f. esp. 167.
20. Suetonius, *Augustus*, 31; Dio Cassius, 55.22; Ovid, *Fasti*, 6.455.
21. See G. B. de Pighi, *de ludis saecularibus* (1965).
22. In general see J. M. Toynbee, 'The Ara Pacis Reconsidered', *Proc. British Academy* 39 (1953) 67–95; S. Weinstock, 'Pax and the "Ara Pacis"', *JRS* 50 (1960) 44–58 maintains that this attribution of the monument has no ancient warrant. On altars see the study by I. Scott Ryberg, *Rites of the State Religion in Roman Art* (1955), *MAAR* 22.
23. Augustus instituted a change from an expiatory sacrifice to 'a triumphant and patriotic solemnity'; see G. Boissier, *La religion romaine d'Auguste aux Antonins* (1884) 1.86f. esp. 87.
24. See W. W. Fowler, *The Religious Experience of the Roman People* (1922) 429, in his chapter on 'The Augustan Revival'; he treats philosophy, Caesar-worship, eastern cults and the old religion as warring elements in a house of discord, instead of seeing them as stages in a process of accretion.
25. See A. J. Toynbee, *A Study of History* (1946, Somervell abridgement of 1–6), 505–15, who compares the Roman and other archaisms and finds that the Augustan revival is 'almost unique in religious history'.
26. Ovid, *Fasti*, 5.145; Dio Cassius, 51.20. For accounts see L. R. Taylor, 'The Worship of Augustus in Italy during his Lifetime', *TAPA* 51 (1920) 116f. and for an analysis of Augustan *numen* see D. M. Pippidi, 'Le numen Augusti', *REL* 9 (1931) 83f.
27. The festival of Lug, the 'Irish Mercury', was celebrated on August 1 both in Ireland and at Lyon. See F. Benoît, *Mars et Mercure* (1959) esp. 176–7. But its significance for the growth of ruler-cult is disputed; see D. Fishwick, 'Provincial Ruler Worship in the West', *ANRW* 16.2., 1201f.
28. P. Gros, *Aurea Templa* (1976) 32–3 gives a list of temples with known dates of the former *dies natalis* and the Augustan days. There was a change in just over half the cases.
29. Augustus has often been applauded for his understanding of religious psychology; see e.g. M. Grant, *Roman Imperial Money* (1954) 219, with a discussion of anniversaries of temple-foundations. For sympathetic appraisals see J. Bayet, *Histoire politique et psychologique de la religion romaine* (1957) 169–93 and R. M. Ogilvie, *The Romans and their Gods* (1969) 112–23.

CHAPTER FOUR

1. Aulus Gellius, *Attic Nights*, 16.13.8 explains the difference between *coloniae* and *municipia*, observing of the former that they appear to be 'the tiny effigies and images' of the grandeur and majesty of the Roman people.
2. A. Alföldi (*Die monarchische Repräsentation im Römischen Kaiserreiche*, 1970, reprinted from *MDAIR* 49 (1934) and 50 (1935)) refers succinctly to two opposing tendencies involved in approaching the emperor: (1) treating the *princeps* as a member of the senatorial élite; (2) separating the master of the world (*dominus*) from human society on religious grounds; see *op.cit.* esp. 25f. and 29f. For veneration of the imperial purple ('the attitude towards it became almost mystical') see W. T. Avery, 'The adoratio purpurae', *MAAR* 17 (1940) 66–80. For Diocletian and Maximian see *ILS*, 629.
3. On the temple of Augustus see Suetonius, *Tiberius*, 47 and *Caligula*, 21 (but Tacitus, *Annals*, 6.45 implies that Tiberius completed the temple though he did not dedicate it); Martial, 4.53. On Flavian policy see K. Scott, *The Imperial Cult under the Flavians* (1936) and for a good discussion that takes in the Antonines, see M. Hammond, *The Antonine Monarchy* (1959) esp. ch. 6, 'Religious Elements in the Position of the Emperor', 203–43, with full references.

   On the emperor Tacitus see *HA, Tacitus,* 9.5, and for the consecration of the place 'which the deified Augustus first touched at his birth', see Suetonius, *Augustus*, 5.
4. Dio Cassius, 56.46; on the many aspects of Augustus' religious standing see W. Deonna, 'La légende d'Octave–Auguste', *RHR* 83 (1921), ch. 3 n.4 above. Dio Cassius, 51.20 makes the point that the Romans paid divine honours to their rulers after death 'though they could not bear to call them kings while they were alive'. A good emperor who was declared a *divus* for the state was still an ancestor for his family. Hence E. Bickerman, 'Consecratio', in *Le Culte des Souverains dans l'Empire Romain* (1972) in *Entretiens Hardt* 19, 3–25, makes the point that Livia and the emperors after Augustus (as family, so to say) honoured the anniversary of Augustus' *death* 'whereas *divus Augustus* was honoured at the anniversary of his *birth*' (*ibid.* 17).
5. For Tiberius and the precedent of Minos, Suetonius, *Tiberius*, 70; on Claudius, Suetonius, *Claudius*, 11. For the piety of Antoninus see *HA, Ant. Pius*, 2.6, *Hadrian*, 24.10, and the useful analysis by J. Beaujeu, *La religion romaine à l'apogée de l'empire* (1955) 279–91.
6. The study by M.P. Charlesworth, 'The Virtues of a Roman Emperor', *Proc. British Academy* 23 (1937) 105f. sets piety among the other virtues with the reminder that 'it is the most difficult to define'. For the Ciceronian definition, Cicero, *de officiis*, 2.11 and cf. *Nature of the Gods*, 1.116; for Macrinus' 'piety' see *HA, Macrinus*, 5.
7. The dynastic idea has been well described by J. Gagé, 'Divus Augustus', *Revue Archéologique* 34 (1931) 11–41. For Nero's titulary, *ILS*, 229; the names referred to are those of *divus* Augustus and *divus* Claudius.

8. For Severus see *ILS*, 8806[b] and *HA, Severus Alexander*, 10. For Julian's tribute to Gordian, see Ammianus, 23.5. Notice that Augustus did not encourage indiscriminate piety to gods that were or seemed alien; he praised Caius for not offering prayers at Jerusalem – Suetonius, *Augustus*, 93.
9. On building see, for in and near Rome, F. W. Shipley (1931 ch. 3, n.8 above) and H. G. Ramsay, 'A third century a. C. building program', *Antiquité Classique* 4 (1935) 419–47; for the provinces see the sketch by R. MacMullen, 'Roman Imperial Building in the Provinces', *Harvard Studies in Classical Philology* 64 (1959) 207–35. For instances of imperial conduct at sacrifices see Suetonius, *Tiberius*, 70; *HA, Hadrian*, 13; Suetonius, *Augustus*, 90f; *Nero*, 56; Marcus Aurelius, *Meditations*, 6.30.
10. On gratitude to benefactors in general see M. P. Charlesworth, 'Some Observations on Ruler-Cult', *HTR* 28 (1935) 5–44 esp. 8–16. For an example of gratitude carried to extremes see Dio Cassius, 56 fr. 2 '... a man told his heirs to sacrifice because he left Augustus still alive'.
11. J. F. Gilliam, 'On *Divi* under the Severi', *Hommages Renard* (1969) 2.284–289 suggests that 'Faustina's honors as a *diva* may have been eliminated or reduced by Caracalla ... ' See *HA, Caracalla*, 11.5f. *ILS*, 5074 records an offering to 'Augustan Mars, protector of our master Gordian ... ' On Augustus as an epithet see the valuable material collected by A. D. Nock, 'Studies in the Graeco-Roman Beliefs of the Empire', n.73 in Nock (1972) 1.42.
12. Lucian, *sacrifices*, 11.
13. *ILS*, 6088 xxvi gives an example of an oath 'by Jupiter and *divus* Augustus and *divus* Claudius', and so on to the Genius of Domitian. For the Gytheum inscription see Ehrenberg and Jones, *Documents*[2] 102; and A. Garzetti, *From Tiberius to the Antonines* (1974) 570 for a bibliography.
14. J. A. O. Larsen takes two Gallic assemblies as the starting-point of his discussion about provincial assemblies in the west; see his *Representative Government in Greek and Roman History* (1955) 126f. For the Iberian and Celtic background to the cult see R. Etienne, *Le culte impérial dans la péninsule ibérique* (1958) esp. 49f. For Africa see T. Kotula, 'Les origines des assemblées provinciales dans l'Afrique romaine', *Eos* 52 (1962) 146f.
15. *ILS*, 6811 commemorates a priest of the cult in Africa; D. Fishwick, 'The Institution of the Provincial Cult in Africa Proconsularis', *Hermes* 92 (1964) 342–63 sums up in favour of a Flavian rather than an earlier date. See A. Mócsy, *Pannonia* (1974) 175 and 214; and J. J. Wilkes, *Dalmatia* (1969) 166; 200; 253; 292.
16. In general see L. Cerfaux and J. Tondriau, *Le culte des souverains* (1957) and J. Deininger, *Die Provinziallandtage der römischen Kaiserzeit* (1965). On the whole subject of 'giving for a return' see A. R. Hands, *Charities and Social Aid in Greece and Rome* (1968) esp. 26–61. For the disaffected priest see Tacitus, *Annals*, 1.57; on Claudius' temple *Annals*, 14.31.6 and Seneca, *Apocolocyntosis*, 8.
17. See P. A. Brunt, 'Charges of Provincial Maladministration under the Early Principate', *Historia* 10 (1961) 189–227, esp. 212, for the view that 'the

primary business (*sc.* of the *concilia*) seems to have been the celebration of the imperial cult'; and see too J. A. O. Larsen (1955, above n. 14). But J. Deininger, *Die Provinziallandtage der römischen Kaiserzeit*, (1965) 161f. argues that political functions were inherent from the start in this organization.

18. In Spain the native practice of *devotio* to a military leader meant that loyalty to Romans such as Sertorius and then Augustus was accompanied by a religious sentiment. For examples see Plutarch, *Sertorius*, 14 and Dio Cassius, 53.20 (a tribune who 'devoted' himself to Augustus in the Spanish style 'and put a like oath to the people in spite of Augustus' objections'). For a comparison of Spanish and Roman *devotio* see R. Etienne (n. 14 above, 1958) 75f. esp. 77. In the case of Gaul the thesis 'that Augustus was building here on native religious practice' is more doubtful; see D. Fishwick, 'Provincial Ruler Worship in the West', *ANRW* (1978) 16.2. 1201f. esp. 1204.
19. Suetonius, *Augustus*, 18. On the link with Dionysus, the work it seems of Ptolemy Philopator, see P.M. Fraser, *Ptolemaic Alexandria* (1972) 201–7; and for the dynastic cult there, 213f.
20. The distinction made in the text is valid for many, but not all, of the phenomena, and is probably, I suggest, of most service for an understanding of emperors' caution in pressing their religious claims within the city of Rome. Hellenistic Greeks, however, had long been used to hyperbole in these matters; it is not surprising therefore that Caius, adopted son of Augustus, was in AD 2 honoured at Athens as 'new Ares' – see *Inscriptiones Graecae* 2.3.3250.
21. On the reluctance of Probus see *HA, Probus*, 10 and W. T. Avery (n.2 above); on Marcus Aurelius and Jupiter's games see *HA, Marcus*, 21.5; for knowledge of formulae, *Marcus*, 4; on restoration of temples, see *HA, Severus*, 23; on condescension to pontiffs, *HA, Alexander Severus*, 22.5. On the 'moderation' of Augustus himself see above ch. 3. esp. nn. 14 and 15; even Antonians could make an Augustan beginning – see Herodian, 1.7.6 on Commodus.
22. For Caligula see Philo, *Embassy*, 81f and Suetonius, *Caius*, 22; on Commodus as Hercules, *HA, Commodus*[8]; on sacrifices, *HA, Didius Julianus*, 7.10; on Nero, Tacitus, *Annals*, 14.13. Pliny, *Letters*, 4.11 criticizes Domitian's treatment of the pontiffs, and *Panegyricus*, 52 is especially important for its views on imperial religious decorum.
23. On Augustus see above ch. 3 n.14 and Dio Cassius, 52.35; on Domitian's 'pollution' Pliny, *Panegyricus*, 52; on Baetica, *ILS*, 103; on C. Vibius Salutaris at Ephesus see *ILS*, 7193–5 and the discussion in M. Rostovtzeff, 'L'empereur Tibère et le culte impérial', *Revue Historique* 163 (1930) 1–36 esp. 13.
24. Mucianus (Tacitus, *Histories*, 2.76) emphasizes the fact that the political time is right; religious confirmation of his judgment follows (*ibid*., 2.78). See also Suetonius, *Vespasian*, 5 and Tacitus, *Histories*, 4.81f., on Vespasian as a healer at Alexandria. For the complaints about Nero, *Annals*, 15.67. Some causes of imperial misconduct are outlined by *HA, Aurelian*, 43, and include *licentia*, extravagance, and bad advisers.
25. Domitian rebuilt the temple of Jupiter (dedicated in 82) and held games; for Jupiter Custos see Tacitus, *Histories*, 3.74 and Suetonius, *Domitian*, 5. See K.

Scott, *The Imperial Cult under the Flavians* (1936) esp. 91–2; also F. Sauter, *Der römische Kaiserkult bei Martial und Statius* (1934) 31f.

26. Tacitus, *Annals*, 4.14 and 37. L. R. Taylor, 'Tiberius' refusals of divine honours', *TAPA* 60 (1929) 87–101 points out that the publicity given to Tiberius' refusals should not be allowed to obscure the fact that he accepted many honours.
27. See Tacitus, *Annals*, 3.18, 36 and 66; Apuleius, *Metamorphoses*, 6.4; *Digest*, 21.1.17.12 and 21.1.19.1; Suetonius, *Tiberius*, 53. K. Hopkins, *Conquerors and Slaves* (1979) 221f. discusses taking refuge at statues as an instance of the emperor's 'living presence'.
28. See M. Rostovtzeff, *Revue Historique* 163 (1930) 3f. esp. 7 and K. Scott, 'Notes on Augustus' religious policy', *ARW* 35 (1938) 123.
29. On vows for Pompey, see Cicero, *ad Atticum*, 8.16.1; and L. W. Daly, 'Vota publica pro salute alicuius', *TAPA* 81 (1950) 164–8. On supplications see G. Freyburger, 'La supplication d'action de grâces sous le Haut-Empire', *ANRW* (1978) 16.2, 1418–1439 and cf. above ch. 2. n.6.
30. The theme has recently been explored by J. R. Fears, *Princeps a diis electus* (1977), though the references to it in imperial literature are not that many: see the review by P. A. Brunt in *JRS* 69 (1979) 168–74. Divine choice was sometimes predicated of Vestals (*ILS*, 4935) and is the subject of a remarkable essay by A. D. Nock, '*A diis electa*', in Nock (1972), 1.252–270.
31. See Tacitus, *Annals*, 13.10 on Nero's refusal. The general point to be made is that flattery, which has been condemned by many ancient (and some modern) critics as morally objectionable, was also an important vehicle of expressing, and to some extent making, social change.
32. Tacitus, *Annals*, 2.34 remarks that by time-honoured custom the Vestals gave their evidence in open court; *Annals*, 1.62 gives Tiberius' criticism of Germanicus; for Domitian and the Vestals see Pliny, *Letters*, 4.11. Ceremonial minutiae: e.g. after the conviction and death of Libo in AD 16, Tacitus, *Annals*, 2.32 mentions the proposal (by senators) that there should be a supplication, that offerings be made to gods and that the day of Libo's death be a *dies festus*; the ironical contrast is between the grim power allegedly exercised by Tiberius and the immoderate honours that were all the senators could bestow.
33. Tacitus, *Annals*, 3.64. Perhaps the archaism which did most to associate senators and rulers was the company of the Arval Brethren: G. Henzen, *Acta Fratrum Arvalium* (1874). Brief discussion in F. Millar, *The Emperor in the Roman World* (1978) 356.
34. On the priesthoods as a medium of imperial patronage see F. Millar (1978) n. 33 above, and cf. above ch. 2 n. 21. Seneca, *de ira*, 3.31.2 gives the (imagined) words of an ambitious man who complains that he has been co-opted (by the emperor) into only *one* college.
35. See Pliny, *Letters*, 3.4; 4.1; and 10.8. J. H. W. G. Liebeschuetz, *Continuity and Change in Roman Religion* (1979) 186 remarks that Pliny's 'munificence looks like the performance of social rather than religious duty'. It is inextricably both

of these. For a general discussion of senatorial religion see J. Beaujeu in *Hommages J. Bayet* (1964) 54–75.

36. On Claudius' marriage see Tacitus, *Annals*, 12.8. M. W. H. Lewis, *The Official Priests of Rome under the Julio-Claudians* (1955); *MAAR* 16, 17 n. 52 points out that there were only four instances after 44 BC in which the pontiffs' advice was asked; see *Annals*, 1.10; Dio Cassius, 48.53; and *Annals*, 11.15.
37. Nearly all the evidence is from inscriptions. The difference between Augustales and seviri Augustales has been much discussed; see L. R. Taylor, 'Augustales, Seviri Augustales and Seviri', *TAPA* 45 (1914) 231–53; A. D. Nock, 'Seviri and Augustales', in Nock (1972) 1.348–356; R. Duthoy, 'Les Augustales', *ANRW* (1978) 16.2. 1254–1309. Nock (*ibid.*, 350) describes the position of the sevir as quasi-magistratual, 'implying membership of a college of officials with equal powers'; but I have used the term quasi-magistratual of Augustales precisely because they, like those in traditional posts, provided official bounty from their own pocket. For a literary description of a sevir Augustalis see Petronius, *Sat.*, 29 and 65f. and scholia to Horace, *Satires*, 2.3.281.
38. *ILS*, 7213 gives the charter of Aesculapius and Hygia; see *CIL*, 11.126 for Neptune at Ravenna. The dining activities are well brought out by J.-P. Waltzing, *Étude historique sur les corporations professionelles chez les Romains* (1895) 1.210f. The names of the meeting-places varied; some were non-religious such as *curia* or *domus*, but we also find *templum* (*CIL*, 5.2864, for a college of *centonarii*) and *aedes* (*CIL*, 3.5659, a college of *fabri*); see Waltzing, 1. 224.
39. For a useful introduction to army religion see C. Martin, *History Today* 19 (1969) 255–63. On the sources see Valerius Maximus, 6.1.11 for the centurion; Josephus, *Jewish War*, 3.81f. describes the *praetorium* as like a temple and calls the camp an improvised city; Vegetius, 2.6 calls the emperors' imagines 'divina et praesentia signa'. For an instance of troops worshipping local gods as well as the legion's *genius* see *CIL*, 8.2527–8 and 10760 (Lambaesis). R. Cagnat, *L'armée romaine d'Afrique* (1892 edn) 421f. argues that in Africa the officer-class paid cult to Roman and oriental deities whereas other ranks preferred local or African deities.
40. Augustus himself (Suetonius, *Augustus*, 71 and 75) enjoyed the holiday aspect of *feriae* and would expect his troops to celebrate them likewise; see *YCS* (1940) 165f; A. D. Nock, 'The Roman Army and the Roman Religious Year' in Nock (1972) 2.736; J. F. Gilliam, 'The Roman Military Feriale', *HTR* 47 (1954) 183–96. The *Feriale Duranum* was probably set up by Augustus and (so Gilliam says) 'tells us more about Augustus than Severus Alexander.'
41. See M. I. Finley, *The Ancient Economy* (1975 edn) 175 on the two 'classical' ways of coping with too great a population: (a) sending out colonies, and (b) acquiring wealth from outside.
42. Cf. above ch. 1. n. 16. The elegiac lament for the earlier Roman religion; the ambivalent attitude to oriental cults, betraying both a Roman fear of the exotic and also an exaggerated regard for them as *personally* satisfying; and lastly the

assumption that paganism was all wrong anyway, these are *three* preconceptions which have often made it difficult for modern scholars to be other than patronizing about civic religion at Rome. See ch.2. nn. 1, 41 and 46.

43. On control of gladiators see *ILS*, 5163; for the classic attempt to control civic spending see Pliny, *Letters*, 10, on Bithynia.
44. On Jupiter see Seneca, *Benefits*, 4.7–8; on thunder, Seneca, *Natural Questions*, 2.45. F. Sauter, *Der römische Kaiserkult bei Martial und Statius* (1934) 166f. has collected useful material from poets on the subject of the emperor's *numen* and nature.
45. For Pliny's views see esp. *Natural History*, 2.14–18; 7. 147–191; 14. 119. Pliny finds both atheism ('no regard for the gods') and superstition ('regard for the gods that is carried to shameful lengths') objectionable. See the account by Th. Köves–Zulauf, 'Plinius der Ältere und die römische Religion' (1978) *ANRW*, 16.1.187–288; also, on the emperors, K. Scott, 'The elder and younger Pliny on emperor-worship', *TAPA* 63 (1932) 156–65.
46. See Seneca, *Benefits*, 4.31; Tacitus, *Annals* 4.1; 13.17; 16.16. *Histories*, 1.3 makes this view very clear – 'the gods are not concerned with man's happiness but with his punishment.'
47. See Pliny, *Panegyricus*, esp. 1; 3; 10; 16; 52.
48. See Dio Chrysostom, 12.43f. A. Hauser, *The Social History of Art* (1962 edn) 1.102–8 has drawn attention to the relative novelty of Dio's attempt to raise the standing of the craftsman-artist.

CHAPTER FIVE

1. See above, ch. 1, n. 12 and ch. 3, n. 25.
2. Cf. above ch. 4, n. 42 on received ideas about eastern religions. F. Cumont, *Les religions orientales dans l'empire romain* (1929 edn.) 22f. and esp. ch. 1, nn. 11 and 12, summarizes some earlier views on the threat from the east and 'oriental degeneration', and rightly comments that 'they are in reality inspired by this old illusion that Asia under the Empire was inferior to Europe.' He maintains that the eastern cults were less 'primitive' than the old Greco-Italic idolatry and were 'equipped, I venture to say, with more organs'; his classic study was intended to prove this. My brief version here starts from the reminder that the eastern cults did not only release individuals; they were also used to save groups and states.
3. See A. García y Bellido, *Les religions orientales dans l'Espagne romaine* (1967), *EPRO* 5, viiif. He was emphasizing the fact that the oriental religions, including those which were not religions in the strict sense but might be 'superstitions with a pronounced degree of magic', began as peripheral to the Roman Empire and were gradually taken to its geographical and institutional heart.
4. See A. D. Nock in *Cambridge Ancient History* 10 (1934) 481f. 'The Institution of Ruler-Worship'; and for dedications to emperors see his 'Studies in the Graeco-Roman Beliefs of the Empire' (*JHS*, 1925) in Nock (1972), 1. 33–48

esp. 41f. On enthusiasm perhaps the 'locus classicus' in literature (as opposed to inscriptions) is Suetonius, *Augustus*, 98: '... from an Alexandrian ship ... the passengers and sailors, wearing white, crowned with garlands, and offering incense, praised him [Augustus] to the skies, saying that it was through him they lived, through him that they sailed the seas, and through him that they enjoyed their liberty and their fortunes.'

5. Tertullian, *Apology*, 35. 8–10, says bitterly of those who had successfully conspired against certain emperors: 'Every one of them, right up to the moment of the outburst of impiety (i.e. assassination) was offering sacrifice for the health of the Emperor and was swearing by the genius of the Emperor ... ' Religious ceremonies certainly gave access to the ruler (cf. above ch. 4 n.9), but the use or abuse of religion to hedge a political bet is not confined to classical paganism.
6. For Juvenal see e.g. *Satires*, 6. 529f; 12.28; 13.93f. On Seneca's contempt for the noisy sistrum, see *Dialogues*, 7. 26. 7–8 and R. Turcan, *Sénèque et les religions orientales* (1967); Dionysius of Halicarnassus, *Ant. Rom.*, 2.19; on Cybele see below n. 8.
7. See E. W. Said, *Orientalism* (1978) 2f., who distinguishes between kinds of orientalism: (1) as an academic subject; (2) as a distinction between East and West, 'the starting point for elaborate theories', and (3) as 'a Western style ... for having authority over the Orient.'
8. On the coming of Cybele see Th. Köves, 'Zum Empfang der Magna Mater in Rom', *Historia* 12 (1963) 321–47; F. Bömer, 'Kybele in Rom', *MDAIR* 71 (1964) 130–51. Sophocles had received Asclepius just as Scipio (Livy, 29.10), *vir optimus in civitate*, acted as receptionist to Cybele; see W. S. Ferguson, 'The Attic Orgeones', *HTR* 37 (1944) 61–130 esp. 90f. Köves (326f.) examines the political significance of the connection between Scipio and Juventas.
9. A phallic interpretation is rejected by M. G. Carretoni and R. Schilling in the discussion reported in *REL* 51 (1973) 32–4. On baetylia in general see F. Lenormant, 'Les Bétyles', *RHR* 3 (1881) 31–53; for Greek material see E. Maas, 'Heilige Steine', *Rheinisches Museum* 78 (1929) 1–25.
10. See M. J. Vermaseren, *Cybele and Attis* (1977), plate 34.
11. See A. Bruhl, *Liber Pater* (1953) 164 and cf. above ch. 2 nn. 43 and 44.
12. Dio Cassius, 40.47; 52.36 (Maecenas); 53.2 (Augustus' exclusion of Egyptian rites). The religious policy of the late Republic and early Empire is surveyed by M. Malaise, *Les conditions de pénétration et de diffusion des cultes égyptiens en Italie* (1972), *EPRO* 22, esp. 362–78.
13. Dio Cassius, 54.6. See Malaise (cf. n.12 above) 388f., who thinks there is a marked contrast between Augustus' acceptance of Cybele (as now part of the Roman establishment) and his hostility to Isis.
14. For Licinius see Eusebius, *Life of Constantine*, 1.53.
15. Strabo, 467 explains and defends 'religious frenzy' (though his remarks embrace both ecstatic and non-ecstatic types of religion). For an example-study of personal devotion see V. Tran Tam Tinh, *Essai sur le culte d'Isis à Pompeii* (1964) esp. 109f.

16. Cicero, *Laws*, 2.40, on *stips* (cf. ch.2, n.30 above).
17. The assertion may be too positive but Caligula was certainly Egyptophile. See M. Malaise (cf. n.12 above) 395–401 and Platner-Ashby, 283–4. Isis had therefore recovered from the setbacks under Tiberius described by Josephus, *Antiquities*, 18.65–80, Tacitus, *Annals*, 2.85 and Suetonius, *Tiberius*, 36 (with reference to AD 19).
18. See M. Malaise (nn. 12 and 13 above) and V. Tran Tam Tinh, *Essai sur le culte d'Isis à Pompeii* (1964) esp. 60–61.
19. On Commodus, *HA*, 9.6; for Diocletian see *ILS*, 659.
20. See below 120f. and nn. 32–6.
21. For a general study see A. S. Hoey, 'Official Policy Towards Oriental Cults in the Roman Army', *TAPA* 70 (1939) 456–81 and cf. the remarks of A. D. Nock in *HTR* 45, in Nock (1972), 2.747. For the particular case of Mithras see C. M. Daniels, 'The role of the Roman army in the spread and practice of Mithraism', *Mithraic Studies* (1975) 2.249–274.
22. Nock (*HTR* 45, in Nock (1972), 2.736f.) remarks that the days observed in the Dura-calendar 'may be classified in three broad groups': (1) Imperial occasions; (2) ordinary public festivals, such as the birthday of Rome, the Neptunalia, the Saturnalia etc.; (3) military events, such as the day of honourable discharge (*honesta missio*). On religious buildings at Dura see M. Rostovtzeff, *Dura-Europos and its Art* (1938) 33f. esp. 51.
23. At Ostia, for example, there are sites of oriental cults on the outskirts, it is true, but the Mithraea are distributed throughout the town; see figure 27 in R. Meiggs, *Roman Ostia* (1960) 382.
24. See *ILS*, 2193, the relief of Ulpius Chresimus, and M.P. Speidel, *The Religion of Iuppiter Dolichenus in the Roman Army* (1978), *EPRO* 63, 12f. and 46f., on priests of Jupiter Dolichenus in the army, with references to Nock and Hoey.
25. For Ostian Mithraea see Meiggs, *Roman Ostia* (1960) 372f. J. P. Kane, 'The Mithraic cult meal in the Greek and Roman environment', *Mithraic Studies* (1975) 2.313–351, observes that the most important Hellenistic mysteries (such as the Dionysiac) continued the classical tradition of combining worship of god with relaxation for men (e.g. in banquets). He adds, 'I believe that the Mithraists, who were brought up in this religious tradition, would neither have wanted nor been able to reject it.' See esp. 348–9. For a good example of a prayer see *ILS*, 372.
26. See *ILS*, 21, for the dedication to Isis, and the accounts in Meiggs, *Roman Ostia* (1960) of other Isiac dedications (369f) and of Vulcan (337–43).
27. See M. le Glay, 'Les syncrétismes dans l'Afrique ancienne', in *Les Syncrétismes dans les religions de l'antiquité* (1975), *EPRO* 46, 127 and 140 (Mercury Silvanus) and 141 (Neptune).
28. *ILS*, 3094.
29. The dates are conveniently set out in M. J. Vermaseren, *Cybele and Attis* (1977) 113f.
30. See E. N. Lane, 'The Italian connection: an aspect of the cult of Men', *Numen*

22, (1975) 235–9 and his longer study, *Corpus Monumentorum Religionis Dei Menis* (1976) in *EPRO* 19.3.

31. See S. K. Heyob, *The Cult of Isis among Women in the Graeco-Roman World* (1975), *EPRO* 51. She remarks (*ibid.*, 129) that even in large cult centres, such as Athens and Rome, female Isiacs 'did not comprise more than half of all devotees.'
32. On Roman Sol see Varro, *de lingua latina*, 5.74 and Tacitus, *Annals*, 15.41 and 74; for the rising, oriental sun see G. H. Halsberghe, *The Cult of Sol Invictus* (1972), *EPRO* 23, esp. 45f. and cf. Hoey (1939) in n. 21 above.
33. See *HA, Heliogabalus*, 1.6; 3.4; 6.7.
34. On the temple at Emesa see Herodian, 5.3.4f. and on the banishment of the god from Rome, Dio Cassius, 79.21; for a discussion see Th. Optendreck, *Die Religionspolitik des Kaisers Elagabal* (1969).
35. See *HA, Aurelian*, esp. 1.3 and 39.2; for his victory at Emesa, 25. 4–6, and for the board of priests, 35.3.
36. L. P. Homo, *Essai sur le règne de l'empereur Aurélien* (1904) 188f. describes Aurelian as *not* a fanatic and considers that the 'Aurelian reform' was almost entirely political.
37. On the privileges granted by Caesar, Josephus, *Antiquities*, 14. 213–16; *ibid.* 16. 162–5; on these see E. M. Smallwood, *The Jews under Roman Rule* (1976) 134f. and 136f. On the revolts see esp. Smallwood, chs. 14–16 and M. Grant, *The Jews in the Roman World* (1973) 173f.
38. See Josephus, *Antiquities*, 15.1.3f. and E. Schürer, *The History of the Jewish People in the Age of Jesus Christ* (1973) 1.296 and n.27.
39. But Josephus, *Antiquities*, 20.11.1 is extremely critical of Florus and is followed by W. H. C. Frend, *Martyrdom and Persecution in the Early Church* (1965) 169.
40. For Petronius see Philo, *Embassy*, 333f. For Roman attitudes see the collection by M. Stern, *Greek and Latin Authors on Jews and Judaism* (1974) 1 and (1980) 2: 1.193f (Cicero); 1.207f (Varro); 2.1–93 (Tacitus). Esp. important is the excursus in Tacitus, *Histories*, 5. 1–13. According to Stern Seneca was the first Latin writer to show hostility to the Jewish religion; see e.g. Augustine, *City of God*, 6.11 and Seneca, *Letters*, 95.47. There were important differences *within* as well as *between* ethnic groups; see e.g. S. Applebaum, *Jews and Greeks in Ancient Cyrene* (1979) 220 for an example among Jews.
41. I am following the distinctions drawn by F. Pollock, 'The Theory of Persecution', in *Essays in Jurisprudence and Ethics* (1882) 144–75.
42. See J. Juster, *Les Juifs dans l'empire romain* (1914) 1.246 and 2.282; Josephus, *Jewish War*, 7.218.
43. On the *laographia* see V. A. Tcherikower and A. Fuks, *Corpus Papyrorum Judaicarum* (1957) 1.60f., as 'a sign of political and cultural degradation'.
44. For a brief account see H. Musurillo, *The Acts of the Christian Martyrs* (1972) lvii-lxii. For discussion see esp. G.E.M. de Ste Croix, 'Why Were the Early Christians Persecuted?' *Past and Present* 26 (1963) 6–38, and the subsequent

papers by A. N. Sherwin-White and de Ste Croix, both in *Past and Present* 27 (1964) 23–27 and 28–33.

45. 'The servants ... falsely accused the Christians of Oedipodean marriages and dinners in the manner of Ṭhyestes ... '; see 'The Martyrs of Lyons', 14 in Musurillo, *The Acts of the Christian Martyrs* (1972) 67, and cf. Minucius Felix, *Octavius*, 9. 5–7 and Tertullian, *Apology* 7. Perhaps one should compare the ritual murder accusation described in C. Roth, *A History of the Jews in England* (1964 edn.) 21–2.
46. Eusebius, *History of the Church*, 6.41 explicitly blames for the persecution not the imperial edict but 'the nameless prophet'.
47. See Pliny, *Letters*, 10. 96–7; R. M. Grant, 'Pliny and the Christians', *HTR* 41 (1948) 273–4 suggests that Pliny's phrasing is derived from Livy's account of the Bacchanalia. For examples of caution on the part of officials see H. Musurillo, *The Acts of the Christian Martyrs* (1972) 93f. (Apollonius) and 89 (the reprieve of thirty days for the Scillitan Martyrs).
48. M. Simon and A. Benoît, *Le Judaisme et le Christianisme antique* (1968) 131–43 refer to 'conservative and reactionary principles'; see also C. Munier, *L'église dans l'empire romain* (1979) 249f. The number of Christian dead was considerable (Simon and Benoît, 143) but so too was Christian expansion (Munier, 257f).
49. Eusebius, *History of the Church*, 6.28 (Maximin) and 6.39 (Decius); Eusebius refers explicitly to Decius' hatred of Philip, described by him as a Christian (6.34).
50. Cf. F. Pollock, 'The Theory of Persecution', 149.
51. For a sociological analysis of sect see B. Wilson, *Magic and the Millennium* (1975) 11f.
52. On Tertullian see T. D. Barnes, *Tertullian* (1970) 99f. and 133f (on garlands); for Origen see *Against Celsus*, 8.73. The general question is well discussed by R. H. Bainton, 'The Early Church and War', *HTR* 39 (1946) 189–212; see too, on Tertullian and Origen, the article by Leclerq, 'Militarisme', in *DAC*, cols. 1122–30.
53. See Eusebius, *History of the Church*, 6.41 and 8.4. For examples of army Christians see *AB*, 10 (1891) 50–2 on Julius Veteranus, who compares his former loyalty as a soldier with his present loyalty to God; and *ibid.*, 127 on the refusal of Fabius to carry the standards as 'imagines' of the dead; for a refusal of gold offered by an emperor see *AB* 9 (1890) 116–23, Typasius Veteranus.
54. See J. R. Knipfing, 'The Libelli of the Decian Persecution', *HTR* 16 (1923) 345–90.
55. See E. A. Thompson, 'The Passio S. Sabae etc.', *Historia* 4 (1955) 331–8; and for the story of Marinus, Eusebius, *History of the Church*, 7.15.
56. See Sulpicius Severus, *Chronica*, 2.33, and on the respite in Gaul see E. Griffe, *La Gaule Chrétienne à l'époque romaine* (1964) 1.220f.
57. The tentative discussion in Nock (1972), 1.30f emphasizes the individual's need for salvation as well as the appeal of Christianity as a historical religion. I

find his remarks on the social effects of the 'monarchic episcopate' more convincing than the last point.

## CHAPTER SIX

1. In their remarkable book *Les Survivances du culte impérial romain* (1920) Bréhier and Battifol sought to provide comfort for Christians in modern imperial Japan by instructing them in the examples set by their forebears in imperial Rome.
2. The distinction (by E. G. Léonard) is usefully discussed by H. Carrier, *The Sociology of Religious Belonging* (1965) 51, who contrasts 'the church of those who profess their religion' (i.e. those who believe they have the experience of salvation, like Donatists) and 'the church of the multitude' (i.e. membership goes by an external rite like baptism). See too *ibid.* 156f. for later examples of transforming pagan customs into Christian practice.
3. Maximin says to the pagans of Nicomedia that their request (to expel Christians) 'was by no means unanimous'; that people are free to follow their own worship; see Eusebius, *History of the Church*, 9.9a. On paganism among the educated see A. H. M. Jones in *The Conflict between Paganism and Christianity in the Fourth Century* esp. 30f. In *Constantine and the Conversion of Europe* (1972) 85f. Jones calls the Christians 'a tiny minority', but the evidence for this is obscure.
4. The main sources are Lactantius, *Deaths of the Persecutors*, 44.5 and Eusebius, *Life of Constantine*, 1.26f. (Artemidorus, *Oneirocriticon*, 2.34f. discusses dreams of gods). For the interpretation of Constantine's 'vision' as a halo-phenomenon see A. H. M. Jones, *Constantine and the Conversion of Europe* (1972) 99f.
5. For the Edict of Milan see Lactantius, *Deaths of the Persecutors*, 48. On Sun worship see esp. A. Piganiol, *L'empereur Constantin* (1932), 45 and esp. 119f. 'Deux empereurs solaires'. Jones, *Constantine and the Conversion of Europe* (1972) 96 says 'the Divine Power ... is described in studiously vague terms'; see *Panegyrici Latini*, 12.26.
6. 'No Christian is to go up to the idol of the Capitol to sacrifice'; *Concilium Eliberitanum* 59 in *PL*, 84.301. Constantine's reception: see *Panegyrici Latini*, 7.8 and 12.19, and J. Straub, 'Konstantins Verzicht auf den Gang zum Kapitol', *Historia* 4 (1955) 297–313.
7. On the Aventine at this period see A. Merlin, *L'Aventin dans l'antiquité* (1906) 333f. This area had become a centre where pagan aristocrats lived as near neighbours to well-known Christians such as Marcella – for whom see *PLRE*, 1, Marcella 2 and Jerome, *Letters* 47.3. For the comment on the 1st-century calendar see Tacitus, *Histories*, 4.40.
8. On the Hellenistic background to house-worship see A. D. Nock, *Conversion* (1933) 50–4 and R. M. Grant, *Early Christianity and Society* (1978) 146f., who compares the Mithraea in private houses. On Constantine's Rome, R.

Krautheimer, *Early Christian and Byzantine Architecture* (1965) 19f. and 42; but he exaggerates slightly – 'no pagan religious building was adaptable to the needs of Christian worship.'

9. J. B. Ward Perkins, *PBSR* 9 (1954) 69–90, discussing the origin of the Christian basilica, concludes (*ibid*., 87) that 'the audience-halls of contemporary court ceremonial may have been the immediate model for the Constantinian basilicas.' On the house as a meeting-centre see J. M. Petersen, 'House-churches in Rome', *Vigiliae Christianae*, 23 (1969) 264f. C. Thomas, *Christianity in Roman Britain to AD 500* (1981) 157f. describes 'congregational churches' as places organized for formal worship, liturgical use and baptismal instruction, and distinguishes them from extra-mural cemetery churches and estate churches.
10. Overthrow of temples: Libanius, *oratio*, 30.34–38 complains of Constantine and Constantius, and (42) reminds Theodosius that the temples are civic ornaments as well as imperial property. Eusebius, *Life of Constantine*, 3.54–58 refers to shrines at Aphaca, Aegae and Heliopolis.
11. Augustine, *Letters*, 29 describes his attempt to persuade the faithful of Hippo to give up their traditional celebrations in church; cf. Paulinus of Nola, *Letters*, 13.11 on the banquet held by Pammachius for his dead wife. The multi-functionality of the old temples seems alien to the purpose of the new churches, but such practices as incubation, sanctuary, feasting, dancing, selling and meeting persisted; see J. G. Davies, *The Secular Use of Church Buildings* (1968) esp. 207f.
12. On 'walls do not make Christians' see P. Courcelle in *Mélanges Carcopino* (1966) 241f. and Augustine, *Confessions*, 8.2.4 for the remark made by Victorinus to the insistent Christian Simplicianus; see too Pope Gregory, *Letters*, 76.
13. The sources and the secondary literature are immense. For Christian attacks see e.g. Clement, *Stromateis*, 7. 28–29; Tertullian, *On Idolatry*; Arnobius, *Against the Pagans*, 6.8 and 17. A late pagan justification of the statue as a living force is in Asclepius 3.23b (W. Scott, *Hermetica* (1924) 1.338–339); and E. R. Dodds, *JRS* (1947) 63 discusses the use of magical statuettes and relates it to neo-Platonism. K. Majewski in *Hommages Renard* (1969) 2.478–84 comments briefly on the social pressures affecting iconoclasm. Cf. n.14 below.
14. N. Baynes, 'Idolatry and the Early Church' (1955) 116f. esp. 125 shows how our understanding of Christian attitudes to images needs to be rooted in the age of Constantine. For the sources see Eusebius, *Life of Constantine*, 3.54f; Augustine, *Letters*, 47.3 treats *Deuteronomy* 7.25 ('Thou shalt not covet their silver or gold ... ') as forbidding the *private* use of pagan art; see *Concilium Eliberitanum* 41 (*domini* and slaves) and 60 (martyrs).
15. For a brief account of Neptune-bathing see G. J. Laing, *Survivals of Roman Religion* (1931) 114f. (Poseidon-Neptune and Saint Nicholas); and on the subject in general see P. Saintyves, 'De l'immersion des idoles antiques etc.' *RHR* 108 (1933) 144–92. Suetonius, *Augustus*, 16 describes Aug.'s punishment

of Neptune. On incense see Laing, 210f. (Prudentius describes idolaters as the 'incense-bearing crowd') and on hymns see M.P. Nilsson *HTR* 38 (1945) 63–9.

16. For discussions of Constantine's claim see W. Seston, 'Constantine as a "Bishop"' *JRS* 37 (1947) 127f. and J. Straub, 'Constantine as koinos episkopos', *Dumbarton Oaks Papers* 21 (1967) 37–56. See Ammianus, 21.16.18 on Constantius.
17. But Fustel de Coulanges, *La Cité Antique* 462, considered that in the Christianized Empire policy was released from the strict rules that had once been laid down by (polytheistic) religion. He was forgetting the fact that politicians and rulers had often been adept at side-stepping the rules and that the bishops of the Church were more than autonomous intercessors with God for personal salvation, they were required to plead with great men for material assistance in this life. Thus Church and state were formally liberated from each other but intertwined in practice.
18. *Cth*, 16.2.6 lays down that exemption from public service 'shall not be granted indiscriminately to all who petition in the name of being clerics ...' For the comment on Gothic valour see Jerome, *Letters*, 107. Goths were despised by Julian (Ammianus, 22.7.8) but the Christian idealizing of them was a natural if only as a moral contrast to Romans; see e.g. Salvian, *de gubernatione dei*, 7.38 and 107.
19. G. Dragon, *Naissance d'une capitale* (1974) esp. 34f. argues that Constantinople was expensive as a foundation but not because of the churches; see e.g. Sozomen, *History of the Church*, 2.3.5; Libanius, *Oratio*, 30.6 and 62.8.
20. On the reaction to Ambrose's appointment see Rufinus, *History of the Church*, 2.11; Paulinus, *Life of Ambrose*, 8; Ambrose, *Letters*, 21. For the governor-like activities of Synesius see his *Letters*, 69 and 78; for the role of the bishop as a spokesman for petitioners see e.g. Basil, *Letters*, 15, 32 and 37.
21. On Melania and Pinianus see the entries in *PLRE*, 1 and the *Lives* of Melania in *AB*, 8. 19f. and *AB*, 22. 7f. On Pliny cf. ch. 4. n. 35.
22. The massacre at Thessalonica in AD 390: Ambrose, *Letters*, 51; Paulinus, *Life of Ambrose*, 24; Sozomen, *History of the Church*, 7.25.
23. On Christian 'compromise with idolatry' see H. Chadwick, *Priscillian of Avila* (1976) 1–3 whose account is largely based on the canons of Elvira (*Concilium Eliberitanum*). The term 'palaeo-Christians' is used by Leclerq, *DAC*, 13.600 of Christians whose beliefs were in conformity with errors 'which are in part explicable in terms of the paganism from which they had come'.
24. For Christian comments on the exchange of gifts see Augustine, *Sermons*, 197 and 198, and Asterius in *PG*, 40 Homily 6. For the pagan customs see M. Meslin, *La fête des Kalendes de janvier* (1970).
25. The religious modern is Johnson; see Boswell, *Life of Johnson* (1958 edn.) 952.
26. On Victorinus, 'a staunch pagan for many years', see *PLRE*, 1 Victorinus 11 and Augustine, *Confessions*, 8.2.3–5. Augustine's conversion may be said to have taken from AD 372 to 386 – see P. Brown, *Augustine of Hippo* (1967).
27. On Anullinus see Eusebius, *History of the Church*, 10.6.4 and 10.7.1;

translated in A.H.M. Jones, *Constantine and the Conversion of Europe* (1972) 86f.

28. *CTh*, 16.10.21.
29. For Tatianus see *ILS*, 2942; but it is not clear whether his religious offices justify the assertion (*PLRE*, 1 Tatianus 4) that he was a 'keen pagan'. Athanasius explicitly criticized Faustinus for his heresy and his bad character; see the entry in *PLRE*, 1.
30. Bauto and Rumoridus were both *magistri militum*; the latter was certainly pagan (Ambrose, *Letters*, 57.3), the former may not have been, but it is not necessary to suppose that the passage in Ambrose implies that Bauto was Christian; cf. J. Wytzes, *Der letzte Kampf des Heidentums in Rom* (1977), *EPRO* 56, 303–4.
31. Ammianus, 22.10.2 tells how Julian would ask at some inopportune moment what a litigant's religion was, and (*ibid.*, 10.7) complains of the edict directed against Christian teachers of rhetoric. Eutropius (10.16.3) praises Julian but says he was 'religionis Christianae nimius insectator.'
32. The comment is made by P. Petit, *Libanius et la vie municipale à Antioche* (1955) 191f. Libanius' speech *For the Temples* (*oratio* 30) is said to be the 'most positive affirmation of his position in the religious controversies' after Julian; see the Loeb Libanius, 2.92.
33. For the pagan appeal to tradition see Symmachus, *relatio* 3. On the martyrs mentioned see Augustine, *Letters*, 16 and 17; W. H. C. Frend, *The Donatist Church* (1952) 55; and T. D. Barnes, *Tertullian* (1970) 261.
34. See H. Bloch, 'The Pagan Revival etc.' in *The Conflict between Paganism and Christianity in the Fourth Century* (1963) 204f. on Flavianus. Julian in effect waited for the death of Constantius before declaring himself; Julian, *Letters*, 26.
35. Arius, for example, seems to have put his doctrines in the form of popular songs called *Thaleia* (banquets). The crowd turbulence was especially partisan at Alexandria; see H. Lietzmann, *A History of the Early Church* (1961) 3.112f.
36. *CTh*, 16.2.4 lays down that any property may be left to the Church. Augustine, *Letters*, 126 refers to the attempt made by people at Hippo to keep the wealthy Pinianus for their church.
37. See C. B. Welles, *Royal Correspondence* etc. (1934) no. 70. 280f. for a grant made by Antiochus to Zeus of Baetocaece. On the size of temple-lands, T. Zawadski in *Eos* 46 (1952) 83–96.
38. Jerome's circle: see J. N. D. Kelly, *Jerome* (1975) 91f. Masculine virtues are accorded to women in *AB* (1890) 116f.
39. *CTh*, 16.10.3 (AD 342) protects extra-mural temples in order to keep up the regular performance of the traditional amusements.
40. G. Combès, for instance, in *La doctrine politique de Saint Augustin* (1927) 304 says of Julian that he came to the rescue of the Church which had suffered from the policies of Constantius.
41. The prefect Gracchus (Jerome, *Letters*, 107.2) overturned some statues, and

others were moved by Probianus (*ILS*, 9354); see A. Chastagnol, *La préfecture urbaine à Rome sous le bas-empire* (1960) 157f.

42. Eusebius, *History of the Church*, 10.8.9f. and *Life of Constantine*, 1.51 makes the most of Licinius' anti-Christian acts.
43. Eugenius' army: see Augustine, *City of God*, 5.26. On Julian cf. above 153; Augustine, however (*enarrationes in Psalmos*, 124.7), says that the troops obeyed Julian's orders to fight but not his orders to worship the pagan gods.
44. Maximin's priests: see Eusebius, *History of the Church*, 9.4. Julian's ideas are clearly stated in the (fragmentary) letter to a priest (288Bf.) and in *Letters*, 20.
45. Eusebius, *History of the Church*, 9.2.4 says that men in the cities sought to please the emperor by attacking Christians.
46. The main source is Julian's heavy satire, the *Misopogon*.
47. Symmachus' plea is given in his *relatio*, 3. The death of Flavianus is recorded by Sozomen, *History of the Church*, 7.22. On the war with Eugenius see Augustine, *City of God*, 5.25f.
48. For Alfenius Ceionius Julianus signo Kamenius, vicarius of Africa, see *ILS*, 1264 and *PLRE*, 1, Julianus 25.
49. The case for Christian industry in reading pagan authors is well put by A. Cameron, 'Paganism and Literature in Late Fourth Century Rome', *Entretiens sur l'antiquité classique* 23 (1977) 1f. esp. 20.
50. But E. Stein, *Histoire du Bas-empire* (1959) 213f. argues against the common opinion that a pagan reaction had little chance of succeeding by the end of the fourth century; he points out that Christianity soon gave way to Islam in countries where it seemed well-established.
51. On the edict see Julian, *Letters*, 36; *CTh*, 13.3.5; and Ammianus, 22.10.7.
52. Ammianus, 17.7.10 refers to the silence of the pontifical books on the god of earthquakes. Augustine (*Letters*, 91.5) complains bitterly that no amount of allegory can explain away Jupiter's misconduct.
53. See Ammianus, 22.11.4 for bishop George. For Suffectana see Augustine, *Letters*, 50, and for Calama, *Letters*, 90–1, from and to Nectarius; on the sack of Rome, *sermo*, 197.
54. See P. Brown, 'Aspects of the Christianization of the Roman Aristocracy', *JRS* 51 (1961) 10.
55. On the emperor as the counterpart of God see S. Runciman, *The Byzantine Theocracy* (1973), 2f. and for a detailed study of Eusebius see J.-M. Sansterre in *Byzantion* 42 (1972) 131f. and 532f. As regards the western part of the Empire W. Ullmann, *Medieval Political Thought* (1975 edn.) 19f. argues that the church of Rome became established as a governmental institution that could have far more influence on imperial policy than was possible in the East.
56. The expression is from Tertullian, *On Idolatry*, 1 and 14.
57. For Lactantius' arguments see his *Divine Institutes*, 1.1.5 and 2.2–3.
58. Laws against superstition: see e.g. *CTh*, 16.10.2 and 3; Augustine discusses the Ciceronian distinction in *City of God*, 4.30 and denies the Academic any authority in matters religious. A. D. Momigliano in his paper, 'Popular religious beliefs and the late Roman historians' (1972) 1–18 trenchantly

remarks (11) that the 'Christians ... set up their palisade between religion and superstition to coincide with the frontier between Christianity and Paganism.'

59. See esp. Augustine, *Letters*, 138 and 189. E. O. Isichei, *Political Thinking and Social Experience* (1964) 72–80 portrays Augustine's defence of the Empire as more important than 'his scattered attacks on imperialism.'

60. D. S. Wallace-Hadrill, *The Greek Patristic View of Nature* (1968) esp. 101f. contrasts the lack of meaning in (some) pagan writers' references to nature with the approach of the fathers who saw nature 'more as an ordered system which they felt revealed something more beyond itself.'

61. Cicero's view, for example (cf. above ch. 2. n.84), is that modern 'science' has undone the foundations of primitive belief in earlier Rome, *not* that knowledge has corroborated or modified religion. He has no idea of coming to understand the primitive mind and relating it to the contemporary through science, theories of myth and so on. For the modern experience see F. E. Manuel, *The Eighteenth Century Confronts the Gods* (1959) 8f.

62. Eusebius, *History of the Church*, 1.4.10 says that the religion proclaimed through Christ's teaching is none other than 'the first most ancient and most primitive of all religions, discovered by Abraham ... ' whose *floruit* was contemporary with Assyria, before Rome, according to Augustine, *City of God*, 18.2.2.

63. Augustine, *City of God*, 5.25f.

64. Orosius says he was overwhelmed by the misery of the present until he began to investigate the disasters of the past; *Against the Pagans*, prologue 13f. Cf. Augustine, *City of God*, 1.

# *Bibliography*

## 1

This short list refers to those books, manuals and papers which have been my basic works of reference while I was working on this subject.

BROWN, P. 'Aspects of the Christianization of the Roman Aristocracy', *JRS* 51 (1961) 1–11; reprinted in *Religion and Society in the Age of St Augustine* (1972) 161–82.

— *Augustine of Hippo* (1967).

GEFFCKEN, J. *The Last Days of Greco-Roman Paganism*, trs. by S. MacCormack (1978).

GELLNER, E. 'Concepts and Society', in *Rationality*, ed. Bryan Wilson (1977), 18–49.

LATTE, K. *Römische Religionsgeschichte* (1960).

MOMIGLIANO, A. D. (ed.) *The Conflict between Paganism and Christianity in the Fourth Century* (1963).

NOCK, A. D. *Essays on Religion and the Ancient World*, ed. Z. Stewart, 2 vols (1972).

TOUTAIN, J. *Les cultes païens dans l'empire romain* (1907).

WISSOWA, G. *Religion und Kultus der Römer* (1912).

## 2

## List of works cited in the notes

ABBOTT, F. F., and JOHNSON, A. C. *Municial Administration in the Roman Empire* (1926).

ALFÖLDI, A. *Die monarchische Repräsentation im römischen Kaiserreiche* (1970); reprinted from *MDAIR* 49 (1934) and 50 (1935).

ALTHEIM, F. *A History of Roman Religion* (1938).

AMIT, M. 'Concordia', *Iura* 13 (1962) 133–69.

APPLEBAUM, S. *Jews and Greeks in Ancient Cyrene* (1979).

ASTIN, A. E. 'Leges Aelia et Fufia', *Latomus* 23 (1964) 421–45.

AVERY, W. T. 'The adoratio purpurae' (1940), *MAAR* 17.

BADIAN, E. 'Sulla's Augurate', *Arethusa* 1 (1968) 26–46.
BAINTON, R. H. 'The Early Church and War', *HTR* 39 (1946) 189–212.
BARDON, H. 'La naissance d'un temple', *REL* 33 (1955) 166–82.
BARNES, T. D. *Tertullian* (1970).
BASANOFF, V. *Evocatio* (1947).
BAYET, J. *Histoire politique et psychologique de la religion romaine* (1957).
— *Croyances et rites dans la Rome antique* (1971).
BAYNES, N. 'Idolatry and the Early Church', in *Byzantine Studies and Other Essays* (1955) 116–43.
BEAUJEU, M. *La religion romaine à l'apogée de l'empire* (1955).
— 'La religion de la classe sénatoriale à l'époque des Antonins', *Hommages J. Bayet* (1964) 54–75.
— 'Les constantes religieuses du scepticisme', *Hommages Renard* (1969) 2.61–73.
BENOÎT, F. *Mars et Mercure* (1959).
BENVENISTE, E. *Le vocabulaire des institutions indo-européennes* (1969).
BICKERMANN, E. 'Consecratio, le culte des souverains dans l'Empire Romain' (1972), *Entretiens Hardt* (19) 3–25.
BLEICKEN, J. 'Oberpontifex und Pontifikalkollegium', *Hermes* 85 (1957) 345–66.
BLOCH, H. 'A New Document', *HTR* 38 (1945) 199–244.
— 'The Pagan Revival in the West at the End of the Fourth Century', in *The Conflict between Paganism and Christianity in the Fourth Century*, ed. A. D. Momigliano (1963) 193–218.
BOISSIER, G. *La religion romaine d'Auguste aux Antonins* (1884).
BÖMER, F. 'Kybele in Rom', *MDAIR* 71 (1964) 130–51.
BOUCHÉ-LECLERQ, A. *Les pontifes de l'ancienne Rome* (1871).
BOYANCÉ, P. 'Sur la théologie de Varron', *REA* 57 (1955) 57–85.
BRACKERTZ, U. *Zum Problem der Schutzgottheiten griechischer Städte* (1976).
BRAND, C. E. *Roman Military Law* (1968).
BRÉHIER, L., and BATTIFOL, P. *Les survivances du culte impérial romain* (1920).
BRISCOE, J. *A Commentary on Livy 31–33* (1973).
BRUHL, A. *Liber Pater* (1953).
BRUNT, P. A. 'Charges of Provincial Maladministration under the Early Principate', *Historia* 10 (1961) 189–227.
— Review of Fears, *JRS* 69 (1979) 168–74.
BUCKLAND, W. W. *A Text-Book of Roman Law* (revised Stein, 1966).
BURKE, P. *Popular Culture in Early Modern Europe* (1978).
CAGNAT, R. L. V. *L'armée romaine d'Afrique* (1892).

CAMERON, A. 'Paganism and Literature in Late Fourth Century Rome', in *Entretiens sur l'antiquité classique* 23 (1977) 1–31.

CARCOPINO, J. *Histoire romaine* (1950) vol. 3 pt. 2.

CARRETONI, M. G. 'Séance du 13 Mars 1973' in *REL* 51 (1973) 32–4.

CARRIER, H. *The Sociology of Religious Belonging* (1965).

CERFAUX, L., and TONDRIAU, J. *Le culte des souverains* (1957).

CHADWICK, H. *Priscillian of Avila* (1976).

CHARLESWORTH, M. P. 'Some Observations upon Ruler-Cult', *HTR* 28 (1935) 5–44.

— 'The Virtues of a Roman Emperor', *Proceedings of the British Academy* 23 (1937) 105–34.

CHASTAGNOL, A. *La préfecture urbaine à Rome sous le bas-empire* (1960).

COMBÈS, G. *La doctrine politique de Saint Augustin* (1927).

COMBÈS, R. *Imperator* (1966).

COURCELLE, P. 'Parietes faciunt Christianos?', in *Mélanges Carcopino* (1966) 241–8.

COURTNEY, E. 'Notes on Cicero', *Classical Review* NS 10 (1960) 95–9.

COUSIN, J. 'La crise religieuse de 207 avant J–C', *RHR* 126 (1943) 15–41.

CRAWFORD, M. *Roman Republican Coinage* (1974).

CUMONT, F. *Les religions orientales dans l'empire romain* (1929).

DAGRON, G. *Naissance d'une capitale* (1974).

DALY, L. W. 'Vota publica pro salute alicuius', *TAPA* 81 (1950) 164–8.

DANIELS, C. M. 'The role of the Roman army in the spread and practice of Mithraism', *Mithraic Studies* (1975) 2.249–74.

DAVIES, J. G. *The Secular Use of Church Buildings* (1968).

DE AZEVEDO, M. C. 'I "Capitolia" dell' impero Romano', *Atti della Pontificia Accademia Romana di Archeologia, Memorie 5* (1941) 1–76.

DEININGER, J. *Die Provinziallandtage der römischen Kaiserzeit* (1965).

DELLA CASA, A. *Nigidio Figulo* (1962).

DEONNA, W. 'La légende d'Octave-Auguste', *RHR* 83 (1921) 32–58 and 163–95, and 84 (1921) 77–107.

DE PIGHI, G. B. *De ludis saecularibus* (1965).

DE STE CROIX, G. E. M. 'Why Were the Early Christians Persecuted?', *Past and Present* 26 (1963) 6–38.

— 'A Rejoinder', *Past and Present* 27 (1964) 28–33.

DODDS, E. R. 'Theurgy and its relation to NeoPlatonism', *JRS* 37 (1947) 55–69.

— *The Greeks and the Irrational* (1951).

DUMÉZIL, G. *Archaic Roman Religion* (1970).

DUTHOY, R. 'Les Augustales', *ANRW* 16.2 (1978) 1254–309.

EHRENBERG, V. and JONES, A.H.M. *Documents Illustrating the Reigns of Augustus and Tiberius*[2] (1976).
ETIENNE, R. *Le culte impérial dans la péninsule ibérique* (1958).
FABRE, P. 'Minime romano sacro', *REA* 42 (1940) 419–24.
FARNELL, L. R. *Cults of the Greek States* (1907).
FEARS, J. R. *Princeps a diis electus* (1977), *MAAR* 26.
FERGUSON, W. S. 'The Attic Orgeones', *HTR* 37 (1944) 61–130.
FINER, S. E. *The Man on Horseback* (1976).
FINLEY, M. I. *The Ancient Economy* (1973).
FISHWICK, D. 'The Institution of the Provincial Cult in Africa Proconsularis', *Hermes* 92 (1964) 342–63.
— 'Provincial Ruler Worship in the West', *ANRW* (1978) 16.2.1201–53.
FOWLER, W. W. *The Roman Festivals of the Period of the Republic* (1899).
— *The Religious Experience of the Roman People* (1922).
FRANK, T. 'The Sacred Treasure and the Rate of Manumission', *AJP* 53 (1932) 360–3.
FRASER, P. M. *Ptolemaic Alexandria* (1972).
FREND, W. H. C. *The Donatist Church* (1952).
— *Martyrdom and Persecution in the Early Church* (1965).
FREYBURGER, G. 'La supplication d'action de grâces sous le Haut-Empire', *ANRW* 16.2 (1978) 1418–39.
GAGÉ, J. 'Divus Augustus', *Revue Archéologique* 34 (1931) 11–41.
GARCÍA Y BELLIDO, A. *Les religions orientales dans l'Espagne romaine* (1967), *EPRO* 5.
GARLAN, Y. *La guerre dans l'antiquité* (1972).
GARZETTI, A. *From Tiberius to the Antonines* (1974).
GILLIAM, J. F. 'The Roman Military Feriale', *HTR* 47 (1954) 183–96.
— 'On *Divi* under the Severi', *Hommages Renard* (1969) 2.284–289.
GJERSTAD, E. *Early Rome* (1960 etc.).
GOAR, R. J. *Cicero and the State Religion* (1972).
GRANT, M. *Roman Imperial Money* (1954).
— *Roman Myths* (1971).
— *The Jews in the Roman World* (1973).
GRANT, R. M. 'Pliny and the Christians', *HTR* 41 (1948) 273–4.
— *Early Christianity and Society* (1978).
GRIFFE, E. *La Gaule Chrétienne à l'époque romaine* (1964).
GRODZYNSKI, D. 'Superstitio', *REA* 76 (1974) 36–61.
GROS, P. *Aurea Templa* (1976).
HAHM, D. E. 'Roman Nobility and the Three Major Priesthoods 218–167 B.C.', *TAPA* 94 (1963) 73–85.
HALKIN, L. *La supplication d'action de grâces chez les Romains* (1953).

HALSBERGHE, G. H. *The Cult of Sol Invictus* (1972), *EPRO* 23.
HAMMOND, M. *The Antonine Monarchy* (1959).
HANDS, A. R. *Charities and Social Aid in Greece and Rome* (1968).
HANSON, J. A. *Roman Theater-Temples* (1959).
HARDY, E. G. *Roman Laws and Charters* (1912).
HARRIS, W. V. *War and Imperialism in Republican Rome* (1979).
HAUSER, A. *A Social History of Art* (1962).
HENZEN, G. *Acta Fratrum Arvalium* (1874).
HEURGON, J. *Trois études sur le 'ver sacrum'* (1957).
HEYOB, S. K. *The Cult of Isis among Women in the Graeco-Roman World* (1975), *EPRO* 51.
HOEY, A. S. 'Official Policy Towards Oriental Cults in the Roman Army', *TAPA* 70 (1939) 456–81.
HOMO, L. P. *Essai sur le règne de l'empereur Aurélien* (1904).
HOPKINS, K. *Conquerors and Slaves* (1979).
ISICHEI, E. O. *Political Thinking and Social Experience* (1964).
JONES, A. H. M. 'The Social Background of the Struggle between Paganism and Christianity', in *The Conflict between Paganism and Christianity in the Fourth Century,* ed. A. D. Momigliano (1963) 17–37.
— *Constantine and the Conversion of Europe* (1972).
JUSTER, J. *Les Juifs dans l'empire romain* (1914).
KANE, J. P. 'The Mithraic cult meal in the Greek and Roman environment', *Mithraic Studies* (1975) 2.313–51.
KELLY, J. N. D. *Jerome* (1975).
KNIPFING, J. R. 'The Libelli of the Decian Persecution', *HTR* 16 (1923) 345–90.
KOCH, C. 'Gottheit und Mensch', in *Religio*, ed. O. Seel (1960).
KOTULA, T. 'Les origines des assemblées provinciales dans l'Afrique romaine', *Eos* 52 (1962) 147–67.
KÖVES, TH. 'Zum Empfang der Magna Mater in Rom', *Historia* 12 (1963) 321–47.
KÖVES-ZULAUF, TH. 'Plinius der Ältere und die römische Religion', *ANRW* (1978) 16.1.187–288.
KRAUTHEIMER, R. *Early Christian and Byzantine Architecture* (1965).
KUHFELDT, O. *De Capitolis Imperii Romani* (1883).
LAING, G. J. *Survivals of Roman Religion* (1931).
LAMBRECHTS, P. 'Auguste et la religion romaine', *Latomus* 6 (1947) 177–91.
LANE, E. 'The Italian connection: an aspect of the cult of Men', *Numen* 22 (1975) 235–9.
— *Corpus Monumentorum Religionis Dei Menis* (1976), *EPRO* 19.3.

LARSEN, J. A. O. *Representative Government in Greek and Roman History* (1955).

LE BONNIEC, H. *Le culte de Cérès à Rome* (1958).

— 'Aspects religieux de la guerre à Rome', in *Problèmes de la guerre à Rome*, ed. J. P. Brisson (1969) 101–15.

LECLERQ, H. Articles in *DAC* s.vv. Militarisme and Paléo-Chrétiens.

LE GLAY, M. *Saturne Africain* (1966).

— 'Les syncrétismes dans l'Afrique ancienne', 123–51 in *Les Syncrétismes dans les religions de l'antiquité*, ed. F. Dunand and P. Lévêque (1975), *EPRO* 46.

LENAGHAN, J. O. *A Commentary on Cicero's Oration de haruspicum responso* (1969).

LENORMANT, M. F. 'Les Bétyles', *RHR* 3 (1881) 31–53.

LEWIS, I. M. *Ecstatic Religion* (1971).

LEWIS, M. W. H. *The Official Priests of Rome under the Julio-Claudians* (1955), *MAAR* 16.

LIEBESCHUETZ, J. H. W. G. *Continuity and Change in Roman Religion* (1979).

LIETZMANN, H. *A History of the Early Church* (1961).

LUCE, T. J. 'Political Propaganda on Roman Republican Coins 92–82 BC', *AJA* 72 (1968) 25–39.

MAAS, E. 'Heilige Steine', *Rheinisches Museum* 78 (1929) 1–25.

MACMULLEN, R. 'Roman Imperial Building in the Provinces', *Harvard Studies in Classical Philology* 64 (1959) 207–35.

MAJEWSKI, K. 'Les images de culte dans l'antiquité', *Hommages Renard* (1969) 2.478–84.

MALAISE, M. *Les conditions de pénétration et de diffusion des cultes égyptiens en Italie* (1972), *EPRO* 22.

MANUEL, F. E. *The Eighteenth Century Confronts the Gods* (1959).

MARTIN, C. 'The Gods of the Imperial Roman Army', *History Today* 19 (1969) 255–63.

MEIGGS, R. *Roman Ostia* (1960).

MELLOR, R. *Thea Rōmē: the worship of the goddess Roma in the Greek world* (1975).

MERLIN, A. *L'Aventin dans l'antiquité* (1906).

MESLIN, M. *La fête des Kalendes de janvier* (1970).

MICHELS, A. K. *The Calendar of the Roman Republic* (1967).

MILLAR, F. *The Emperor in the Roman World* (1977).

MÓCSY, A. *Pannonia* (1974).

MOMIGLIANO, A. D. 'Popular religious beliefs and the late Roman historians', in *Studies in Church History* 8 (1972) 1–18.

MOMMSEN, T. *Handbuch der römischen Altertümer* (1887).
MONTANARI, E. 'Mens', in *Religioni e Civiltà* 2 (1976) 173–235.
MORGAN, M. G. 'The Portico of Metellus', *Hermes* 99 (1971) 480–505.
MUNIER, C. *L'église dans l'empire romain* (1979).
MUSURILLO, H. *The Acts of the Christian Martyrs* (1972).
NILSSON, M. P. 'Pagan Divine Service in Late Antiquity', *HTR* 38 (1945) 63–9.
NOCK, A. D. *Conversion* (1933).
— In *Cambridge Ancient History* 10 (1934) 481 f.
NORTH, J. A. Review of Weinstock, 'Praesens Divus', *JRS* 65 (1975) 171–7.
— 'Conservatism and Change in Roman Religion', *PBSR* 44 (1976) 1–12.
OGILVIE, R. M. *A Commentary on Livy 1–5* (1965).
— *The Romans and Their Gods* (1969).
OPTENDRECK, TH. *Die Religionspolitik des Kaisers Elagabal* (1969).
PARKE, H. W. *Festivals of the Athenians* (1977).
PERKINS, J. B. WARD, 'Constantine and the Origins of the Christian Basilica', *PBSR* 9 (1954) 69–90.
PETERSEN, J. M. 'House-churches in Rome', *Vigiliae Christianae* 23 (1969) 264–72.
PETIT, P. *Libanius et la vie municipale à Antioche* (1955).
PICHON, R. 'Le rôle religieux des femmes dans l'ancienne Rome', in *Conférences au Musée Guimet* (1912) 77–135.
PIGANIOL, A. *L'empereur Constantin* (1932).
PIPPIDI, D. M. 'Le numen Augusti', *REL* 9 (1931) 83–112.
PLATNER, S., and ASHBY, T. *A Topographical Dictionary of Ancient Rome* (1929).
POLLOCK, F. 'The Theory of Persecution', in *Essays in Jurisprudence and Ethics* (1882) 144–75.
RAMSAY, H. G. 'A third century a.C. building program', *Antiquité Classique* 4 (1935) 419–47.
RAWSON, E. 'Scipio, Laelius, Furius and the Ancestral Religion', *JRS* 63 (1973) 161–74.
— 'Religion and Politics in the Late Second Century BC at Rome', *Phoenix* 28 (1974) 193–212.
ROBERT, L. 'Études sur les inscriptions et la topographie de la Grèce centrale', *BCH* 59 (1935) 193 f.
ROBERTSON, R. *The Sociological Interpretation of Religion* (1970).
ROMER, F. E. 'A Numismatic Date for the Departure of Caesar', *TAPA* 108 (1978) 192–6.
ROSE, H. J. *Ancient Roman Religion* (1948).

ROSTOVTZEFF, M. 'L'empereur Tibère et le culte impérial', *Revue Historique* 163 (1930) 1–36.

— *Dura-Europos and its Art* (1938).

— *The Social and Economic History of the Hellenistic World* (1941).

ROTH, C. *A History of the Jews in England* (1964 edn).

RUNCIMAN, S. *The Byzantine Theocracy* (1973).

RYBERG, I. SCOTT, *Rites of the State Religion in Roman Art* (1955), *MAAR* 22.

SAID, E. W. *Orientalism* (1978).

SAINTYVES, P. 'De l'immersion des idoles antiques aux baignades des statues saintes dans le Christianisme', *RHR* 108 (1933) 144–92.

SANSTERRE, J. M. 'Eusèbe de Césarée et la naissance de la théorie "césaropapiste"', *Byzantion* 42 (1972) 131–95 and 532–93.

SAUTER, F. *Der römische Kaiserkult bei Martial und Statius* (1934).

SCHILLING, R. *La religion romaine de Vénus* (1954).

— 'La place de la Sicile dans la religion romaine', *Kokalos* 10 (1964–5) 259–83.

SCHÜRER, E. *The History of the Jewish People in the Age of Jesus Christ*, rev. Vermes, Millar and Black (1973).

SCOTT, K. 'Emperor-Worship in Ovid', *TAPA* 61 (1930) 43–69.

— 'The Significance of Statues in Precious Metals in Emperor-Worship', *TAPA* 62 (1931) 101–23.

— 'The Elder and Younger Pliny on Emperor-Worship', *TAPA* 63 (1932) 156–65.

— *The Imperial Cult under the Flavians* (1936).

— 'Notes on Augustus' religious policy', *ARW* 35 (1938) 121–30.

SCOTT, W. *Hermetica* 1 (1924).

SEGUIN, R. 'La religion de Scipion l'Africain', *Latomus* 33 (1974) 3–21.

SESTON, W. 'Constantine as a "Bishop"', *JRS* 37 (1947) 127–31.

SHATZMANN, I. *Senatorial Wealth and Roman Politics* (1975).

SHERWIN-WHITE, A. N. 'Why were the Early Christians persecuted? an amendment', *Past and Present* 27 (1964) 23–7.

SHIPLEY, F. W. *Chronology of the Building Operations in Rome from the Death of Caesar to the Death of Augustus* (1931), *MAAR* 9.

SIMON, M., and BENOÎT, A. *Le Judaisme et le Christianisme antique* (1968).

SIMPSON, C. J. 'The Date of Dedication of the Temple of Mars Ultor', *JRS* 67 (1977) 91–5.

SMALLWOOD, E. M. *The Jews under Roman Rule* (1976).

SPEIDEL, M. P. *The Religion of Iuppiter Dolichenus in the Roman Army* (1978), *EPRO* 63.

STAMBAUGH, J. E. 'The Functions of Roman Temples', *ANRW* 16.1 (1978) 554–608.

STEIN, E. *Histoire du Bas-Empire* (1959).

STERN, M. *Greek and Latin Authors on Jews and Judaism* (1974) 1 and (1980) 2.

STRAUB, J. 'Konstantins Verzicht auf den Gang zum Kapitol', *Historia* 4 (1955) 297–313.

— 'Constantine as koinos episkopos', *Dumbarton Oaks Papers* 21 (1967) 37–56.

STRONG, D. E. 'The Administration of Public Building in Rome', *BICS* 15 (1968) 97–109.

SZEMLER, G. J. 'Religio, Priesthoods and Magistracies in the Roman Republic', *Numen* 18 (1971) 103–31.

— *The Priests of the Roman Republic* (1972).

—'Sacerdotes Publici and the Ius Sententiam Dicendi', *Hermes* 104 (1976) 53–8.

TAYLOR, L. R. 'Augustales, Seviri Augustales and Seviri', *TAPA* 45 (1914) 231–53.

— 'The Worship of Augustus in Italy during his Lifetime', *TAPA* 51 (1920) 116–33.

— *Local Cults in Etruria* (1923).

— 'Tiberius' Refusals of Divine Honours', *TAPA* 60 (1929) 87–101.

— *The Divinity of the Roman Emperor* (1931).

— 'The "Sellisternium" and the Theatrical "Pompa"', *CP* 30 (1935) 122–30.

— 'Caesars' Colleagues in the Pontifical College', *AJP* 63 (1942) 385–412.

— 'Symbols of the Augurate on coins of the Caecilii Metelli', *AJA* 48 (1944) 352–6.

— *Party Politics in the Age of Caesar* (1949).

TCHERIKOWER, V. A., and FUKS, A. *Corpus Papyrorum Judaicarum* 1 (1957).

THOMAS, C. *Christianity in Roman Britain to AD 500* (1981).

THOMPSON, E. A. 'The Passio S. Sabae and Early Visigothic Society', *Historia* 4 (1955) 331–8.

TOYNBEE, A. J: *A Study of History*, Somervell Abridgement of Vols 1–6 (1946).

— *An Historian's Approach to Religion* (1955).

— *Hannibal's Legacy* (1965).

TOYNBEE, J. M. 'The Ara Pacis Reconsidered', *Proceedings of the British Academy* 39 (1953) 67–96.

TRAN TAM TINH, V. *Essai sur le culte d'Isis à Pompeii* (1964).

TUDOR, H. *Political Myth* (1972).

TURCAN, R. *Sénèque et les religions orientales* (1967).

ULLMANN, W. *Medieval Political Thought* (1975).

VAN DOREN, M. 'Peregrina Ṣacra', *Historia* 3 (1954) 488–97.

VERMASEREN, M. J. *Cybele and Attis* (1977).

WALLACE-HADRILL, D. S. *The Greek Patristic View of Nature* (1968).

WALTZING, J-P. *Étude historique sur les corporations professionelles chez les Romains* (1895).

WATT, W. M. 'The Place of Religion in the Islamic and Roman Empire', *Numen* 9 (1962) 110–27.

WEBER, M. *The Sociology of Religion* (1971 edn).

WEINBROT, H. *Augustus Caesar in 'Augustan' England* (1978).

WEINSTOCK, S. *Divus Julius* (1971).

— 'Pax and the "Ara Pacis"', *JRS* 50 (1960) 44–58.

WELLES, B. *The Royal Correspondence of Hellenistic Kings* (1934).

WHITEHEAD, A. N. *Religion in the Making* (1926).

WILKES, J. J. *Dalmatia* (1969).

WILSON, A. J. N. *Emigration from Italy in the Republican Age of Rome* (1966).

WILSON, B. *Magic and the Millennium* (1975).

WYTZES, J. *Der letzte kampf des Heidentums in Rom* (1977), *EPRO* 56.

*Yale Classical Studies*, 'The Feriale Duranum', by R. O. Fink, A. S. Hoey and W. F. Snyder (1940).

ZAWADSKI, T. 'Quelques remarques sur l'étendue et l'accroissement des domaines des grands temples en Asie Mineure', *Eos* 46 (1952) 83–96.

ZWAENEPOL, A. 'L'inspiration religieuse de l'impérialisme romain', *Antiquité Classique* 18 (1949) 5–23.

# Index

## Principal Names and Themes


Aelian Fufian Laws, 45
Aeneas, 5, 7, 11
Aesculapius, 3, 55, 99
Alexandria, 90, 124, 127, 131, 160
Ambrose, St., 146, 148, 152, 155, 161
Ammianus Marcellinus, 160
Amphiaraus, at Oropus, 47, 55
Anthropomorphism, 2f., 23, 35, 54, 106, 163
M. Antoninus Pius, 82
M. Antonius (triumvir), 52, 56, 63, 68, 91
Apollo, 68, 70, 72, 91, 120
  at Delos, 16
  games for, 36
  temple at Rome, 92
Apollonius of Tyana, 160
Apotheosis, 81f., 86, 93, 104
Archaism, 20, 31, 55, 71, 95, 130, 166
Army (Roman), 99, 115, 119, 131
Arnobius, 143
Arval Brethren, 72, 145
Asylum, 16, 93f.
Athena, 5, 38
Attis, 112, 119
Augurs (augury), 14, 18, 24, 67, 97
Augustales, 76, 98
Augustine, St., 43, 144, 149, 161–2, 164
Augustus, 7, 18, 28, 55, 66, 77, 90
  altar of, 14
  Augustanism, 64f., 67
  as god, 81, 84, 87
  his gods, 49f., 68, 91, 120, 144
  and Jews, 124
  and Roma, 76, 87
Aurelian, 102, 115, 121
M. Aurelius Antoninus, 59, 85
Aventine, 8, 14, 42, 70, 140

Bacchanalia, 40, 113, 118
Bellona, 10, 71, 159
Bona Dea, 14, 46

Caecina, Aulus, 47
Caesar, C. Julius, 5, 7, 15, 24, 28, 31, 43
  cult of, 51f., 55, 69
  and deification, 44, 60
  his games, 24
  on Gauls, 58
  and Jews, 124
  as pontiff, 32
  religious aims, 63
  and Roma, 50
Caligula, 82, 91, 105, 114, 127
Capitol, 11, 15, 29, 34, 39, 172
  triad on, 11, 50, 119
  vows on, 91, 138
Caracalla, 83, 84, 93, 120
Cato the younger, 39, 167
Ceres, 3, 5, 8, 37
Christianity, 49, 58, 101, 112, 133, 151
  and Constantine, 139, 173
  offshoot of Judaism, 108, 123, 142
  and oriental religions, 122
Cicero: *see* Tullius
Claudius, 26, 82, 88, 95, 115, 119
Clement of Alexandria, 143
Cologne (oppidum Ubiorum), 77, 88
Commodus, 91f., 115
Concord, temple of, 34, 44, 51, 70
Constantine, 135f., 161, 167
  and the church, 145, 151
  conversion of, 137f.
Constantinople, 141, 146

Constantius II, 145, 157
Cybele, 34, 40, 111, 119, 121, 159

Decius, 130–1
Demeter, 3, 37
Diana, 14, 42, 70
 at Ephesus, 16
Dio Chrysostom, 107
Diocletian, 81, 128, 130f.
Dionysius of Halicarnassus, 111
Dionysus (see also Bacchanalia), 5, 40, 90, 112, 123
Dioscuri, 42, 91
Divus Julius, temple of, 52, 94
Domitian, 60, 82, 93, 96
Donatism, 146
Druids, 59
Dura calendar, 100, 116

Elagabalus, 84, 93, 120
Ephesus, 50, 92, 128
Epulones, 30
Etruria (Etruscan), 12, 19, 47, 62, 104, 119, 159
Eugenius, 156f., 159
Euhemerism, 55, 85, 133, 164
Eusebius, of Caesarea, 129, 136, 141, 144, 161

Fetials, college of, 9, 20, 48, 71, 96
Flamines, 16f., 24, 56
 flamen Dialis, 17, 30, 48, 64, 72f.
 of Mars, 32
 of Quirinus, 17
Flavianus (Virius Nicomachus), 153, 159
Fortuna, 73, 104
 temple of, 49

Galerius, 128, 167
Games (*ludi*), 14, 24f., 91, 100
 Megalesian, 26
 Plebeian, 26
 Roman, 26, 36
 Secular, 64
Genius, 76, 99, 128, 160
Gordian, 84, 86
Gracchi, 28, 30, 42f., 51
Gratian, 155, 167
Gregory I, Pope, 143

Hadrian, 50, 83, 124
Hannibal, 22, 33, 37, 39, 45
Hellenization, 23, 35, 37, 125
Hercules, 7, 29, 55, 86, 91, 130, 161
Herod the Great, 125
Homer, 107
Honos and Virtus, temple of, 18, 28, 34, 49

Isis, 108, 111, 118, 123
 temple of, 113–4

Janus, temple of, 71
Jerome, St., 147
Jerusalem, the Temple, 123f., 133, 142
Jews (Judaism), 54, 58, 65n.3, 142, 166
 persecuted, 123f.
 of the Diaspora, 124, 126
Jovian, 167
Julian the Apostate, 84, 99, 147, 152, 155
 at Antioch, 158
 his paganism, 157, 160
Juno, 3, 5
 Moneta, 11
 Regina, 5, 38
 of Veii, 3
Jupiter, 10, 28, 51, 80, 86, 90, 126, 130, 157
 Capitolinus, 10, 35, 42, 103
 Custos, 93
 Dolichenus, 109, 117, 118
 Latiaris, 6
 Optimus Maximus, 4, 6, 13, 39, 69f., 118
 Stator, 104, 106
 Tonans, 68
 his adultery, 160, 165
 and banquets, 19, 30
 and Christ, 133
 on coins, 29
 games, 91
 punishes the wicked, 62
 and sacred spring, 36
 as sky-god, 2f., 12
Juvenal, 111, 117

Lactantius, 137, 162
Lares, 29, 76
Lectisternium, 36
Libanius, 152f.
Liber, 40, 112, 159
Libertas, temple of, 28, 44
Licinius, 113, 137, 156
Livy, 9, 17f., 30, 37f., 41, 52
Lucian, 86
Lucretia, 166
Lucretius, 53, 56f.

Ma, 114
Maecenas, 66, 92
Marius, 28, 30, 42, 49, 52
Mars, 5, 12, 17, 80
  Ultor, 3, 68f., 74
Maxentius, 137f.
Maximin Daia, 136, 156f., 160
Maximinus, C. Julius, 16, 130
Men (deity), 119
Mens, temple of, 34
Mercury, 118
Metellus, portico of, 28
Minerva, 5, 39, 60, 91, 93, 100
Minucius Felix, 62, 105
Mithras, 108, 115, 117, 120, 159
Monotheism, 3f., 121f.

Neptune, 4, 91, 100, 118, 144
Nero, 15, 60, 82, 85f., 92, 95
Nerva, 97
P. Nigidius Figulus, 47
Numa Pompilius, 54, 166

Olympus, 2, 85, 169
Origen, 131
Ostia, 117
Ovid, 43, 70

Palatine, 68, 69, 112
Peace, 71, 118
Pessinus, 34, 112, 115
Petronius, 98
Philip the Arab, 84
Philo, 127
Piety, 8, 20, 37, 110
  dynastic, 83, 87
Plato, 53
Pliny the elder, 104
Pliny the younger, 97, 105f., 129, 147
Polybius, 53
Polytheism, 2, 118, 164, 170
*Pomerium*, 11, 113, 135, 140
Cn. Pompeius Magnus, 7, 26, 29, 49, 94
Pontifex (pontifices), 13f., 18f., 24, 97
  college of, 31, 43
  political influence of, 32f.
  of Sun, 121
Probus, 91
Ptolemies, 90
Pudicitia, 9

Quindecemvirs (*sacris faciundis*), 30, 72
Quirinal, 120
Quirinus, 17

Robigus, 1f.
Roma, cult of, 50, 76f., 87f.
Romulus, 16, 61, 104, 166

Sacrifice, 36, 56f.
Saturn (Saturnalia), 10, 35f.
Scipio the elder, 29, 39
P. Scipio Nasica, 112
Seneca the younger, 62, 104, 111
Septimius Severus, 84
Severus Alexander, 84, 86
Sibylline books, 16, 19, 36, 72, 146
Statues, 92, 95, 106, 125, 143f., 162
Stoics, 53, 61, 104
Suetonius, 60, 66
Sulla Felix, 19, 24, 29, 31, 42, 68
Sun (*Sol*), Invictus, 109, 115, 118, 120f.
  temple of, 102, 120
Superstition (opp. religion), 39, 57, 85,
    162f.
Supplication, 8, 27, 37–8, 94, 173
Symmachus, 152, 159
Synesius, 147

Tacitus, 13, 15, 88, 96
Tacitus, the emperor, 82
Tellus, shrine of, 47
Temples (*templa*), 15, 43, 72f., 114
  functions of, 10, 93
Tertullian, 110, 131, 143
Theodosius I, 148, 156, 159, 162, 167

Tiberius, 18, 70, 74, 82, 93
his moderation, 93f.
his sacrificing, 83–4
Titus, the emperor, 99, 124
Toynbee, A. J., 5n, 33, 71n, 143
Trajan, 85, 92, 97, 99, 127, 129
M. Tullius Cicero, 5, 27, 31, 44, 47, 53, 56
as augur, 19, 97
on Cybele, 114
on doubt, 171
*Dream of Scipio*, 55
on Greeks, 94
his *Laws*, 54
on piety, 83
on religion, 39, 47, 57, 60f., 104, 164

Valentinian I, 147
Valerius Maximus, 15, 52, 99
Varro, M. Terentius, 2, 47, 77, 106
on gods, 53, 62, 104
Venus, 5, 7, 12, 29, 91
of Eryx, 12, 34, 48
Genetrix, 66
Victrix, 26, 49
Vespasian, 82, 92, 104, 125
Vesta, 10, 43, 69, 121
Vestal Virgins, 13f., 37, 43, 72, 96, 121, 158
Victorinus, 143, 149
Victory, altar of, 120, 152, 155, 158
Virgil, 4, 11, 38–9
Vitruvius, 12
Vulcan, 12, 73, 117

Women: and Christianity, 154
in supplications, 38, 41

Zeus, 2, 107
Capetolios, 50